In the Country of Women

In the Country of Women

A Memoir

Susan Straight

Some of these chapters have appeared, in different form, in *The New York Times Magazine*, *Los Angeles Times*, *Salon*, *Oxford American*, *Granta*, *McSweeney's*, *The Believer*, *The Best American Essays 2010*, and on National Public Radio's *All Things Considered*.

Grateful acknowledgment is made to Linda Hogan for permission to reprint a portion of her poem *Walking*.

Unless otherwise credited, all photographs are provided courtesy of the author.

Photograph on title page: Rosie Morris and Alberta Sims

ISBN: 978-1-948226-22-6

Jacket design by Nicole Caputo
Book design by Wah-Ming Chang

Catapult titles are distributed to the trade by Publishers Group West
Phone: 866-400-5351

Library of Congress Control Number: 2018965034

Printed in the United States of America
10 9 8 7 6 5 4 3 2 1

For General and Alberta Sims,
and John and Gabrielle Watson

Author's Note

Memory is a sixth sense, or seventh—and so belongs in specific truth to the people who told me these stories over a span of fifty years. I've written them here as they were given to us—people whose lives were not documented by history but by their own persistence in retelling all of us, again and again, how we came to be.

For the six generations of women in this book:

"Your crown has been bought and paid for.
All you must do is put it on."

—JAMES BALDWIN

Contents

PART IV

In the Country of Women

Prologue

Homerica

To my daughters:

They never tell us about the odysseys of women. They never say about a woman: "Her passage was worthy of Homer . . . her voyage a mythic quest for new lands." Women don't get the Heroine's Journey.

Men are accorded the road and the sea and the asphalt. The monsters and battles and the murders. Men get *The Iliad* and *The Odyssey*. They get Joseph Campbell. They get *The Thousand Faces of the Hero*. They get "the epic novel," "the great American story," and Ken Burns documentaries.

But our women fought harder than men—they fought men! Men who claimed to love them, to protect them, to help them—men who trapped and tried to kill them. They fought for sons and daughters, they had the battalions of their sisters and mothers and aunts. Some bad-ass aunts. The women used their cunning and their bullets, the power of their ancestors and of the other women in the wagon or the truck with them. They survived passages that would have made a lot of men quit.

Sometimes the men did quit. Sometimes the women quit the men—to stay alive.

The women might have wanted to return home. But they couldn't. They were not Odysseus, with rowers and soldiers, returning after conquer and plunder. These women had to travel to new worlds—pioneers and explorers, mythic as goddesses of war and love and intellect—because the old world was trying to kill them, starve them, or bury them alive.

Our women were not in history class, or film, or the literature of "the canon." Our women survived the men who survived the cannons of war, and those were hard men. We hung out with hard men. Weak men. Good men. We married them. We got the babies. The violence. The guns. More babies. The laundry. The pots. Dancing. Pigs. The barter—sex and beds and sheets. The chickens. The bread.

We kept the nation alive.

The women who came before you, my daughters, were legends. Their flights lasted decades, treks that covered America, after they arrived here from the continents of Africa and Europe and married into the indigenous peoples of this continent. They crossed countless rivers. They were, like Odysseus, imprisoned and seduced and threatened with death. They slept with lotus-eaters and escaped monsters like the Cyclops and Charybdis, and sometimes they battled other women who were Sirens or who tried to steal their children.

Because they always had their children on the boat, and even other women's children for whom they had become responsible. Odysseus survived everything to return to his wife and son, but he didn't have little kids on his boat. Though he kept losing his soldiers, he started out with a damn army, and instead your female ancestors had endless brigades of foolish and jealous men trying to stop them.

These women had murder and marrow on their minds. They shed blood for us.

Fine, who was your father's great-grandmother, utterly alone after her enslaved mother died when she was six or seven. No sailors on her ship, no gods to capture winds in a leather pouch and deliver them to her for speed when she fled the violence of Reconstruction in Tennessee.

Daisy, your father's grandmother, a lovely trickster who kept secret the identities of the men who fathered her four daughters—even, as they say, taking their names to her grave. A woman with a smile so incandescent she was threatened with death if she took her face away from her first husband. Her single captain was Aint Dear, a fierce goddess of retribution herself after they fled Mississippi.

Ruby, my paternal grandmother, her hopeful travels in a Model A Ford with a battalion of five sisters, from Illinois to Colorado and then marriage to someone she fled again and again—the sisters her aid, the husband her love and her enemy, until the Rocky Mountains claimed her.

Rosa, my mother's stepmother, a woman from a Grimm's fairy tale, a stern and tireless general who with no assistance kept my feckless grandfather and his children alive by leading them to Fontana, California.

The promised land. All the women ended up in Calafia, a mythical island ruled by a warrior queen, whose inhabitants were black women. It is said our state was named for her.

The Odyssey was an epic poem meant to be declaimed aloud to people assembled for hearing the tale of harrowing travels home, for loyalty and love. We heard our stories spoken cautiously, or whispered. Here are the women. The origin bodies for thousands of Americans, including you, my daughters.

My mother gave me my first book when I was three. I read

the Greek and Roman myths when I was five, in D'Aulaire's wonderful illustrated anthology, because a kindergarten teacher was kind to me and let me sit in the corner with books. I was mesmerized by the pantheon of gods and goddesses, memorized their powers, fascinated by *The Odyssey*, by the monster Scylla and the beautiful Sirens. I imagined myself running like Diana the Huntress when I was attacked by boys or men, actually prepared perfect scathing rebukes, like Athena, who sprang from her father's head fully formed and intellectually whole. My father was gone, and my mother was working, but I sprang from the pages of books fully formed, though I was so small and thin and ugly I was often invisible, except for when I was hunted as a girl and young woman, as so many of us were then, and I had to use what I'd learned in books to escape.

Sometimes the women in our family didn't escape.

The women crossed thousands of miles of hardship so that when I was fourteen and your father was fifteen, he could walk one mile from his house to the end of my street—no one had cars, no one had any money for a date, we met only in parks—where he bounced a basketball in the playground of my elementary school. I walked there to meet him. We sat on the wooden bench against the chain-link fence that separated the playground from the railroad tracks twenty feet away. His shirt: white waffle-weave long underwear with the sleeves cut off for a tank top. I remember the smell of freshly laundered cotton and Hai Karate even now. My shirt: a halter top I'd sewn from two red bandannas, from a pattern I found in *Seventeen* magazine. We talked for a long time in the darkness, played a few games of H-O-R-S-E (I wondered why it was always horse and never something more entertaining, like platypus or elephant or anaconda), and returned to the splintery bench. We kissed for the first time.

His arms were the color of palm bark—brown with a glossy red underneath—and his fingers so long and elegant that when he put my palm against his, my whole hand barely came to the middle knuckles. My arms should have been pale, but this was 1975—some girls rubbed Johnson's baby oil onto their skin and lay at the beach or beside pools to get brown. I had the baby oil—but no beach or pool. I mowed lawns and lay in the bed of my dad's truck while he drove us to the desert.

Your father pointed to the dark brown dot on the skin below my collarbone. "What's that?" he said quietly.

Was I supposed to say *mole*? *Mole* sounded terrible. A blind animal nosing out of the earth. I was so nearsighted I could barely see the playground, because I'd left my glasses at home. "Beauty mark?" I said.

He laughed. "That's if you paint it on your face."

"Who says?"

"All my aunts."

I remember too the smell of sulfur in the rocks along the railroad tracks, and the pepper trees nearby with their spicy pink berries.

Thousands of miles of migration—from slave ships arrived to America, from boats leaving Europe after World War II, from indigenous peoples, hardened ranchwomen, and fierce mothers. The women moved ever west, fled men, met new men, made silent narrow-eyed decisions in the darkness, got on buses and in cars and walked for miles to survive. West until there was no more west.

We were born here, to more dreamers of the golden dream, the ones you never hear about. We moved through the streets of southern California, still with no money, but we had more than those women did when they were girls. We shared one burrito four ways, we rode eight to a car in a Dodge Dart or crowded the bed of a Ford pickup, we partied in the orange groves or in a field by the towering cement Lily Cup, where our friends' parents worked at the plant making paper cups that Americans used to hold at the water cooler.

More than a year later, your father finally picked me up in the Batmobile, a 1961 Cadillac with vintage paint oxidized brown as faded coffee grounds, with huge fins as if sharks would chaperone us down the street. The sound was like a freight train. Sitting in the passenger seat, I saw a dark stain along the inside of the door. It was cold, and I asked your father to roll up the window, but he didn't want me to see the spiderweb cracks around the bullet hole in the glass. Some guy had been leaning against the car window when he was shot. The stains were reminders of his blood. General Sims II, your grandfather, had bought the car from under a pepper tree where it had sat since the murder, covered in California dust. Your father drove me a mile and a half, to General and Alberta's house, and in the driveway Alberta held out her hand and said, *Come and make you a plate*, and my life changed.

That is how you, our three daughters, became California girls. Via the Batmobile. You are the apex of the dream, the future of America, and nearly every day of my life I imagine the women watching you, hoping they—the ancestors—won't be forgotten.

In the country of women, we have maps and threads of kin some people find hard to believe. The women could not have dreamed that in this promised land we would still have bullets and fear and murder. Fracture and derision and assault, sharp and revived.

I was born here, and I am still here, and I didn't leave, which doesn't feel very heroic. You three have laughed at me for looking out the kitchen window of our house toward the hospital where I was born, where your father was born, where you were born. My daily life is a five-mile radius of memory and work and family. You three daughters know this in your genes: You love only orange-blossom honey, because you grew up with that scent and those flowers, that fruit and those bees. You long for Santa Ana winds and sunflowers, tumbleweeds and the laughter of people eating at long unfolded tables in a driveway. We bury descendants of the women, and we serve funeral repasts in church halls built by some of California's black pioneers. The women in our family are everything: African-American, Mexican-American, Cherokee and Creek, Swiss, Irish and English, French and Filipino, Samoan and Haitian. Some of their heritage remains a mystery.

I was not beautiful, and I never went anywhere. But I'm the writer. When I was seventeen, and left for college in Los Angeles, one of my first class assignments was a Xeroxed copy of Joan Didion's famed essay "Some Dreamers of the Golden Dream." I read it three times, actually breathless. Her sentences were lapidary and precise. She dissected the place where we live with lovely caustic prose: "This is the country where it is easy to Dial-A-Devotion, but hard to buy a book. This is the country in which a belief in the literal interpretation of Genesis has slipped imperceptibly into a belief in the literal interpretation of *Double Indemnity*, the country of the teased hair and the Capris and the girls for whom all life's promise comes down to a waltz-length white wedding dress and the birth of a Kimberly or a Sherry or a Debbi and a Tijuana divorce and return to hairdressers' school. 'We were just crazy kids,' they say without regret, and look to the future. The future always looks good in the golden land, because no one remembers the past."

I was stunned.

She was writing about us, except for the Dial-A-Devotion. (I never knew anyone who did that.) My mother and all three of my aunts had been "divorcees." One aunt had been married three times. One was recently divided from a Fontana Hell's Angel biker. My stepmother was divorced when she met my father; she was now his third wife. My friends—black and white and Japanese-American and Mexican-American—were named Kimberly and Sherry and Debbie. We lived amid the citrus groves described in the essay, with low walls built of riverbed stone.

I went home that weekend, passing through the places Didion's essay made famous: Ontario, Fontana, and Rialto. Finally I got to Riverside, and in my mother's kitchen, standing at the Formica counter I had spent half my life scrubbing, I tried to explain the piece to my mother. She was distracted, cooking, not interested until I read part of a paragraph out loud, wherein the cheating wife pushes a burning Volkswagen that contains her unconscious husband into a lemon grove. My mother looked up at me then, and said, "That was Lucille Miller. Your aunt Beverly lived across the street from that woman when it happened. She always said Lucille was going to kill someone."

I was further stunned.

I went outside to look at the palm tree in our front yard, whose stair steps of gray dessicated bark I had climbed when I was five, everyone shouting at me to get down. I knew a version of us, of the girls and women here, that was not in the essay. Debbie Martinez, Deborah Adams, Deb Clyde. Girls descended from Mexican and black families arrived in the 1920s, and white families arrived from Arkansas after the Korean War. Our mothers and grandmothers remember their pasts.

I wanted to write about us.

Your father and I took our first journey three days after we were married in the oldest black church in Riverside, Allen Chapel African Methodist Episcopal, founded in 1875. (The afternoon of our wedding, we were driven around the city lake in another Cadillac, belonging to our friend Newcat, a car with a broken horn, so that your uncle General III stood in the open sunroof, his arms spread wide, shouting to people, *Honk, honk, goddamnit, these two fools just got married!*) We drove across the country from California to Massachusetts, in a Honda Civic—a truly tiny car back then, in 1983, and your father was six feet four inches and 195 pounds, so it was no joke sleeping in the front seats at rest stops.

In Amherst, we found a mattress and some furniture on the street and lived in a studio apartment while I learned to be a writer and your father worked nights in a correctional facility. But we met James Baldwin, my teacher and mentor. His driver, Rico, and his secretary, Skip, were tall black men who wanted to play basketball with your father. So everyone came to dinner in our bleak front room with two card tables we'd borrowed, the gray linoleum scrubbed, and the tiny red television my brother had won by selling newspaper subscriptions when he was twelve, which he'd given me for Christmas seven years earlier.

James Baldwin said the apartment reminded him of old days in Harlem. He walked the floor slowly holding a glass of Johnnie Walker Black Label, leaning toward my small blue typewriter on the windowsill, reading the handwritten note I had taped to the glass:

> *With the rhythm it takes to dance through*
> *what we have to live through*
> *you can dance underwater and not get wet.*

He turned to me, his voice precise and resonant as ever but with the wonder he always allowed himself (I already knew that was who I wanted to be—someone endlessly willing to look at something new and feel continuous wonder), and said, "That's the most extraordinarily profound thing I've read in a long time. Who wrote this?"

George Clinton, we told him. On our ancient black boombox kept on the windowsill, too, we played a cassette tape of "Aqua Boogie" for James Baldwin, the song whose refrain kept me going in the cold snowy nights when I missed oranges and friends and pepper trees. We told him about home. He said to me, "This is remarkable. This is what you must write about. Your lives."

I was twenty-two then. But I wasn't ready.

Now mourning and love shape this memoir. Our elders are dying, and our young people, too. Your great-aunts, your aunts, and your cousins. Our country feels as if it has gathered itself at a cliff and is studying the long scree of loose rock, deciding whether to slide down and descend completely again into open hatred. This is a different memoir than the one I thought I would write when you three girls were small, when you were Our Little Women, and this was our Orchard House, though our orchards were orange trees.

You three daughters have left us, your father and me, and many of the women we loved are gone as well, so we are here with our kin in the city where we were born, still sitting under the trees in the searing heat near the big grill where entire slabs of ribs smoke for hours, and then we women chop them into single bones with hatchet and ax so the kids can hold one curve of glistening meat and hear again about how their great-grandfather General II didn't want to eat squirrel ever again after Oklahoma.

All of American history is in your bones. In your skin and hair and brains and in your blood. Your kin family numbers five hundred or more. When your cousin Corion died last year, at twenty, our grief was depthless. He was a skateboarder,

Dwayne Sims, Skip ("I'm the secretary"), James Baldwin,
Rico ("I'm the driver"), at Baldwin's rented house in
Amherst, Massachusetts, 1984

walking home, having just passed the driveway where our family's heart has gathered for fifty years, and so I see him walking still. At his funeral, I read this poem, by Linda Hogan, Chickasaw poet of Oklahoma and Colorado, two places where our stories originate. It seems the right way to begin:

Tonight, I walk. I am watching the sky. I think of the people who came before me and how they knew the placement of the stars in the sky. Listening to what speaks in the blood. I am listening to a deeper way. Suddenly all my ancestors are behind me. Be still, they say. Watch and listen. You are the result of the love of thousands.

And thousands of miles, by foot and boat and train.

I see the women moving about in the darkness, not because I was in that darkness with them, but because the air was dim or dust around us when the stories were told. The people who spoke to me looked off into the distance, or out a car window, their voices low and rough talking about the night or day when life was altered in a moment. Many stories had a beautiful woman, a murder or tragic death; many had a terrible man.

One afternoon, sitting by the living room fire, our knees inches apart, her crimson lipstick gleaming, winged eyebrows drawn together and then rising in surprise, my mother-in-law, Alberta, waited for me to hand her Gaila—my first daughter, finally fallen asleep with milk on her lips. Then Alberta spoke softly about Sunflower County, Mississippi.

Other days, under the eucalyptus trees shedding their creamy beige bark around us, their leaves like silver sickles, our cousins and uncles would hold paper plates of barbecued meat on their laps, speaking of Denton, Texas, and Tulsa, Oklahoma.

In the dry-grass-scented night of the Colorado prairie, in a tiny house moved from a ghost town fifty years earlier to Nunn, a town going ghost now, five elderly cousins of my grandmother told me for the first time about a country dance.

On a November evening, my mother crying, the wooden clock from Switzerland clacking implacably above us, the clock from the tiny village in the Alps where she was raised, like Heidi, where when she was nine, her mother died, just like Heidi's, and my mother told me she went down in the night to see her mother's body in the living room, and now her life was ruined here in Glen Avon, California.

When I went outside the next day, the chain-link fences were white with feathers heaped onto the wires like insanely monstrous snowflakes, and the Santa Ana winds were blowing, and I tried to figure out how someone would lay a dead woman on a table. I was three years old, and felt as if not just me but our entire street could be lifted up and moved to a different world by that wind, which always blew west, into my face, so that I had to close my eyes.

I

I

Little House in the Thistles

Glen Avon, California, 1963

Here in the land of tumbleweeds so immense and fiercely mobile, a windstorm in November sent so many skeletal balls of thorn blowing across the fields that the small house where my mother and I lived was buried in brown. It was a valley of granite boulders and turkey ranches. Tumbleweeds six and eight feet across packed in drifts around the windows, which were coated with dust from the famous Santa Ana winds. "It was like a snowstorm," my mother told me years later. "I couldn't even open the door."

My mother, Gabrielle Gertrude Leu Straight Watson, grew up in the Swiss Alps, in a chalet built in the 1800s, the wood nearly black with age, the balconies carved with floral designs, and in winter the snow reached the roof. She told me stories of skiing to school, the beauty of glittering icicles, drifts of sparkling white crystals nearly blinding in the sun. But when her mother died and her father remarried, he took them to Canada, a place about which she told me no stories except these: she worked in the fields, her stepmother,

Rosa, tried to marry her off at fifteen to a pig farmer, and my mother ran away.

My father, Richard Dean Straight, grew up in the Colorado Rockies, in rough wooden ranch outfits built in the 1800s, the wood nearly black with age, but no balconies or flowers, just corrals filled with cattle and sheep, and his feet damaged by frostbite, his memory damaged by terror. His mother, Ruby, left his father again and again, but always returned. My father went from Colorado to California, from remote ranch to the city of Los Angeles, and back to the mountains. He was born for leaving, as the cowboy songs go, but when he left my mother and me, he didn't go wandering on a horse back to the ranch. He never came back for more than five minutes at the curb, once a month, while I climbed into his Mustang and went to his house for two days. Never longer than that.

It's stunning to gather the stories now and see the parallels in their lives, my parents, and to think they spoke about twelve words to each other in the last fifty years.

In November 1963, I was three years old. The tumbleweeds were everywhere. My mother was crying, and I was trying to climb up onto her lap, but there was no lap because she was eight months pregnant, so I sat near her feet. The Santa Ana winds blew incessantly and dust filtered through the cracks around the windows until a golden sparkle of haze moved on the floor in the light from the streetlamp.

My mother had brought few things from Switzerland. She was allowed one small trunk on the boat to Canada. How she came into possession of the wooden clock, I don't know. But three things she had are now mine: a black lacquered bowl painted with Swiss wildflowers, one pair of silver scissors she used to cut our fingernails, and a strange little folder of cloth into whose pages are inserted sewing needles of all sizes. I was taught to sew, knit, crochet, and embroider when I was seven.

My mother had spent her childhood darning socks for her father and brothers, and knitting new ones. She taught me to knit in the way that her mother had taught her: I sat across from her, holding the heavy loop of yarn as it came from the store, and she pulled the yarn to make a large ball. Now and then she wove yarn tightly around pieces of Brach's hard candy, which could be bought cheaply by the pound, butterscotches and peppermints and oblong toffees, all in bright cellophane or foil. She wrapped yarn so fast her hands were nearly invisible, and the strands covered the candy like a sped-up cartoon.

Then I sat in a chair and knitted, the ball of yarn at my feet—exactly as she had. My head was bent, my hair was in a braid, and I was required not to touch the ball of yarn, even when I saw a flash of foil or yellow cellophane. The piece of candy had to fall out onto the floor, after I had knitted enough to remove those strands of yarn. I was always glad when the cats batted the damn ball and the candy fell out early.

She told me she hated the darning of socks. I knew I didn't have to learn to darn because we lived in a place where it was over 100 degrees for weeks at a time, and my siblings and I went barefoot until our feet were so dark and callused we were proud to not require shoes to walk on glass and thorns.

She had made it all the way to southern California to get a job, get married, buy a small house, plant roses, and have a baby. Me.

She worked as a teller at Household Finance Savings and Loan in Riverside. One day in 1955, a man came in to apply for a $50 loan. He was on strike from Boeing Aircraft, living in his car for the moment, and recently divorced, he said. Why she agreed to go out with him is an enduring mystery to me.

Richard Straight. Why she married him is even more confusing. But he was handsome.

They lived in a tiny wooden bungalow behind a larger house on Tyrolite Street in Glen Avon, an unincorporated community people called Okietown. My mother was very good at saving money. After four years, they bought her dream house, an eight-hundred-square-foot stucco cottage off Pyrite Street. The new freeway and poultry ranches and granite quarries to the north; to the east, the Santa Ana River. My mother still had her job. But my father had met another woman, and he was gone.

Now she was abandoned. On the west side of the river, fifty miles from Los Angeles, we lived in an area where white people had arrived from dust bowl farms, Mexican people from Michoacan and Zacatecas, black people from Mississippi, Oklahoma, and Louisiana. Japanese-American strawberry farmers and Spanish-Mexican native Californians had been there for decades. My mother was the only one from Europe.

We had oatmeal and a can of beans. I recall the oatmeal, but in a vague way. My mother says we had a conversation on the third day of oatmeal. My mother: "I told you to eat the oatmeal, and you said you wouldn't. I slapped you so hard the oatmeal flew off the high chair. You said, 'You can hit me again but I won't eat it.'"

She shook her head. "You only wanted your book."

I had one book. I knew all the words. I wanted another book.

All my life, my mother had told me two versions of how she taught me to read in a single weekend, when I was three. The first: My father was gone, she had to go to work, and she didn't want me to bother the babysitter by talking (I'd been dropped on my head once by an inebriated caretaker), so she taught me to read and sit quietly in the corner. Believable. The second:

She didn't think American kindergarten accepted children unless they could already read, and she was eager for me to go to school and not pay for babysitting. Also plausible.

But I asked her again in 2017, laying out the two stories. For the first time, she said with some bemusement: "No—you taught yourself to read. I read you the first book, maybe three times, and then you knew the whole thing and you wanted another one. We were so poor, but you just wanted a book, and I went to Stater Bros. [the local grocery] and spent my last quarter to buy one of those little books with the gold at the edges."

I was so surprised.

She'd bought me a Little Golden Book. Maybe *Poky Little Puppy*, she thought. Then President John F. Kennedy was shot and killed, a public murder so graphic and visible on television, shocking to the nation. My mother sobbed and grieved in front of the small black-and-white television, and I lay on the floor listening.

My mother had become an American citizen in November 1960 so that she could vote for John F. Kennedy in the presidential election. Before that, for five years, she had been an immigrant with a green card. "I wasn't in any hurry to become a citizen," she told me the other night. "Not until I saw John F. Kennedy."

"You didn't vote for—" I blanked.

She called to my stepfather, John—"Who was before Kennedy?"

"Eisenhower," he replied dryly.

She waved her hand dismissively. "No," she said to me. "I didn't feel any reason to vote until President Kennedy. He was different."

She was pregnant with me, in late 1960, when she began the citizenship class at the Riverside courthouse. "You had to renounce your other citizenship, back then," she said. "I didn't want to lose my Swiss citizenship, but I really wanted to vote for him. It wasn't hard at all, back then, to become a citizen," she said. "We learned some history."

She had me in October. The following month, she said, "We went to the courthouse. Dad and me. We just happened to be there at the same time."

That dad was not my father, Richard Straight, whose name my mother never ever said aloud. That was John Paul Watson, my future stepfather, born in Saint John, New Brunswick, Canada. They became citizens together, taking the oath in the same room.

She was truly an American then, when she cast her vote for John F. Kennedy in a white skirt and blouse, her hair carefully risen in a Jackie Kennedy bubble.

But by the night of November 23, 1963, she was on her own, two weeks overdue in her pregnancy. "I had taken the week off from work, because your brother was so late," she told me. "But he didn't come, and I couldn't afford to take any more time off. I had no money. I was desperate. I was watching television, and there they were, he and Jackie, and then he was shot. It hurt me to the quick. I just cried and cried, I couldn't stop crying."

I remember the crying, the black-and-white images going past my face, which I held close to the thick curved screen where the static from the constant dry wind would shock me so hard I could feel it inside my nose.

"I couldn't stop crying, and your brother wouldn't come. I went to see Grandma."

That was her stepmother—Rosa. I said, "Where was I? I didn't go."

My mother frowned. "Where were you? I took you to the

neighbors. I drove to Fontana and Grandma said the best thing when your baby is late is to walk. That's all she told me. So I walked all around Fontana. I didn't know what to do."

She went into labor and the following morning she had my brother. In 2017, telling me this story, she sat in her sixth house, each one a bit bigger than the last, but all within a ten-mile radius. I ladled out the chicken and rice I brought on many Sundays. "Then the TV was on in my hospital room, and I saw that man shoot Lee Harvey Oswald. Who was that man?" she called to my stepfather.

"Jack Ruby," he replied.

She said to me, "I saw the whole thing. Over and over again. That was terrible, too."

The next day, Rosa drove her from the hospital with my brother, and dropped her off at the dream house. "She didn't come inside. She said, 'You made your bed. Now you must lie in it.' That's what she told me. Then she drove away." My mother was quiet for a moment.

I knew this part. I said, "The neighbor had left our door unlocked and the wind blew it open."

"I took him inside and there was dirt everywhere. I was so tired. And I had to get out the vacuum."

That door faced east, into the brunt of Santa Ana winds screaming down off the foothills. The door was wide open and the house full of dirt from the fields. My mother, though abandoned, had spent the last weeks feverishly knitting a new layette for the baby—soft yellow jacket and booties. She had a new bassinet. These were the things she cared about most, having spent all those years knitting thick woolen socks for her Swiss father and brothers, and now knitting fine booties for her son. The bassinet and its lining, the layette she'd left displayed there, for herself, if no one else—all of it was filthy, and the wind was hot as hell.

My baby brother, Jeffrey, was screaming, his fists held on either side of his face all clenched tight and red, like puckered tomato bottoms three in a row. Then he threw up all over the bassinet. (His hands were fists for the rest of his life—larger than the rest of his body, so powerful, knuckles and wrists swollen with work, scarred from fighting and farming and burning old paint off buildings.)

I had my book.

She was broken. It is the only time my mother ever described to me feeling as if she were defeated and could not go on. No food. Swimming in dirt and thorned weeds. My brother blind with fury. I had my book.

Rosa Leu's words seem particularly ironic and cruel, since my mother had slept only two nights in the hospital, and she sure wasn't going to be lying in her bed, alone, while her three-year-old and three-day-old children lay in the dancing dust on their blankets.

She went back to work the next day. We went to the babysitter. I read my book. While my brother's hands remained fists, my eyes remained the hungriest part of me. As long as I had a book, or a Sears catalog, or a cereal box, or a Betty Crocker recipe book, I would eat what I was given. As long as I had something to read, I could imagine I was somewhere else, speaking with the strangely colonial Mr. Quaker Oats with his long gray curls, wearing new Sears dresses with smocking, while Betty Crocker with bouffant hair served us lattice-crust pie on a checkered tablecloth.

Nothing was ever the same for my mother. The motorcade, the beauty and hope and pillbox hat and handsome jaw, the accent so patrician, the way her president spoke, and his wife with her clean smile and cheekbones. Then that wife held her husband's brains in her hand. She was alone.

My mother was alone, too, with two children. Her president was buried. She never missed work. At the branch was John Watson, from the citizenship ceremony, who had worked with her at Household Finance before Richard Straight came in for that damn loan. (My mother's dating pool was apparently very small—men inside the savings and loan building.)

She left us, my baby brother and me, with a babysitter who lived at the edge of the orange groves, and married her friend from Canada. I loved him because the first time he met me, he gave me a Tonka truck. He had asked what I wanted, and I didn't say doll, but truck. Earthmoving seemed important where we lived—that is what I saw every day, bulldozers and tractors and turkey feathers and trucks hauling oranges. We lived in an unincorporated community, not even a town. I moved a lot of dirt in that yard, after my stepfather married my mother. Less than a year later, she had another baby—another boy, John Jr.—and we moved across the Santa Ana River to the city of Riverside.

We were feral children, as were most of us then, in the 1960s and '70s, and our wild kingdom was the orange groves. The other kids threw fruit as missiles and set up bunkers in the irrigation towers. But after the wars, I sat under the white blossoms that fell like stars, and I read.

That night I asked my mother how I learned to read, she looked into the distance and added, "I was an immigrant, and I had no money, and I could never buy enough books for you. But I wanted you to go to school and do well."

She took me to the Riverside Public Library, where I attempted to check out twenty-two books. She limited me to ten.

That fall, I was not yet five. My mother walked me down the street, turned left, walked another long block, and took me into the kindergarten classroom, where Mrs. Dalton, a kind and generous teacher, allowed me to sit in the corner and read. She did not force me to take a nap with the others. I refused to sleep when there were so many books.

The next day, my mother said, "You know the way," and I was overjoyed to be alone on the sidewalk, along the dirt path through the foxtails and wild mustard, and then into the classroom. I have felt this way for the rest of my years.

I read Laura Ingalls Wilder, *Little House in the Big Woods*. Their log house was buried not by tumbleweeds but by snow. The entire Maud Hart Lovelace *Betsy-Tacy* series set in Wisconsin, with snow and muffs into which girls put their hands before skating; *Caddie Woodlawn* and the *Nancy Drew* mysteries (what the heck was a sedan?). In 1965, my stepfather had adopted my brother, Jeffrey. But Richard Straight would not consent to my adoption, and I became the rift that never healed. Every three weeks, he picked me up, alone, and we drove to his new family. There, I was the youngest of five children. My stepsiblings, Jim, Dick, Pam, and Tricia, were ten to fourteen years older than me. From them I learned to macramé, listened to Gary Glitter and the Rolling Stones, and saw my stepbrothers go off to Vietnam.

But in 1966, my mother brought two foster children home. We went to the county juvenile facility to pick them up, at night. It was dark and terrifying. It was a jail. Then we were stair steps, and I was the oldest of five children: Susan, Bridget, Patrick, Jeffrey, and John Jr.

It was a strange place to be—in the middle of two families, step and half and foster siblings, and my brother who now had a different last name than mine.

I know now my mother wanted to give other kids a safe place to live. We all wore the same home-sewn T-shirts and shorts. We each held a hot dog in a bun. We sat in a row on the hot metal tailgate of the Country Squire station wagon. But decades later, my mother said to me, "I never asked how you all felt about it. You didn't ask children how they felt."

And my stepfather, John, called out, "You never asked me, either! I'd come home from work and there were two more kids at the table and they stayed for years! You never said a word."

My mother grinned, and shrugged. My dad and I knew she was the small intractable engine of our lives—she always got what she wanted. She wanted life to be better for those kids. Bridget and Patrick stayed for three years, until they went to live with their grandparents. Only a short time later, my mother found Sandy and Chris, exactly the same age in relation to us, in shelter care, and they came to live with us for five years. The controlled chaos of our house was all we ever knew—we stole oranges and my mother quartered them onto our plates, never tired herself of the magical sections of skin-held juice; we rode skateboards and left our knee-skin on the sidewalk, and she dispensed the rusty-hued pain of Mercurochrome and told us not to flinch or cry. If anyone made fun of us at school, she was staunch in our defense. My stepfather worked six days a week, and came home to look longingly at the dinner table, where we ate a lot of hot dog casserole, tuna casserole, and potatoes.

I cared nothing about our clothes or the single hot dog. Only books. Story was the escape. Cloth diapers and pins that stuck my thumb rather than fat baby brother thighs, weeds and tomato worms I dropped into coffee cans, sliding glass doors with fingerprints like swarms of ghostly beetles I sprayed with Windex the blue of ocean in *Anne of Green Gables*. I looked at my stepfather and imagined Prince Edward Island, close to his birthplace. I read *Heidi* and looked at my mother, imagining the Alps. I hid in closets, in hedges and trees, and under beds to read.

In my rough neighborhood, where one man six houses up from us shot a peephole into his front door, and kids set the foothills on fire for enjoyment of the spectacle, I read other worlds, and never imagined anyone had written about a place like mine until I found *A Tree Grows in Brooklyn*, by Betty Smith, when I was eight.

At the library, I checked out this novel and stepped into a mirror that made me feel almost lavishly dizzy. Francie is also the dreamy impractical eldest daughter of an impoverished, stern immigrant mother. Francie hates cleaning, and her thrill is the library, where she works her way alphabetically through the shelves. Back at her apartment, she arranges peppermint wafers on a blue plate, and sits outside on the fire escape to immerse herself in another world.

I put one Oreo on a plate, climbed the fruitless mulberry tree in our backyard, lying on a branch above the exposed roots and dirt where my three brothers had set up elaborate military maneuvers with hundreds of olive-drab plastic soldiers, and while I was shot with mud clods, entered 1900s Williamsburg: pickles, carts and horses, men who wore celluloid collars, boys who died of tuberculosis. *Brooklyn*, I whispered.

That we could control death and violence by writing about it was transforming. I had seen drug deals, wildfires, a man who held a woman so tightly by her hair that her temple puckered. Sometimes I was terrified. There was the man waiting on the narrow dirt path on the way to school, who opened his coat, a clichéd pervert (who the hell wears an overcoat when it's 100 degrees?), but I'd read *A Tree Grows in Brooklyn* four times by then, and Francie's mother shoots the pervert (he's called the pervert) in the groin, so I just glanced at him (pale and gross and oddly just like the novel) and ran into the weeds, wishing I had Francie's mother or her gun.

The summer of 1970, the bookmobile arrived in far-flung

neighborhoods like mine. No one wanted to accompany me, and I was thrilled. I walked alone through fields of wild oats, past the pepper trees under which older kids smoked marijuana and drank Coors and listened to Grand Funk Railroad and James Brown on transistor radios, across the railroad tracks, down into the steep arroyo where a green trickle of water was my creek, and up into a grocery store parking lot where for two hours inside the air-conditioned hum of a converted bus, I read about death. I found S. E. Hinton's *The Outsiders*, with desperate, joking, hardworking boys as close to my own neighborhood as anything I'd ever read, and then, shaken, walked back home as the branches of the pepper trees shivered with electric guitars and laughter. *Tulsa*, I whispered.

By then, I'd worked my way through the children's shelves downtown, and kids didn't wander the adult sections. But in the bookmobile, no one paid attention to me lying near the mystery shelves while I read Alfred Hitchcock, wherein people were stabbed, strangled, shot, and poisoned, all scary but less likely than drowning by bathtub. A man killed women by surprising them while they bathed, grabbing their ankles and pulling, rendering them unable to clutch the slippery sides while the water overcame them. We had no shower in the bathroom. At home, I drained the bathtub water after my siblings were finished, crouched under the faucet, and shivered.

When I was eleven, I read James Baldwin's *Go Tell It on the Mountain*. It altered everything. John, wielding a carpet sweeper on a rug, was with me while I swept the endless windblown leaves on the sidewalk. He was a boy trying to please a father who cannot escape his terrible past, watching his brother and other boys fighting themselves and the world. I was failing to please my mother, and my brother came home bleeding.

Just after that, I saw a slim paperback in a rotating rack, on the cover a pensive young woman with brown skin, a flowered dress, and a yellow rose. She looked like an older sister of a girl in my class. But she was Sula. The voices of the women in *Sula* were like those of the mothers and grandmothers who came to our elementary school auditorium, the women cheering in the bleachers at the Little League games where my brothers played. *Medallion*, I whispered.

Along the iridescence of the railroad tracks, abandoned shopping carts lying on their sides in the arroyo, covered with water grass like green fur, I saw all those fictional children like me. I walked home through the wild mustard dried to rattle at my knees.

By the time I was thirteen, books were my addiction, as powerful as the alcohol, Marlboros, and marijuana joints my friends and the neighborhood boys held in their hands. Kids were drinking Everclear and Olde English. I partook of the Marlboros and beer. I was afraid of everything else. I spent my time under the pepper tree branches, and in the vacant lots where parties were held (think *Dazed and Confused*, but with way more black and Chicano teenagers, and additions of Con Funk Shun, Parliament, and Tierra). But even at the moment when the police helicopters came, or my friends fell off their platforms, lit embers floating in darkness like constellations of red and gold, I was waiting to be somewhere else. Reading a novel.

Back in 1965, my stepfather bought the laundromat next to the market where my mother had spent her quarter on my first book. For the next ten years, we kids swept the floors of landed clouds of lint, restocked the little boxes of detergent. I watched the people move about, descendants of Okies and slaves and braceros and Japanese strawberry farmers. These were the parents of my friends. We drank in vacant lots, Boone's Farm strawberry wine in Lily Tulip cups, near the Lily Tulip plant with its actual giant concrete cup. (The world's largest paper cup!) Then we married each other, and our children are American babies, despite what some people think.

A few times a year now, I walk near the old Lily Tulip Cup, the towering cement painted white and blue, near the last orange groves. As a child in the laundromat, I must have known my life would be about language, and place, because I saw people's baskets full of stories, the way their hands moved when they held up a shirt, their eyes narrowed with private legends of the man or baby or mother to whom it belonged.

But every night, I walk along the Santa Ana River, and up into the steep small foothills along the riverbed. From the rocky slopes, I can see my whole life. That is not an odyssey. I am the woman who left briefly and then came back right away, who has never left home since.

Looking west, I can see Mission Boulevard, the street that leads to the house where I was born, and the lights of the laundromat, in the small place called Rubidoux. That place was rancho land taken from the Cahuilla peoples by the Spanish Californios, and sold to Louis Robidoux, a French-born fur trapper who married a young Spanish woman. Dwayne's cousins still live near the river in a family compound built by Henderson "Gato" Butts in the 1920s, after he left Oklahoma.

Looking north, I see the Cajon Pass, which everyone in our family navigated when they came to California. My grandmother Ruby and my father, only seven, came down the pass in a bus, down onto Route 66, where all roads led away from her husband: San Bernardino, Ontario, and Echo Park. Dwayne's great-grandmother Fine, born just after the Civil War, sent all her grandchildren across that same desert and down the same pass to Los Angeles.

Turning east, I see my childhood neighborhood and

Dwayne's, the old tract homes from the 1960s. The avenue I drive every single day to work, that passes the street of Dwayne's parents, General and Alberta Sims, and the driveway where I learned to be a good human, and the houses of all my relatives and friends.

Turning the last quarter, looking south only half a mile, I see my own house, where I've lived for thirty years this spring, where I've raised three daughters. In historical photos, acres of citrus and walnut groves covered the land for miles, broken only by a few farmhouses. Mine is one of those. A bungalow with green shingles and burgundy window frames, once solitary in the trees, but now anchoring the corner of my block. A house that my eldest daughter's friends told me I could not paint a different color, because they wouldn't be able to find their way to the place where they could always be sure of food and a couch on which to sleep, and the right book to take with them in the morning.

My house—which I made into the home from Robert Frost's poem: "When you go there, they have to take you in."

I learned that from my marriage family, from Alberta and General Sims.

Every night, I stand there for a moment with my dog, the brittlebush quivering in the wind, thinking that all those years, no matter which way I looked, I was never alone.

The women who brought us here were utterly alone. Sometimes they had only what they held inside to call company. Even as children, they had no one but themselves.

2

The First Bullet

Fine, Near Murfreesboro,
Tennessee, 1876

She was

called Fine when she was orphaned. Then her name changed
for each man in her life, for seventy years. She became Fin
Hofford, Viney Rollins, Fannie Rollins, Tinnie Kemp, Fanny
Kemp, and finally, in letters carved onto her headstone in a
historic black cemetery outside Tulsa, Oklahoma:

BELOVED GRANDMOTHER
FINEY KEMP
1874–1952

nothing but

a new possession to the white people who took her from the
former slave cabin in the countryside northwest of Nashville,

where she was born maybe in 1869, only four years after the Civil War ended, according to an 1870 U.S. Census document, or maybe in 1874, according to information written on an application for social security just before her death.

It doesn't matter. By the time she was five or six, Fine was a child bereft. Adrift.

Like countless children during Reconstruction, a violent maelstrom of greed and revenge and ruined land, Fine moved through the world alone. Small wanderers were everywhere along the roadsides, among the trees, in the edges of the yards.

Bereft of all love and care. Bereaved is what we feel when someone dies. Bereft is when we are left without anything.

Henry Ely, her father, had been "run off by the law," Fine told her grandchildren, said to have made his way to Texas. Shortly afterward, her mother, Catherine, died in the place where she and her own sister had been enslaved for their entire lives. Fine was the youngest of five children. Imagine the children in the cabin doorway, watching wagons enter the yard to take them away.

Fine told the story of her life to her daughters and her grandchildren in Oklahoma and California; as her grandchildren became our elders, they recounted the details at family gatherings, and now the last surviving grandson of Fine, our beloved uncle John Prexy Sims, is eighty-two years old and tells her story to our own children.

"They took her by herself," he said. "Her mother was dead and her father was gone. There was no one to contest the white people who came and picked the little ones out like puppies. The family that took her called her Fine simply because she looked strong and healthy." She never saw her family again.

John said, "Her father was a Cherokee man, and he was in love with two sisters who were slaves. They were so beautiful he couldn't pick one. So he loved them both."

Family legend: Catherine and her sister lived together in one slave dwelling. Henry Ely was a free man, not allowed onto the plantation, so he dug a tunnel from the forest at the boundary of the land and under the fence. He planned the tunnel to open up into the dirt floor of the cabin of the sisters. (Like a fairy tale of a prince and two princesses—the fairy tales we were all told of captive women and a man whose love might rescue them. But this was 1850s Tennessee.)

Free men of color were often killed or forced out of the area by slaveowners or vigilantes. New laws made the very presence of men like Henry illegal. If Henry was Cherokee, his life was endangered by President Andrew Jackson's Indian Removal Act. Jackson wanted the west, and Tennessee was then part of the west. Manifest Destiny—painted landscapes with white angels wearing white garments hovered over the wagon trains of white settlers as they crossed the Appalachian Mountains into Tennessee. The indigenous peoples known as the Five Civilized Tribes, Cherokee, Chickasaw, Creek, Choctaw, and Seminole, were forcibly removed by American militia from Tennessee, Georgia, Mississippi, Alabama, and Florida, sent on the winter death march known as the Trail of Tears to Oklahoma Territory.

Whoever Henry Ely was, he called Catherine his wife, and they had six children. (The names of her sister and the children of that sister, and whether they were fathered by Henry are unknown.)

By the time her family disintegrated, when Fine was about five, Reconstruction meant violence, starvation, and murder for freedmen and freedwomen. The Freedmen's Bureau made reports such as these, in 1866, in Murfreesboro, near the place where Henry and Catherine lived, where a "colored" man gave testimony:

July 28, 1865: "Ben (col'd) says on the 29th of June, 'Beverly

Randolph beat my wife with his fists then caught her by the chin threw back her head pulled out his knife swore he would cut her throat'—(the woman was large with child at the time.)" Randolph was fined $50.

The Freedmen's Bureau reported further: "The freedmen are daily driven from their homes without a cent after having been induced to work the year with a promise of a share of the crop. Husbands are not permitted to claim their wives or parents their children, women have been struck to the ground and choked."

"A freedman living twelve miles south came in last night, covered with blood, with severe cuts on his head—his former master had beaten him with a heavy stick while his son-in-law stood by with a pistol, because the freedman had said that he intended to go and hunt up his children, whom he had not seen in four years."

This is the world Fine was born into.

She had lived in a small cabin with her people. Then there was a wagon—she either rode or walked behind. Did she cry and scream, when she saw her siblings taken away? Or was she taken first? She went alone. She never saw again the brothers and sisters with

Skin

that looked like hers and now her life was filled with cruelty, especially at the hands of an elderly matriarch to whom emancipation meant nothing.

John Sims's voice still resonated with hurt when he talked about Fine: "She told me many stories about her life with the family that took her. Her food was scraps from the plates of the family, or whatever wild nuts, fruits, and berries she could find. Her clothes—castoffs from the family. She found that she could earn a little money by selling the wild blackberries that she picked (five cents a gallon). This little money she would save in hopes of buying a pair of shoes, but in spite of her efforts to find a safe hiding place, the family would find the money and take it away. Beatings came at the least little thing, from all members of the family, especially from the old woman, who was nearly bald and suffering from mouth cancer."

Fine wanted shoes. She wore rags, chopped wood, brought water from the well, and still the old woman beat her as if the beatings were the old woman's work, the schedule and imprint of her former life. Maybe she had beaten children all her life, or maybe she chose to beat only this one child, who would not be subdued.

Fine was in tatters and cold. She was hungry. Inside, she was a furious whirl of anger. She was skin

and Bone

in the yard: well and woodpile, field and house. The woodpile. The insatiable need for wood to cook and wash clothes and always more wood. Her bare feet. Her anger.

One day there was a glint of metal on the ground.

A bullet. All those bullets, balls of lead aimed at the heads of soldiers on both sides, and then freedmen and women, the countryside near Murfreesboro littered with bullets and cannonballs and bones and even unburied bodies. Decades of war and retribution. Hunting and killing of animals and humans.

Fine put the bullet into the pocket of her apron. It was her talisman. She was about eleven years old. In her mind, having not a single human to help her, she was capable of murder. She didn't know anything about gunpowder or firing pins. She only knew people died from bullets.

John Sims said, "Grandma (we pronounced it *Gramaw*

and still do) was out picking berries (she never went to school!) and came upon a cartridge lying by the side of the road. She thought it to be a weapon all by itself. With great care, she hid it away for just the right moment. One day while chopping wood for the family stoves, the old woman came out to watch her . . . Gramaw told her, 'These wood chips flying and you liable to get hit!' The old woman told her to shut up and get to work. Soon the opportune moment came. When the old woman was looking away, Gramaw took the bullet out of her apron pocket. With all her might, she threw it at the old woman's head. It landed flush on the temple. A bloodcurdling scream from the old woman that could be heard all around the farm brought the rest of the family on the run. Gramaw told them she said to watch out for the wood chips, but she still got a beating, which was the least of her pain. The one weapon she thought would give her a taste of revenge was a bitter disappointment. How can it be? she wondered. I know it hit her. Why didn't she die?"

She had cheekbones like ledges of slate under her eyes, and black hair thick and long. She was thirteen. She wanted shoes. She headed to the blackberry thickets along the edges of the woods, picking buckets of berries to sell to people passing by in wagons. It was 1887. She met a young man by the roadside. Robert. He might have been seventeen or eighteen. Fine fell in love. (The word is always *fell*, not leaped or landed or rested or dived. *Fell.*) She ran away with him, and he took her to an old shack in the woods built for migrant workers. Soon she was pregnant.

No one ever says whether the white family tried to find her, or how far she had gone to be with Robert. When she grew bigger with child, Robert left, but someone in the area helped Fine give birth to her first daughter, Jennie. The father was listed as Robert Hofford. Fine was listed as Fin Hofford.

Shortly after, alone with the baby, Fine was up and about, picking cotton, picking and selling wild berries. Robert returned with the season, and left again, twice more. Fine gave birth to a son, Mack, and the following year, to another son, Floyd.

Her husband never returned. She was maybe sixteen or seventeen.

She lived in a series of migrant camps in the woods with three children. There was no way to survive, out in the wild between Murfreesboro and Nashville, where the landscape is full of mountains, hollows, creeks, forks, branches, and a vast area called the Barrens. The countryside had not recovered from the war, and the roads were full of people who had no work, no money, and no hope.

She believed there was only one human who would help her. For three years, she picked crops and wild berries, sold whatever she could, wore rags and fed the children, until she'd saved enough for train tickets to Texas. She had heard her father, Henry Ely, had gone to Denton.

Fine and the three children made it to Denton, which by 1900 was a city of five thousand people. She wandered the town, asking people about Henry Ely. No one knew anything about this man. The possibilities of what may have happened to a free man of color, whether he was Cherokee or part black, are endless. The Freedmen's Bureau accounts of murder and kidnapping, of bodies dumped in rivers and woods, are only those of people who actually reported the crimes to government officials. The skeletons of freedmen and women were everywhere.

She was overcome by everything, at the end of the first day. She and the children had not a single penny left, no food, and nowhere to sleep. She sat on a log near a piece of land just at the edge of town, crying.

A man saw them from his farmhouse porch. She was sitting on the road below his land. His name was Zack Rawlings, or Zach Rollins, or several variations of those. He was fifty years old. She was maybe twenty-two. She was a beautiful young woman in desperate circumstances. He went outside to ask her whether she and the children needed a place to stay.

She gathered up her children and followed Zack Rawlings inside. She had no idea of the violence that would ensue here—a continuation and catalyst that would change her life again.

There is a single photograph of Fine, from the 1940s. Her cheekbones are high and wide, her hair curled carefully, her eyes large and brown, her lips held closed over her teeth. As a teenager, hearing these stories at my future husband's house, in the driveway where her grandchildren were adults of immense physical presence, holding the ribs of pigs, talking about how she saved their lives, I imagined her as large and powerful. But she was slight and cautious. Watchful and intent. There was inside her a core of fury and independence and self-preservation, the genetic heritage of survival.

McMinnville to Nashville, Tennessee, to Denton, Texas: 714 miles, not counting the miles walked from the woodpile and the well to the house of the woman who beat her, or the miles walked in the forest picking blackberries and selling them in pails along the road.

3

The Dance

Ruby Triboulet,
Colorado Prairie, 1921

It's the story we all heard, you three girls all saw in movies and on television and in songs, the fantasy and marriage: *I fell in love with her the first time I laid eyes on her. The minute I saw her, there could never be another woman for me. Just one look, that's all it took. I had to have her. I made sure no one else could have her.*

Romantic. It's what we girls are given as true love—first sight, and no other suitors. When I finally heard the story of how Ruby Triboulet, my grandmother, met Robert Straight, my grandfather, I was fifty years old, the same age as she was when she died in Colorado. I had finally gone to visit my relatives in Nunn, on the prairie flatlands of northeast Colorado, near the borders of Wyoming, Kansas, and Nebraska, where the wind blows every day.

In the small front room of a tiny house, night fell with absolute darkness as if a velvet blanket had dropped from the wide sky onto the dirt lanes of Nunn. There were only three hundred people left in town, down from fifteen hundred in the 1950s.

Dale Barnaby, whose mother, Vara, was Ruby's sister, had moved this house in 1952 from the abandoned prairie town of Purcell. Dale was eighty-six years old, and his wife, Kahla, born in Nunn, was eighty-seven. Because I had come to stay with them, they'd called his brother Galen, seventy-seven, his younger sister Toots, seventy-four, and his sister-in-law Fuzz, seventy-six, to join us.

These five people hadn't seen me for thirty years. In 1982, my brother Jeff and I drove across the country, and we slept one night at this tiny house. Now they stared at me. I had asked about my grandmother Ruby. They kept glancing cautiously at one another as if to decide whether I was old enough to hear this. Their voices were rough and hesitant. They didn't even want to say my grandfather's name.

"Well, it was right over there in Purcell, I'd say, at the schoolhouse," Kahla said. "They had a dance, and four of the sisters went."

"And he had a gun," Dale said. He moved his mouth from side to side, looking at me. I was a Straight. Descendant of the man whose name no one liked to mention, even then. I felt so strange, thinking that this terrifying blood was my blood, even though my father had nothing but fear in his own bones.

"Bob Straight," Dale finally said. "He had a gun in his coat."

"Mom said he seen Ruby right away, she was so little and pretty, and she'd just gotten here from Illinois. Where they were from. The sisters," Toots said.

Dale said, "He went all around the dance floor tellin' every man not to dance with her, and he shown 'em his gun. She was just alone all night, she was real sad, and no one asked her to dance. Only him. He finally asked her and she danced with him. Then after that they got married."

My father was Ruby's youngest child. Richard Dean Straight.

Until I was eighteen, I saw him once a month. Maybe once or twice a year, he talked about his mother, Ruby, in very short cryptic tales, almost like fables. In our part of southern California, we lived very close to the heat of the desert, but also within sight of the mountain ranges whose spines ran the length of the state. I lived in Riverside, and my father lived with his new family twenty-four miles away, near Pomona, at the base of the San Bernardino Mountains. My father's young life had been so turbulent, dangerous, and unsparing that he could never pull himself away from those memories, and each strange scene he gave me was out of context, like a Picasso where I was staring at noses and elbows and then a knife. He told me he ate sheep that had been dead for days. A gray-white grizzly bear that he and his father cut into pieces. We ate Wonder Bread smeared with margarine, and he told me this bread had once been a miracle to him.

He had been raised in the coldest place in America—Fraser, Colorado, elevation 8,573 feet in the height of the Rocky Mountains. In winter, he took me to the snow here in California, and when I marveled at the crystalline shimmer and the whiskers of ice inside my nostrils, he said that in Fraser, the snow would bury their ranch cabin, and ice would coat his blanket, coat the iron rims of the bed where he slept in the barn, seal their cooking water inside the bucket.

I spent one weekend a month at his house—without fail. No matter whether I missed birthday parties or trips to Disneyland or a school event—without fail. When I was small, and one time forgot to flush the toilet, he said that he never lived in a house with inside plumbing until he was twelve, and I was five, and I had always had a toilet. If I forgot to turn off a light, he said he had never lived in a house with electricity until he was twelve, and I was seven, and had always had wall switches.

But he taught me to fish. He taught me to cook a trout at the edge of the lake. At night, he bent to check the night-light near me. A night-light in each room. He was obsessive about that. Even then, I realized how much my father, so intimidating to me, was afraid of the dark.

Ruby Triboulet was the third of six sisters, born in 1901. She was small, just five feet tall, with soft waves to her dark hair. Soft eyes. Soft wide mouth, not quite a smile. Soft cheeks. Her picture, taken when she was leaving for Colorado, at nineteen, shows no bones—no sharp shelves of cheek, no bump on her nose, no prominent forehead or collarbones. Not like her mother, Amanda, or her sisters Hazel, Vara, and Emma. They are all bones. Ruby looks apprehensive, dreamy.

The Triboulet girls—Hazel, Vara, Ruby, Emma, Genevieve, and Helen—and their only brother, Carl, were born on a farm at Bear Creek, in Hancock County, Illinois. (It's possible other babies died.) The land belonged in 1859 to their grandfather, Francois Edouard Triboulet, who had come to America from France in 1850. The farm was near the confluence of three creeks, about forty miles from the Mississippi River, which formed the border with Iowa. Their father, Francois "Frank," born in 1872, and mother, Amanda Baldon, born in 1874, were married in 1890. Francois sounds like a gentle, hapless man whose house was full of women; Amanda's face, which was always angry according to my father and in the two photographs

Francois Triboulet, Genevieve Triboulet, Amanda Baldon Triboulet,
Emma Triboulet, Carl Triboulet, Ruby Triboulet; in front, Helen Triboulet.
Hancock County, Illinois, around 1920; Ruby and Emma are going west.

I've seen, was replicated in the faces of four daughters with the pointed chins and hatchet cheeks and classic gaunt features of rural hard-life women. Only Ruby and her baby sister, Helen, had the round cheeks and constant curving smiles of their father.

The weather was often bad, the land flooded, the crops were poor, and the daughters would inherit no land.

Hazel, the eldest, paved the way for all her siblings to move west. She'd gone bravely to the prairie drylands of northeastern Colorado, where antelope outnumbered people in the big square counties. She became a schoolteacher, and wrote to her sisters about the abundant land, the farming and ranching, the prairie schoolhouses, and the climate without humidity or drenching rain. Hazel and Vara had married two cousins, Charles and Armon Barnaby, and they all went out in 1915 in a Model A Ford to Nunn, Colorado, a tiny town on the railroad where people raised dryland crops, depending on rain. White wheat and sugar beets. Beef cattle and dairy cows.

Vara's husband, Armon Barnaby, was a big rough dark-haired man. They didn't live in town, but on a series of windblown ranches where Vara had ten children. Places with no water or electricity, with snow drifted inside the attics where the children slept, with deer shot in fall up on the Poudre River, and antelope shot for dinner any day on a bad week. But Armon Barnaby said that in the dry sweet air and constant wind, he could breathe for the first time in his life.

After a time, the sisters sent for Ruby, Emma, and Genevieve. (Only Helen, who was seven, stayed in Illinois.) Now there were five young women out on the prairie, loading up in the Model A Ford and heading up the Poudre Canyon to the Rockies, driving backward because those old gas tanks would empty out the other way. Picnics and fishing. Church on Sundays—they had all joined the Foursquare Gospel Church of

Aimee Semple McPherson, and became Sunday school teachers. In each tiny prairie town, the first ranchers to fence land would construct a small church, a white spire to break the endless horizon of green grass and big sky.

The sisters were five young women with heart, with what used to be called *verve* and *grit* and *spunk*. Those midwestern and prairie words that came from odd places themselves. They loved their few dresses, their hats, their tablecloths, and singing. They were romantic and sentimental. They always had one another.

Ruby lived with Hazel when she first arrived in Colorado. Then she went to the dance at the schoolhouse in Purcell.

I have a map of America here at my desk, and for years I've traced with pencil the long journeys of our ancestral women. Fine was born outside Murfreesboro, Tennessee, during the same three-year period that Alice Amanda Baldon, Ruby's mother, was born at Bear Creek, Hancock County, Illinois. They were five hundred miles apart—but their states were south and north, their skin black and white, their lives defined by immigration and enslavement. Then there were the men.

What changed women's lives was not just a man, but having a baby with that man. Who married a girl, who slept with a girl, who hunted a girl and took her, who accidentally met a girl, who was told to marry a girl for her land, for her car, who was told not to marry a girl.

Fine met Robert Hofford in the blackberry thickets.

Ruby Triboulet danced with Robert Straight because no one else asked her.

Robert Straight was the man he was that night, in Purcell, because his own father had just stolen his girlfriend and married her.

———

My grandfather, Robert Bates Straight, was the tenth generation of Straight men to be born in a territory farther west than the previous one—from pre-Revolution Massachusetts to Weld County, Colorado. My own father, Richard, said he knew none of this. None. He had hated his father, and knew little about his father's father. What scraps he finally told me were in the last five years of his life, the memories often unmoored by painkillers or anesthetic, so that while I was in a hospital room with him, or driving him around the landscape of his teenaged years here in southern California, or talking to him late at night on the phone, all the scary pieces of his youth came flying at me in random fashion, like T-shirts shot out of a cannon; I'd catch them at high speed and later smooth out the material and read what was written on the chest.

Those fragments were always about his desperation and fear, of being unwanted, of being beaten, freezing, and abandoned.

I spent two years finding the previous ten generations on Ancestry, and when I finally wrote down all the names in order, in blue pen on a yellow legal pad, and told my father I'd bring them to him when we ate breakfast, he didn't want to see the pages. They are right here. He never knew any of the names that came before Daniel Casca Straight, the father of his father, a man he remembered as being very intelligent, manipulative, having a steel plate in his skull from combat in World War I. My great-grandfather, my grandfather, and my father had engineering and mechanical skills that should have led them to great success. But those three generations of Straight men had tempers and no capacity to take orders from anyone, so they worked for themselves, and then quit themselves in disgust, to start a new enterprise.

My great-grandfather Daniel Casca "DC" Straight, born

in 1876 in St. Croix, Wisconsin, was brought to Clay County, Nebraska, in 1880 and raised on a ranch. At twenty-two, he married Laura Bates, who was eighteen. Their oldest son, my grandfather, was born that same year, in 1902, in Loveland. Laura had ten children who lived, and at least two who died, in sixteen years. On November 1, 1918, when the youngest baby was only a year old, Laura died.

By 1921, when Robert was nineteen, he had a girlfriend named Ethel Dickerson. But in June of that year, DC Straight, who was forty-three, married Ethel, who had just turned twenty.

They had two children. Robert left the mountains of Loveland and went to work on the ranches down in the prairie, in Ault and Eaton and Greeley. One night, he went to the dance at Purcell.

The schoolhouse doubled as social hall, meeting room, and community center for those scattered prairie communities, so the Triboulet girls knew everyone. The building was crowded with young men and women, some already married, some not. The young men were ranch hands who rode the prairies rounding up heifers, or milked cows daily in freezing barns, or plowed miles of earth for wheat seed, or harvested sugar beets and transported them to train cars. The sons of Vara Barnaby spent their lives on threshing machines, cutting down wheat.

Ruby stood against the wall and waited. She wore her best dress. Though the young men all danced with other girls, they averted their faces and didn't even look her way. She was nineteen.

If you dance with her, I'll wait until you get outside and I'll kill you.

Song after song. Did he watch her face? The hopefulness and lifted chin, the glimmer in her eyes when the music began and boys came to girls with one hand outstretched, the other holding a hat. Do you want to dance? Song after song, and she was invisible. Did her face grow softer and crumble, or did she lift her chin higher? How did this man, who was only twenty, know what he wanted? Did he want to crush her from the moment he saw her face, and then judge how her face changed? Was that the way he'd observed his own father, or other men? Had Ethel's face changed when she saw his own father, or had his father made her face change with a threat or compliment? Was this way of hunting a woman, of choosing a wife, embedded in his genes?

Whether he'd decided on a particular song to end her torture (every one of us knows how it feels to be left alone on a wall, or a bench, or a folding chair, while music plays) or judged this exactly to the amount of desperation and longing and hurt on her face, he finally stood in front of Ruby Triboulet. Not a year later, in April 1922, they signed a marriage license at the courthouse in Greeley, Colorado.

The first thing he did was take her away from her sisters and the wide-open prairie where everyone knew one another in that grid of county roads, could see every truck and horse and wagon that passed and even the dust that moved along with them, every ranch or farm known by the number, and if you didn't know the horse or vehicle, you could find out at the schoolhouse or the church picnic.

They went to the Rocky Mountains, where Robert Straight had been born. Not the romantic ideal of the mountains, of ranching and the west, of cowboys and the frigid beauty of one of the loveliest places in America. Robert Straight's life had always been high-altitude isolation, snow and ranch, horses and sheep and grizzly bears, hard work and violence, and always, a gun. No one, not wife or children, would ever change that.

Ruby and her four children never changed that. By the time my father, Richard, was born, things were so bad that Ruby kept leaving, taking her youngest son to California. But each time, she went back to Colorado.

My father only ever got the leaving part down. When he left someone, he never went back.

Bear Creek, Hancock County, Illinois, to Nunn and Fraser, Colorado: 936 miles, not counting the times she went up and down the steep narrow highways of the Rockies to the prairie, to the leased ranches where Ruby had her babies, closer to her sisters.

4

The Country Squire

When I was twelve, my mother was at the wheel when our 1966 Ford station wagon, the Country Squire, ran over me. This was at Yogi Bear Campground in the San Bernardino Mountains, and I lay on Boo Boo Lane. I couldn't make that up.

The ultimate car of motherhood, used to ferry all her children—the three she bore, the five foster children she cared for over eight years—all of us used to lie on our bellies in the taupe metal storage area playing cards and sharing one box of Crackerjack. I remember the oily darkness of the undercarriage when the wheels thumped over me, and the smell of the asphalt under my cheek. My poor mother, seeing me crumpled there. She hadn't wanted to take me down the mountain to cheer camp. She never wanted me to shake pompons, because then I'd act dumb even though I wasn't, and I'd probably get pregnant.

When she was fifteen, her stepmother had tried to marry her off to a pig farmer in Canada. The worst fate my mother could imagine was being pregnant.

For my mother, cheerleaders and pompon girls were the kind who cared about beauty, and beautiful girls caused trouble.

At twelve, I had nothing going for me other than my national prize from *Reader's Digest* for speed-reading, and a four-year record of perfect spelling tests. In my neighborhood, those were liabilities. It was the time of Farrah Fawcett and Pam Grier—big hair and boobs mattered in junior high, and it looked like I'd never have either. My chest was flat, and the summer of 1973, my hair was a disturbing shimmery green.

I was a girl who already imagined entire novels in which bodies were discovered in idyllic locations, moss-covered waterfalls and pine glens where the tree trunks glistened with golden sap. A girl detective had to figure out that a killer was always watching, and find out how the victim died, while keeping herself hidden from the killer. On hot nights, I lay with my face close to the screen of my bedroom window hearing teenaged boys walk past with stolen beer, hijacked construction materials, and money from marijuana deals. I figured neither Nancy Drew nor Agatha Christie had been offered weed in sixth grade.

Clearly, my reading was now dominated by the murder mysteries in my two sole sources for books: the bookmobile, and my parents' single bookcase, which held only the 1970 *Encyclopedia Britannica* collection, meaning I knew thousands of random facts about arachnids, Constantinople, and zoology, and the Reader's Digest Condensed Novels, meaning every month I read a new crime novel.

I had no idea how to look acceptable. We five kids grew up in matching T-shirts my enterprising mother sewed from double-knit fabric she got on sale from TG&Y. Boy-style crew-neck

T-shirts—only one pattern. The fabric was horizontally striped or in sad small patterns of chevron or stick figures. We each got a single pair of Toughskins jeans per year, from Sears. When we were small, she actually put small Tupperware bowls—milky green or white plastic—on our heads to cut the hair of my foster sisters and me. In spring, the boys were shorn with clippers.

All young boys were shorn in spring this way in my neighborhood, no matter their race or age. Boys needed only skulls, as far as I could see. But other girls had braids and ribbons and curls and barrettes. By sixth grade, some girls had eye shadow.

Not me. My mother hated the entire concept of natural beauty conferring upon a woman more value than her hard work, or of mild attractiveness enhanced in not-natural ways. My mother hated makeup and nail polish.

Three boys in the tub, and then two girls. We washed our hair under the faucet, neck bent awkwardly so it always felt like I was offering myself up for sacrifice as the water hit my forehead. A showerhead didn't occur to her. My mother had a lot to do, feeding us, keeping us alive, and trying to attend classes at the city college. She'd never been able to graduate from high school in Canada.

Our neighborhood, a tract of houses between orange groves and boulder-strewn foothills, was full of people from somewhere else. Most of our neighbors were military men stationed at the nearby Air Force base, and many had foreign-born wives. The moms in my neighborhood were from Japan, the Philippines, England, Germany, and nearly every state in America. My close friend since kindergarten was Delana (not her real name). We both got glasses in fifth grade, and were teased mercilessly. But aside from her glasses, Delana was beautiful. Her Filipina mother bequeathed her tawny gold skin and thick wavy black hair, and her American military father his large amber eyes and perfect teeth.

I was elfin and useless to boys with my flat chest, terrible hand-crocheted vests, and tragic attempts to tie a thrift-store silk scarf around my throat like models I saw in my stepsisters' *Seventeen* magazine. I wouldn't let my mother cut my hair now, and it grew past my shoulders, so I braided it in a crown around my head, the way Anne Shirley did in *Anne of Green Gables*. I looked like a tiny French grandmother. The new glasses made things worse. At least Delana got tortoiseshell rectangles. I got blue-framed cat-eye glasses, which are very much in fashion now—definitely not back then.

I was the size of a Chihuahua compared to other girls. For three months of summer, my hair was alien green from swimming in the heavily chlorinated city pool. My black and Chicana classmates thought this comic and mildly frightening, and referred to me as a Martian. I had the cat-eye glasses, miserable teeth—a gap between my front teeth, one of which was already chipped from constant roughhousing with my siblings, and one fang perched visibly way up in my gum line. My legs were so thin they resembled peeled mulberry branches.

Just before summer, Delana took off her glasses, in class, and put them away. She never wore them again. I was stunned, not by her lack of camaraderie. "How can you see the blackboard?" I whispered, and she replied, "I don't care what the blackboard says. It doesn't matter. We're going to junior high."

It didn't matter what was on the blackboard. It mattered that we become cheerleaders, to get boyfriends and survive junior high.

The first weeks of summer, we walked through the orange groves and over the canal to the newly built junior high, where the eighth-grade girls studied us with disdain and impatience, sternly demonstrating the complicated tryout routines.

"Cheerleaders are brainless fools, jumping up and down like idiots," my mother said, when she saw my arms moving robotically in the backyard. "It's not a sport. It's a beauty contest and I don't want you doing it."

I had spent years going to my brothers' Little League baseball games, but though we girls played ball in the park, and I could hit, girls couldn't play baseball, or Pop Warner football, or any other organized sport, in 1973. I was allowed to work the snack bar, where I'd been maneuvered under the bleachers and pushed into the dark supply room and felt up by older boys. That wasn't a sport I wanted to continue.

I made the pompon squad only because the older girls needed a Chihuahua-size mascot who could climb to the top of the pyramid and stand with little feet on the shoulders or thighs of other girls. I was told to put away my glasses, do something with my hair, and get measured for a uniform.

I went to the house of Mrs. Yoshiko Smith, from Japan, who would sew uniforms for the pompon squad. My mother didn't like the cost of cheerleading. She made odd pronouncements about the older girls: *Pretty but brainless. Spoiled rotten and won't ever work. She'll have a baby in a few years and she'll never go anywhere.*

We were twelve and thirteen. How could she deduce these things by simply observing my friends? She never talked to them. Our class president wore velvet hot pants, thigh-high boots, and her long hair was ironed straight. Other girls wore hip-hugger jeans and baby-doll shirts, their hair curled back and sprayed into permanence as if they were facing forward from a ship's prow, flying in the breeze.

During one visit to my father, I'd seen my stepsisters actually ironing their hair, on an ironing board, their cheeks pressed to the fabric while the iron's point traveled near their ears. I held my breath. At home, I starched bathroom curtains and delicately moved the iron's point into the ruffles.

And rather than going to Disneyland, where the eighth-grade

cheerleaders had organized a group outing, we packed our small travel trailer, pulled by the old station wagon. We went every year to Yogi Bear Campground because my mother loved the mountains. My brothers loved Yogi Bear and Boo-Boo. We were the apex of uncool.

I never thought about how much my mother missed the mountains of her childhood, which she lost as quickly and silently as a coffin lid closed over the face of her own beloved mother.

My mother, Gabrielle Gertrude Leu, grew up in Burgistein, Switzerland, a tiny village in the Swiss Alps, on the slopes of steep mountains in a narrow valley. Their chalet was named Sunnenschyn—Swiss houses always had names carved into the balconies. That house was Sunshine.

When my mother was six, my grandfather Paul Leu tried running a sauerkraut factory. The valley grew cabbage well, and the shredded cabbage was salted and placed in large wooden vats with boulders holding down the wooden lids; my mother remembers the vivid overwhelming smell of that failure, and the constant work of pressing moisture out of the cabbage and fermenting the leaves. He and his wife, Frieda, then had two small sons, and my mother spent her time working in the garden, darning socks, and skiing to school.

She was tiny, my mother, and excelled at theft. She told us about walking home from school, stealing cherries and pears from trees in the farms along the road. She stole Tobler chocolate from the small store her mother ran on the house's first floor. My mother hid the bars in the precisely stacked woodpile all Swiss men keep beside the house. She sold the chocolate to American soldiers who came through the village in Jeeps during World War II.

Frieda, her mother, was always smiling, a gentle, dark-haired

Gabrielle Gertrude Leu near Wohlhusen, Switzerland,
wearing her apron, 1939

compact woman who loved to draw and paint. When my mother was nine, Frieda Leu grew ill with ovarian cancer. There was no cure—she was sent home from the hospital. "She was bedridden," my mother told me, and I imagined that terrible word—a disease rode my grandmother's body while she lay helpless in the sheets. The illness lasted for months, and a stern young nurse named Rosa Erb was hired—essentially to ease Frieda into death, and to take care of the three children. When Frieda died, my mother crept down the stairs to see her mother's body lying on the kitchen table. Frieda was thirty-nine years old, and my mother was nine.

She told me about these years only in fragmented shards until she turned eighty, when these memories began to spill out. Now, every week, she remains incensed by this loss, and retells me the story.

Shortly after Frieda's burial, Rosa Erb, twenty-eight, was married to Paul Leu. No man took care of his own children back in 1943 in Switzerland. My mother says her stepmother treated her as a small plain burden useful only for hard work, until she could be rid of her. The way my mother described her life in the Swiss forests and snowy mountains, her stepmother might as well have been roaming the woods looking for a huntsman to take my mother's heart.

I have one photo of my parents shortly after their marriage, taken in Las Vegas—it is a postcard taken by the casino that my father addressed to himself, at their tiny house behind a real house. My mother looks as she does in every picture, stoic, sturdy, and suspicious. Her hair is short and brown. No-nonsense. One wave of curl near her forehead. She wears sensible clothing. Her lips hold half a smile.

I didn't realize that was because she had already lost all her top teeth, due to the poor hygiene common to 1940s Europe, and a California dentist who told her he would just pull them

Christophe Leu, Rosa Erb Leu, Paul Leu, Gabrielle Leu,
Thun, Switzerland, 1944

Gabrielle and Richard Straight, Las Vegas, Nevada, 1956

all and give her a denture. She was only twenty. Who does that? She was an immigrant, her English wasn't great, and he probably wanted the money. When I was little, her teeth—pink and white and floating in a glass by her bed—were terrifying. But it wasn't until I was grown that I thought about the sadness of that plastic.

Richard Straight left her for a lovely woman named Ruth Catherine—my stepmother, my father's third wife, told me many times she'd been an Ivory Soap model in Texas, where she was born. She was seven years older than my father. Taller than my mother, with black hair, green eyes like alexandrite, red lipstick, "a full bosom," as she liked to say, and carefully gracious mannerisms. I know she had been born on a hard-luck ranch in rural Texas, and that a tornado had tossed her into a tree trunk when she was a child; her left arm still held scarring at the elbow, and she always wore long sleeves, even in summer, which made her seem ever more exotic and polished to me. She put mandarin oranges and almonds in green salad. I had never eaten a mandarin orange in my life.

She loved jewelry and clothes and makeup and nail polish and shoes; my mother was four feet eleven, had trouble finding women's shoes that fit, didn't get her ears pierced until she was sixty-two, and gave me her wedding ring when I was a teenager, saying she hated rings, along with weddings.

My stepmother worked as a receptionist in a dentist's office, in a sad irony for my mother; when my father went in for a filling, Ruth Catherine told him she studied astrology and she had seen their love in the arrangement of the stars. She was divorced, and lived in Pomona. He fell in love instantly, and loved her passionately and obsessively until she died in 2004. He kept her ashes on his dresser until he died in 2018.

I have no idea whether my mother had ever seen this woman, but she hated the accoutrements, accessories, and aspirations of beauty more than anything else in the world. On my weekend visits, my stepmother and stepsisters had painted my nails. Now I was carrying bedraggled blue-and-white pompons everywhere.

On the third day of camping, the day of the Disneyland trip, I mutinied. My mother didn't want to drive me the hour down the mountain highway, but I argued long and hard. At dawn, there was heavy cold fog all around the campground, and my mother, with a mix of anger and resignation, started up the old battered Country Squire. My youngest brother got into the front seat to keep her company on the way back. Poker-faced, hating my old clothes, I got into the back seat and opened my book.

I can't remember what I was reading. A library book. I was so engrossed that I didn't notice the engine stalling repeatedly in the cold. My mother finally backed out onto the steep downhill campground road. The station wagon died again, rolling backward, gaining speed. (That model of Country Squire weighed 4,300 pounds, and was the last model without a system to circumvent brake failure.) My mother says she tried to pump the brakes, then yanked on the emergency brake, which stripped immediately. In the rearview mirror, she saw a deep ravine at the end of the road. She shouted for us to jump, but I was reading. My little brother, who was eight, opened his front door and threw himself out. My mother yelled at me again, and then she jumped out the driver's door, accidentally wrenching the steering wheel.

I felt a swerve. I pushed down with my elbow on the handle of the back right door, and the car swung sharply, throwing me out. Then the station wagon curved gracefully, front wheel thumping over my crossed legs, and the long car backed itself

gently into another slot in the campground and died on Boo
Boo Lane.

The femur is the largest bone in the body. I didn't learn that
until my left femur was snapped in two. I remember the pain
shaking my body as if a dog held me in its jaws. I remember the
smell of the asphalt. I remember being put into the ambulance
and blacking out a few times on the hour-long ride down the
twisting road to the Riverside hospital where I'd been born.
They didn't give children painkilling medication back then.
Not for the whole ride. Not in the emergency room where I
spent the night on a gurney alone, while a shadowy night nurse
hissed at me to stop crying so loudly because I was waking up
the baby in the crib nearby, a middle-aged woman in her terrifying winged cap telling me in a German accent to be quiet
and stop moving around and my broken bones would stop rub-
bing against each other, or she would give me something to cry
about. She sounded exactly like my grandmother, Rosa Leu,
Nurse-in-Charge, who always frightened me. I blacked out
again.

Traction in 1973 was pretty primitive. I lay on my back in a
bed, my left leg strapped into a device with weights at the end
of my foot to hold the pieces of bone perfectly still while they
knitted themselves back together. This was for seven weeks.

I learned all the Latin names for bones from the orthopedic
surgeon. My femur was snapped in half between the hip joint
and the patella; the tibia and fibula and phalanges remained
intact, though covered with blood. The weights were attached
to tape stretching along the sides of my lower leg, tape changed
frequently when it pulled off my skin and slid down toward my

feet. I had bloody stripes along my lower leg. I could move only my head and arms. I had a bedpan. I was not a child, but not an adult. I was supposed to be learning how to be a teenage girl. My various roommates were grown people who arrived and disappeared in the day and the night, whose ailments and surgeries entailed their moaning and crying and shouting. Sometimes I believed they died in the night, when a nurse pulled the curtain around their screams.

I was terrified. My mother was terrified of hospitals, too, maybe because of her own mother's death. For the first few days, she came at visiting hours, but she had my three brothers and one sister at home, and children were not allowed to visit the orthopedic wing.

Then it got worse. My father wanted to visit. My mother and father could not be in the room together. My father insisted on renting a small television to hang near my right side. My mother was furious. She hated television. She listened to the Dodgers on the radio while knitting.

The second week, my stepmother brought me a makeup kit, on a Saturday. She knew my love for the thirty shades of beauty in tiny compartments—glittery gold and purple and green and blue, cream blushes in bronze and mauve.

My long hair was filthy. That evening, Miss Ledesma, the young Chicana LVN who checked on me every night, saw me with the kit. Her makeup and hair were always perfect. She brought a plastic basin and gently lowered my head into warm water, while I stared up at the ceiling. She lathered my head, her fingernails long and careful on my scalp, and I closed my eyes. No one had been that tender to me in many years. She rinsed out my hair, and combed it through, and blow-dried it. Then she helped me put on eye shadow, blush, and pink lip gloss.

My thin face, the dark circles of pain under my eyes, the

scaly grime gathered in rings around my throat: in the hand mirror Miss Ledesma brought me, I was hideous.

On Sunday my mother walked in with yarn. Since I was laid up, she thought I should crochet granny squares for a blanket or new vest. She must have seen the sparkly powders on my face like a violent sunset. She handed me a hot washcloth and told me to scrub off that junk because it made me look like a hooker.

That week, my mother brought to my room the woman who cut her hair short every month. Too much trouble to take care of waist-length hair in the hospital. Her friend sheared my hair to my ears. Now I was a hideous elf. Without any sun or fresh air, my hair darkened to ash, and my skin looked like wax.

I was a completely different human.

When school began, a tutor was sent to my hospital room. I read all day, but there were not enough books. The skin on my left shin and calf was disappearing, long bleeding stripes turned to scabs and then reopened. My muscles were withered by disuse, and the bones reknitted themselves with a ball of calcium that stuck out as if a doorknob had been inserted into my upper thigh.

It was September. I watched hours of televised college football, hating the cheerleaders so much that I paid attention to the games. Football was complex and inventive, the formations intricate, and I was never bored by the passing routes, the offensive line blocking. When people asked what I wanted to be, as a girl of that time, I was given two choices: teacher or nurse. By now, I didn't want to be a nurse, a woman who yelled if I didn't eat the gooseberries in my fruit cocktail. Who the hell wanted to eat gooseberries? Why would you name them that? They looked like veined green eyeballs.

I decided to be a sportswriter. In my notebook, I wrote articles for each game, the plays and yardage, star quarterbacks and leaping catches and even the way the light hit the field.

I returned to junior high in November, wearing a body cast. It wrapped around my waist and contained my entire left leg, except my filthy toes. For weeks I'd had a bedpan; now I had to slant my body on the toilet and use a cup. My siblings found this hilarious.

I had crutches. No one remembered me. Everyone stared. Guys whispered to girls about sex, but the only thing guys asked me was how I went to the bathroom. I did not mention the cup. Not sexy.

My friends had swelling curves, tight jeans with two-inch zippers, and platform shoes. I had baggy pants that could stretch over plaster, sarcastic signatures near my knee, and really strong arms.

After two more months, the cast was sawn off. I stood in the hospital parking lot on my crutches, crying. My left leg was so thin and helpless that when the winter wind blew, my foot swung of its own volition. My calf was scarred deeply from the traction tape, with stripes of brown as if someone had spilled hot chocolate down my shins. It took weeks of physical therapy until I could walk again.

My grandmother Rosa paid a professional visit to inspect my leg. She said with detachment, "He did a good job, that orthopedic. He could have put screws. I thought her leg would be two inches shorter than the other. I thought you would have to pay for the special shoes—the ones that would make her normal." Then she turned away.

Since she felt no love for us, I tried to study Rosa with my own literary detachment. She was a combination of Great-Aunt

March in *Little Women* and the grandfather in *Heidi*. I knew by then my mother was like Francie's mother in *A Tree Grows in Brooklyn* combined with the mothers of Toni Morrison's novels *The Bluest Eye* and *Sula*. I didn't fully understand those women, but their soliloquies about illness and laundry and hardship were monologues I heard while I ironed or sorted my brothers' jeans with dried mud like small hubcaps at the knees.

There is a watercolor painting here in my house: a still life of wine bottle and gathered fruit. My mother kept it in a folder that we children only glimpsed a few times. When I was an adult, and she moved, I rescued the painting from the trash. She said to me, "I took a painting class at the YWCA. Then I found a book—teach yourself to paint. My mother was an artist. She made beautiful sketches of our garden and our house in Switzerland." She studied her watercolor, and said dispassionately, "Just after I finished this, I had you, and then I never painted anything again. My life was over."

Also in the trash, I found the teach-yourself-to-paint book, with her last, half-finished still life of fruit and flowers. I have it here in my office.

I cannot draw anything. But I loved paintings, sketches, and photography. Maybe I got that from my mother's mother, Frieda. Because I inherited nothing from Rosa, the only grandmother I ever knew.

5

Nurse-in-Charge

Rosa Leu, Aeschlen,
Switzerland, 1944

In the tiny village of Würzbrunnen, in the central mountainous German-speaking part of Switzerland that is called the Berner Oberland, which looks like a tourist brochure come to life—the brown cows with huge bells ringing as they walk and flower garlands around their creamy necks, the grass full of wildflowers and the wooden houses perched on the steep slopes—there is a very small church famous in Switzerland.

The Wolf Church, it is called by our Erb relatives, the family of Rosa Erb Leu. The Erbs have been in this part of Switzerland since the 1600s, in the village of Aeschlen and surrounding area. This church is beautifully simple, pale wooden interior carved with flowers and garlands and biblical verses, no flourishes or gold. It is Anabaptist, the precursor to the Mennonites, plain and devout. But in the base of the stone walls, plastered over with white, are interred the bodies of four women.

Their names are inscribed on the exterior foundation. They were four mothers who all died within the space of a year, just after giving birth, their bodies wracked by fever and infection spread by a traveling doctor who never washed his hands or sterilized his equipment, back in the early 1800s. They would have been better off with a midwife. The babies had to be raised by others.

Rosa Erb was a distant descendant of one of those women. Her relatives told us this place was called the Wolf Church because the last wolf in Switzerland was killed near here. There are no large wild predators in Switzerland now—no wolves or bears, because they were all hunted a century ago. Cows and goats and sheep were always how farmers survived in the mountains. The Erb family has the most successful chicken hatchery in the area.

I remember standing in this place, the dark forest all around us, the vision of wolves and dying mothers and babies bundled in cloth and given to someone else. It felt like I had stepped inside the Grimm's fairy tales that my mother read to us with commentary, unlike most other mothers. She had lived in the forest. She had walked with a wooden basket. She had a little apron. She had a stepmother who wished she would disappear.

My mother has returned to Switzerland only briefly, three times since she left in 1950. The first time, my stepfather sold his laundry business and took all of us to the place where she was born, which she hadn't seen for twenty-eight years. We tried to find her mother's grave in Wattenwil, in a tiny cemetery. We walked the rows again and again, as her face crumpled. No stone with the name Frieda Leu. On the narrow lane through the village, an older woman told my mother that after a few decades, another person is buried on top. "There is no room," the woman said, holding a wooden basket filled with cheese.

A week later, we went to the Wolf Church with Marie Erb, who married Rosa's brother Fritz and had six sons. The Erbs had become our Swiss family, though Rosa Erb Leu never went back home.

Rosa was born in August 1916 in Oberdiessbach, the ninth of ten children. Her mother died when Rosa was three. Her step-mother, whom the children had to call Mrs. Erb, hated the girls. Too many daughters in that family, and three of the girls were sent off to marry widowers with children. Men who needed a woman to clean and cook and run a house. Rosa had dealt with blood, injury, and disease for her entire life. She never had a chance at love, and in all my years, I never saw my grand-mother smile, touch anyone with joy, or behave in any way as if happiness and pleasure were not terrible ideas, and extremely unhealthy.

Rosa's first job, when she was sixteen, was to train as a nurse in an insane asylum in another valley, about fifty miles from her home. I found this out only when I was an adult, and she was nearly blind. I went to visit her, at her mobile home in Hemet, California, twenty miles from here, a mobile home whose décor had never changed in the thirty years she'd lived in it. I stood close to my favorite painting, the first piece of art I had truly studied, when I was very small. This was the world my mother had left: a scene by the Swiss artist Anker, a woman leading a parade of children down a rural lane with the Alps in the distance. But this afternoon, when I spoke to her about the picture, my grandmother stood beside me and pointed to a building tucked into a fold of the mountain behind the road. "I worked there. That is the krankenhaus for the people ill in their brain," she said. As she got older, half her words went back to Swiss German. "It was a terrible place. That was mein arbeit when I was sixteen. With those terrible people. I was always a nurse."

Then she said, "You can go see if there are tomatoes." For Christmas, she gave us flannel pajamas. We did not live in the snow. We lived in a place where Christmas Day sometimes reached 85 degrees, but she didn't want us to catch cold.

As a child, I loved the homes of parents from other places. Our neighbors were from Japanese cities, and they had rice-paper screens and kimonos; from the rural Philippines, with lemongrass in the garden and the smell of adobo cooking; pueblos in Mexico from which parents brought plaster statues of the Virgen of Guadalupe, veladora candles lit on altars, and pan dulce left as ofrendas for the dead; rural Louisiana, where huge electric cookers would be full of gumbo and the fathers spoke Creole French; Mississippi, where fried chicken and greens were on the stove and blues by Muddy Waters and Howlin' Wolf were on the stereo.

No one knew where Switzerland was, and no one had a mother and grandmother from the land of Heidi, featuring florally accessorized cows, cheese with holes that seemed to emanate stink, and a weird wooden clock.

In the only photo I had ever seen of my real grandmother, Frieda Steiger Leu was wearing the Swiss costume of her canton, smiling widely, leading a parade of schoolchildren down a rural road. Exactly like the famous painting. My mother showed us the photo maybe three times during our entire childhood. Not until I was fifty, and asked a friend to make a digital copy, did my mother point to one child and say casually, "That's me." She is holding her mother's hand.

My grandfather hated mountains. What kind of Swiss man hates the Alps? The Matterhorn in a valley not far away. Chalets, waterfalls, the pristine blue lakes. Paul Leu felt claustrophobic in the deep narrow clefts between the famous mountains.

Frieda Steiger Leu, Burgistein, Switzerland, around 1936

He was tired of working as a train conductor. The war had made survival hard. He wanted adventure. He bought maps and planned to take the family to Venezuela, then the Belgian Congo, then New Zealand, but none of those worked out.

He and Rosa had one daughter now, Christine—blond, blue-eyed, fragile and fairylike. In 1950, he and Rosa and the four children took a train through France, crossed the channel to England, and took a ship to Canada. In Oshawa, thirty miles from Toronto, there were farm jobs.

The Leus were given an ancient wooden house, more like a barn, split in half between their Swiss family and a Czechoslovakian family who were war refugees. My mother worked with her father and stepmother hoeing, weeding, picking corn and strawberries. The younger children went to school.

Did Rosa tell my mother she was unattractive? Not destined for love? Not deserving of love? Not living in circumstances that allowed for love?

My mother only says that shortly thereafter, Rosa told her to marry a neighboring pig farmer. The man came to inspect her. My mother refused. Then she ran away. She told me for the first time, two years ago, "Those people were idiots! My father couldn't even handle a housepainting job. He was too short! He was forty-five years old! They said they were going to America. They were going to buy a trailer and go to Florida. So I packed my suitcase and left. I wasn't going to live in a trailer."

She had been babysitting in Oshawa for a family with three children. "They had a brick house," she told me. (My mother has always loved the finer distinctions of real estate.) "They said I could live there. I babysat the children, I went to school." She had one and a half years of high school, but quit to work as a night waitress in a hotel coffeeshop, where men came in on break from the General Motors auto plant. Men from Poland and Hungary who had been doctors and architects in a former life. Even more, my mother wanted to make enough money to escape poverty.

That year, my grandfather took Rosa, his sons Christophe and Markus and daughter Christine, across the border to Detroit. He bought a Pontiac and a travel trailer. The family headed to Winter Haven, Florida, where he thought he had another great job, but it turned out to be more crop work. Florida was a place of sandy roads, shacks, hard labor, humidity, and spiders the size of pancakes, according to Rosa. After seven months, she'd had enough. She'd seen postcards from southern California, the images famous for drawing immigrants to the Golden State—orange trees loaded with fruit in the shadow of purple mountains capped with snow. Fontana, California. But more important, someone had told her about Kaiser Steel, which was hiring nurses.

They drove across America to Fontana, parked the trailer in a court among other trailers, and Rosa was immediately hired as a nurse. This was 1952, when Kaiser Steel was a huge manufacturing plant, employing thousands of men, many from Kentucky. My uncles remember getting beaten up by Kentucky boys for their German-sounding Swiss accents.

My grandmother was so stern, unflappable, and orderly that she received in short time her plaque, which read:

Rosa Leu, R.N.
Nurse-in-Charge

My mother received a letter from her family, and decided to come to America when she was twenty. She arrived in Fontana to find her family still living in the travel trailer, using a common bathroom in a cement shed. She lasted three months there. She rented a single room in a boardinghouse on Seventh Street in Riverside, and got a job at Household Finance. She was a teller, Swiss-efficient, and soon she basically ran the branch. She wrote a letter to the corporate headquarters of Household Finance stating these facts, alluding to her boss's shortcomings, and received a letter back that said, *It will be a cold day in hell before we let a woman be manager.* This story she told me many times, as evidence that I would have to work twice as hard for half as much.

She lived on the second floor of the boardinghouse, was so poor she ate a banana for lunch, and tried to keep her small transistor radio from being stolen, which it often was. At night she listened to the Dodgers. Vin Scully's melodious, resonant voice, his vivid enunciation, was how she learned perfect English. (This is true of thousands of immigrants in southern California. When Scully retired last year, at eighty-eight, many told this story on televised tributes, people from all over the world. My mother cried.)

Scully's voice was magic. My mother has no accent. No one ever assumes she was not born here in California.

When my grandmother died, at ninety-six, she had left instructions to display her starched nurse's cap and the beloved wooden plaque. Nurse-in-Charge. She always said, "We had only a little cement building at Kaiser back then, and they brought those men to me with broken legs and arms or they were bleeding. I took care of them all." Kaiser Permanente Healthcare became America's first HMO, with millions of enrollees now across the nation. Rosa Leu was the oldest living member, and one night, I sat beside her hospital bed as she gave curt instructions to Filipina- and Jamaican- and Mexican-born nurses who marveled at her stories of the early days. I looked at the faces of all these women—traveled from elsewhere, just like Rosa, their constant ministrations to the bodies in the beds, their eyes narrowed in assessment of IVs and needles. The nurses applied lotion to my grandmother's hands, so crippled by arthritis and hard work that her fingers slanted away from her thumbs like bent wings.

Aeschlen to Thun, Switzerland, to Calais, France, by train; to Dover, England, by ferry; to Montreal, Quebec, by ship; to Toronto by train; to Oshawa, Ontario, to Detroit, Michigan, to Winter Haven, Florida, to Fontana, California: 7,942 miles.

6

Hey Now

Riverside, California,
March 1974

When I could walk well again, it was spring. On rainy days, we ate lunch in the gym, sitting in the bleachers with our sack lunches or cafeteria trays. Someone would pull out the record player—yes, an actual record player, with an album spinning, hooked up to speakers—and music blasted onto the hardwood floor between the basketball hoops. The boys got first choice— they played James Brown, Kool & the Gang's "Jungle Boogie," and "Funky Worm" by the Ohio Players. They locked, the precursor to wild-style hip-hop dancing. They did the Robot, the Worm, handstands and backflips.

But the girls took over and changed the record to the Jackson 5, the Stylistics, and the Spinners. Some of my friends from the pompon squad held out their hands to me. They taught me to dance.

There was a new girl, from Chicago, Michelle Nicholson,

with afro puffs and a big smile, and she took over the squad—said she would give us some Chicago style. After all these years, I still find myself walking down the street softly chanting the first cheer Michelle taught us, which we performed with verses I can't believe any teacher or coach heard us singing on the sidelines of the football games, in 1974. Call and response—Michelle shouted and we sang back.

> *I like peaches (Hey Now)*
> *And I like cream (Hey Now)*
> *And I like the Lobos (Hey Now)*
> *'Cause they so mean! (Hey Now)*

> *I went to the railroad (Hey Now)*
> *Put my head on the track (Hey Now)*
> *Started thinkin' 'bout the Lobos (Hey Now)*
> *Took my big head back! (Hey Now)*

> *I went to the liquor store (Hey Now)*
> *Just to buy me a taste (Hey Now)*
> *Started thinkin' 'bout the Lobos (Hey Now)*
> *Bought a whole case! (Hey Now)*

By eighth grade, I was the tiny mascot. In my yearbook, water damage has erased my face, and I see now that my name is the only one omitted—I am actually listed as "(Mascot)." My glasses had been updated to granny rectangles, and I was called Rabbit because I got so tired of pushing them up onto my nose I just did it by alternating twitches of my cheeks. My untouched leg was bowed and the foot slewed permanently to the right like a duck. My repaired leg was straight and covered with scars. My silly grin displayed the crooked teeth. My hair is still tragic. Your father was running past us on the basketball team, not noticing me at all.

But Michelle Nicholson taught me that it didn't matter what I looked like—as long as I got the words right. As long as we did the song together.

Yearbook photo, Riverside, California, 1974

7

Olympia—One Can Could Get You Pregnant

Riverside, California,
June 1974

By the summer before freshman year of high school, I could run again, and my hair had grown out into a short lion's mane, sunned back to blond after I mowed lawns and washed cars for money. I spent all my spare time with Delana, Dawn, and Tari (not their real names). We lived within three blocks of one another. But during my time in the hospital and then limping through unpopularity, most kids I knew had developed a serious taste in drinking.

Everyone's parents drank, at those '70s backyard parties with fondue and guacamole, but our refrigerator held only a few cans of Coors and Olympia. Other parents had full bars and hard alcohol, and were far more oblivious than my immigrant mother, who was strict, rude to interlopers, and could smell a cigarette from the next block. No one ever spent the night at my house, crowded with kids and chores. We always stayed at Tari's. Her parents were from upstate New York. We spent Friday afternoons mixing their gin, vodka, whiskey, brandy, and vermouth with Cherry Kool-Aid in a huge yellow Tupperware bowl. We called it sangria.

I don't understand how alcoholism works in my family genes, considering how many of my male relatives were alcoholic, but all this liquor had very little effect on me. I was too scared of my mother to be drunk. She required me to be home by exactly 7:00 a.m. Saturdays. My dad had bought an appliance repair shop, which came with a junkyard. Saturdays we cleaned the junkyard office and laundromats. Delana would pass out, Dawn would laugh, and Tari would throw up. I stayed awake until the early hours, holding someone's head as she vomited, firmer in my resolve not to be a nurse or a mother. At dawn I walked home to face dryer lint collected like fallen thunderclouds, and the bathroom of men who patronized a junkyard.

Finally, in the late spring of 1975, two boys waited for my friends and me at the park where my street dead-ended. I was in charge of liquor that night, and I headed toward the front door, sad that my offering would be completely meager. My mother saw the unnatural way I held my jacket, covering two cans of Olympia. All we had, but I thought someone might like the waterfall logo, which was pretty. My stepfather shouted, "Don't you realize you could get pregnant from one can of beer?" He must have had some sangria.

Actually not a terrible version of sex education, since in junior high I knew girls who'd gotten pregnant in eighth grade. Lucky he didn't know who was at the park: two senior guys with a van—yellow, pinstriped, with only the two small windows at the back, like fish eyes. One had given me thirteen marijuana joints in a manila envelope, for my thirteenth birthday. (I was extremely popular for a few weeks, because I smoked one, hated the taste and coughing, and gave the other twelve away.)

I was grounded for three months for two cans of Olympia

and the obstinate belief that I could handle my life. My mother didn't like these things: I had asked for a blow-dryer, I was sewing halter tops and hemming up my shorts, and I wore root-beer-flavored lip gloss as blusher, so sheer I thought she hadn't noticed.

She gave me the ugly talk.

We sat at the maple dining room table she'd bought when she married, the one where I'd done my homework every night, every spelling test and math problem, the imprints of my own handwriting and calculations in the golden wood. Every week I rubbed those smooth edges with lemon oil. My mother said sternly these things: "You don't have a lot going for you. You're not athletic." (I thought, well, yeah, I did have to learn to walk again after the Country Squire.) "And you're ugly." (She insists that she used the word *plain*.)

I know this part by heart, though. "With your looks, you'll probably never get married. The only thing you have going for you is your brain. So you'd better not mess it up with drugs. You'd better use it, because it's all you've got."

I sat there for a moment. Then she got up and went to listen to the Dodgers in the other room. I went into my bedroom, where there were novels, and albums by Chaka Khan, Al Green, and Earth, Wind & Fire.

I believed her. I was still very thin. My healed leg had the huge bump of calcification. During cold foggy weather, the healed place hurt, and I didn't know if it was the hurt of memory, or whether icy moisture got into the ball of new bone. I tried not to limp. I still had no braces, because my twelve-year molars hadn't come in although I was thirteen. (They didn't appear until I was sixteen. I got braces hours before junior prom, and my future husband was quizzical but rather dismissive, except for the blood when we kissed.)

I looked into the mirror. My mother was right. Behind my

forehead was my brain. Weed was supposed to leave black tar residue smeared over your brain cells. Drinking made people pass out and choke on their vomit. And it took constant vigilance to not be raped.

My girlfriends and I, along with every other girl we knew, had been hunted for years. I had survived torn clothes, hands that bruised, violating fingers, pinching and twisting of body parts, random bites inflicted by older teen boys, my hair pulled and throat exposed. This was less than many other girls I knew had experienced.

I wanted to be beautiful. I wanted amplified eyelashes and curled hair, cleavage in a baby-doll smock, a perfect smile with canine teeth tucked sedately where they belonged. Not feral.

Boys didn't know what to make of me, even the young man who'd given me the marijuana. He actually said, "I think I'm in love with you, but you just know too much shit about the world." We leaned against a tree and he laughed. "You read too much. You know shit that doesn't make sense."

I accepted ugly. It seemed safer. I went only two places all summer, while my friends partied. I had the bookmobile. I read two books a day. I started hitting tennis balls against the wall at the local university, and watching our high school basketball team's summer scrimmages. I wrote sports articles in my notebook. But really, I went to see Dwayne.

We had met in the junior high gym one day. Then we met again on the freshman-year school bus heading to a field trip, he and his friends in the rear seat causing trouble, me and a friend in the seat ahead laughing. Very tall, a huge natural, and a gap between his front teeth much wider than my own.

I sat in the bleachers of the college gym in my cut-off jeans, holding my tennis racket, learning about offensive rebounds and defensive boards, waiting after the games for him to meet me under a tree. I walk past that tree every day at the university where I have taught now for thirty years. I try not to tell my students.

By the time we were high school seniors, some friends had moved away, and others got deeper into drugs and alcohol. By then, Delana came to school with rings of purple hickeys around her throat like a lovely blurred choker. When I came out of the locker room, after changing for the tennis team, and waited for Dwayne to finish basketball practice, she and I would talk. Sometimes she held out her hand to show me the contents of her corduroy pockets. Black beauties, red Darvon, blue Tuinal.

I had friends addicted to speed, to cocaine, to Super-Kools, meaning marijuana cigarettes dipped in any liquid thought to be an enhancement to the high: even embalming fluid or liquid angel dust. At a party I met a guy who died the next morning of a heart attack, after smoking a Kool cigarette dipped in PCP. Other friends died in wrecked cars, driving high or drunk, or both. For some friends, both was their favorite way.

I got my first job, at the local theater. I drove the damn Country Squire there until it tried to kill me repeatedly, stalling, jumping curbs at midnight, rolling backward to induce an early heart attack. Then I took the bus or got a ride. I wore my candy girl uniform and sang along to the soundtrack of *Car Wash*, which showed for twelve weeks. I got Dwayne and his friends in free to the balcony. I tried not to limp unless the day was very foggy and chilling, the dense white droplets that I hated shrouding the eucalyptus trees into silver wraiths.

My mother bought me a little blue Smith Corona typewriter for high school graduation.

I went through college and graduate school typing on that little machine, first as a sportswriter, then as a novelist. My first published short stories and first novel were spooled through those old ink ribbons. I met Vin Scully, my mother's idol, the man whose broadcast voice taught her precise and resonant English, while covering a Dodger game for a newspaper. I told Vin Scully my mother loved him, and although she was on her second marriage she would leave any man for him. He smiled.

After I published my first novels, I told the story of the Country Squire, and then the ugly talk, to large audiences of women. They were shocked. I called my mother on this, and she said defiantly, "Well, it worked, didn't it? You're not dead." (Once she even told someone, "Well, if I wanted to kill her, I'd have run over her head, not her legs.") But I knew she was still trembling inside. I didn't think about the words her stepmother, Rosa, must have used to make her feel plain or ugly. And though I vaguely remember being in a church basement gluing macaroni sprayed with gold paint, I didn't know back then that the minister had told my mother her divorce meant she was not fit to raise me or my infant brother. He told her to give us up for adoption.

I wear makeup every day, gold and green eye shadow with glimmer (I never wear matte, because I am still of the working-class women Joan Didion eviscerated, and women like me always choose frost).

My hair now looks exactly as it did during my junior year of high school. My appearance-laziness is well-established in this house, as my daughters will testify. My hair is long because I don't care about it. My friend Tracy trims it twice a year and suggests I come in more often. Some women in academia and publishing have told me that my hair and lipstick make me appear unintelligent. What they mean is that I look like a Sherry or Debbi—and I do. I am a descendant of two Golden Dreamers with no money. I blow-dry my hair by going into the backyard to feed my chickens, while the hot Santa Ana winds race through my orange and apricot trees. I often see my friends named Sherry and Debbi and Kimberly at Target and in school parking lots and at funerals. We didn't leave.

I run my tongue over the canine tooth that inexplicably, now that I am fifty-seven, has decided to edge its way back out of my smile.

What did other mothers tell their daughters? I never knew that. But I see other old girlfriends, in homeless shelters or on sidewalks, and feel the rip of admiration like a cord pulled down my chest, even now. Their hair is still lush, but sometimes their faces are gaunt, and sometimes marred with lunar holes from years of methamphetamine. Sometimes their graceful hands are large and thickened and nearly purple, from years of intermittent homelessness. Their eyes fasten upon mine. We talk about what we drank back in the day, when we were thirteen and fourteen and downed beer before gymnastics practice, doing cartwheels on the streets at dusk, convinced while we were upside down that we saw people looking at us from the sewer drains in the curb, when we should have been afraid of the boys in cars parked underneath the pepper trees.

We always talk about our daughters, who are beautiful.

8

Daisy Belle

Sunflower County,
Mississippi, 1915

You so fine I might just have to kill you. Some other fool is gonna take you away, and I can't have that. Family legend: This is what Daisy's first husband said to her, while he held the gun.

Alberta, my mother-in-law, told me the story of her own mother, Daisy, only once, and it was not until after I had my first baby. Alberta was Daisy's third daughter, named for Daisy's sister. We were sitting knee to knee by the massive ochre-brick fireplace in the fall, when Gaila was four months old. In the living room that was never empty, we were alone that day at lunchtime, on my break from work, while I nursed the baby. Alberta was watching the damp black curls of my daughter, glistening with heat from the flames, her head lolling back as she fought sleep.

"My mother never had a home when she was little. Not after her mother died."

She paused. My mother-in-law's hands were elegant, her nails strong and oval and painted, her eyebrows vivid with pencil, her lips always defined with liner and lipstick. We were sitting in maroon leather club chairs whose arms were rolled and graceful, with brass rivets. Alberta said softly, "They were walking down a road. Her and her mother. Mary. She was holding her mother's hand. My grandmother saw the car coming. She threw my mother out of the way, threw her up where no one could see her, and then the car ran her over."

The driver was a young white man with another young white male passenger; the car plowed into Mary Thomas at great speed and then the driver swerved back onto the road and left her behind. Mary had three children—Daisy, five, Arthur, two, and Alberta, one. It makes sense that only Daisy was walking with her, because the others were so young, but no one can say for certain. The three children had been given the surname of their father: Ford. But no one ever mentions him again, either.

This part stays the same, no matter who tells the story: it was dusk, and suddenly a car was speeding down the narrow dirt lane, raising dust, careering toward them, and Mary knew what was coming, and why, and she threw Daisy up onto the roadbank into the trees, or in the ditch into the weeds.

That day by the fire, Alberta said sadly, "My mother was so little. And after that, she went from pillar to post. Yes, she did. Pillar to post."

Alberta held out her arms for the baby. I had to go back to work, and Alberta would hold her for hours while a procession of women came to visit and watch soap operas and share food and stories and rock this grandchild who was so loved that her cheeks would be whorled red with lipstick kisses when I came to retrieve her at 5:00.

I didn't understand the phrase—*pillar to post*. Alberta

watched my daughter relax back into sleep against her elbow, eyelids sliding shut. She said, "My mother never had a home. Not till she got here."

Pillar to post: when someone has gone from a wealthy home, with pillars at the front, as grand embellishment, to a poorer house, with porch held up by simple wooden posts. But in Sunflower County, Daisy went from farmhouse to sharecropper cabin, wherever relatives would take care of her for a time. Daisy's little sister Alberta went to Mary's sister Margaret, and Arthur went to an uncle. Daisy attended school until the fifth grade, as did Arthur.

That night, I lay awake thinking of the car speeding straight toward Daisy's mother while her small daughter lay on the roadbank. I remember the Country Squire passing over me like a large animal. I shivered, wondering what Daisy's mother felt. She lay in soft Mississippi dirt. Did she die there, with her daughter afraid to come out from where she'd been thrown for safekeeping? Did Mary hear her child crying?

Did she crawl?

Years later, at family gatherings, other relatives would offer:

They were drunk and they killed her, but they were rich white boys and no one in that county was gonna prosecute them.

They were sent to kill her because she knew things. About the rich white men around there. They didn't want her to tell.

They killed her because she was black and walking down the road. And Mary was the prettiest of all the girls. She was beautiful.

There were only about six cars in the whole county—it

was a poor place! The police knew whose car it was. Of course they did.

Imagine Daisy's memory, of her small body being flung by her mother's hands to safety, and where she landed, and how it felt. What she saw and heard after that. It's beyond comprehension. Did the men stop and look at Mary Thomas? Was Daisy so scared she knew to keep hidden in the trees or the weeds? Did she breathe? Did she hear her mother's breath? Did she hear pain or crying? How long did she wait by the roadside, and who drove the next vehicle or wagon that came upon them, and what never left her memory?

Violence like that enters the blood. Changes the DNA. We know this, from accounts by survivors of genocide, of the Holocaust, of war and torture and imprisonment. Reading historical narratives from the elderly people formerly enslaved in the American South, in places like Sunflower County, Mississippi, reminds us of how injury, rape, and psychological pain were endured, and interred, in the bones and brain.

Some Americans have tried to make slavery a single chapter in the nation's history, a finite number of years that ceases influence at the end of the Civil War. Tell this to the family of Mary Thomas, and the thousands of other black men and women killed in carefully planned acts of retribution or for casual sport—from the moment the Emancipation Proclamation was read, through the terrors of Reconstruction, to the countless lynchings between 1900 and the 1950s, to the murders during the civil rights movement, to killings that happen right now. This moment.

By 1989, when Alberta told me that story, her mother, Daisy, had traveled through seven states to make sure Alberta's childhood was rooted deeply and firmly in a radius of three miles, and we sat in the center of that radius. But Daisy's odyssey had been long and arduous, and at the end of it, she had four daughters, and endless secrets.

Daisy Belle Ford Morris Carter remains the mystery woman of our family. We still talk even now about how she never told anyone the identities of the fathers of her daughters. In a time when every pair of high heels chosen for the club, every new hairstyle or cup of coffee is documented in cell phone images with time, date, and exact street location, it seems astonishing that the phrase "she took that knowledge to the grave" could be true. Over six decades, Daisy never told anyone. Maybe those men were so dangerous she knew what she was doing.

Fine as wine and just my kind. Bring your fine self over here. So fine you like to blind me when I saw you.

This is what she heard, again and again. Daisy's first husband is listed in one census document as Calvin Morris, but no one left here has ever said they actually saw him. Daisy's cousin Jesse Wall, who'd also been born in Sunflower County and brought to California, told me back in 2014, when he was eighty, "Oh, Daisy was fine. Back in Arkansas, that man told her over and over, 'You're so fine, some fool's gonna take you away from me, and I can't have that, so I might just have to kill you first.' He had the gun on the table by the bed, and he'd sit there with it in his hand at night. And Daisy had the baby. Mary Louise. She had to wait until one night when he left and she could get away. She took the baby and went to Oklahoma to find Sweet Annie."

That was Daisy's aunt, Sweet Annie Tillman, legendary in her own right.

According to family members, Washington Thomas, patriarch of the family, was brought enslaved from Ethiopia to Haiti and then to Mississippi. His name is very common for postslav-ery times, and it has been impossible to find records that are un-deniably accurate. But family history says this: In 1865, after he was finally free, he was extremely ambitious and, by the 1880s, had at least five children: Jonah, Hine, Margaret, Annie, and Mary. Washington Thomas was determined each would have a trade, even the girls: Hine trained as a carpenter, Jonah studied alternative medicine, Margaret learned midwifery. But Annie became a dancing girl at a young age, and Mary, who died on that road, was only a teenager when she had three children.

Hine's ambition had gotten him nearly killed when he was a young man. Like everyone else, he was sharecropping for a former slaveowner, but he ran his own truck farm, as inde-pendent crops were called, to sell vegetables and make enough money to buy a car. This made local white landowners angry—they didn't like initiative or independence. When Hine returned from a trip to Memphis, where he'd made money on his crops, he had to be hidden in a trunk on the back of his own truck so he wouldn't be lynched. (That story always ends with: "He was a small man, which was good.")

Then he fell in love with a woman local people thought was white, so his life was again in danger. She was Native Ameri-can, but so fair that whites assumed her Italian. They had to flee Mississippi for Oklahoma in 1900 to avoid death.

They went to Wewoka, Oklahoma, where she had tribal land. Hine's sister Margaret was married with her own chil-dren, and she had taken in Alberta, Mary's youngest daugh-ter, and a nephew, Eddie Chandler Jr., whose father had been hanged in a violent lynching. Mississippi was untenable. Jo-nah went to Oklahoma after that, followed by his sister Annie. And by the time Daisy was sixteen or so, a lovely teenaged girl, Sweet Annie Tillman, thirty-one, took her niece on the road.

It was the 1920s, the era of speakeasies, dancing, and

transience for many women. Their passage spanned thousands of miles and lasted for fifteen years.

Daisy's first daughter, Mary Louise Morris, was born in Arkansas in August 1929, when Daisy was nineteen. In 1930, Daisy ran from Arkansas to Wewoka, Oklahoma, where she stayed with Hine, Jonah, and Annie.

In 1931, she had a daughter named Myrtle Lee Morris; in 1933 a daughter named Alberta Marie Morris; and in 1936 a daughter named Rosie Morris.

Our cousin Margaret Chandler, named for her grandmother Margaret Thomas Henderson from Mississippi, told me in 2018: "Myrtle asked her mother for years, until Daisy died, who her father was. She used to cry and cry, wanting to know his name. But Daisy would never say anything. And George Thomas, one of the cousins from Wewoka, Jonah's son, he came to California once and he pointed at Myrtle and said, *I know who your daddy is.* But he wouldn't tell her."

Daisy and Sweet Annie left Oklahoma at some point, maybe with just Mary and Myrtle, maybe with all four of Daisy's babies. They went to San Antonio, Texas, where their car broke down and they stayed for a while with cousins. Then they drove the southernmost route, along the border with Mexico, and made it to Las Cruces, New Mexico, where another cousin had settled. Finally, they made it across Arizona to the California border town of Calexico, a rural place that faced Mexicali.

Hine, Daisy's uncle, and his wife had moved to California in 1930. Oklahoma law, passed in 1909, made it illegal for a black person to be married to anyone not black. Anyone. Hine bought farmland in Colorado, and had a thriving business trucking his hay to ranches from San Diego all the way up to Oxnard. He didn't have to hide in a trunk.

He made enough money to buy his sister Margaret Henderson a house in Riverside, two hours north, where the weather was cooler. She had fled Sunflower County, too. When Theodore Bilbo was elected governor of Mississippi in 1935, Margaret said she would never let her sons and grandsons stay in that state under his racist policies. Jesse Wall was one of those grandsons. He always told me, "My grandmother said I would be raised in California, as a man." (His father, Jesse Wall Sr., became a beloved and powerful minister in Riverside; in 1970, Jesse Wall Jr. became the first black male high school teacher in Riverside, and helped desegregate the school system; after his father's death, he became a minister and preached in the family church until 2018, when he died.)

Daisy Morris arrived in Calexico with four girls, one a baby. Soon afterward, she traveled north to stay with Margaret Henderson on Eleventh Street in Riverside. It was 1936. By 1940, Daisy Morris was renting a house a few blocks away, on Denton Street. She was thirty years old, widowed according to her account, and her daughters were ten, eight, six, and four. Listed as birthplace for the three younger girls: California. Daisy had reinvented herself and her family—she was a new woman.

(Alberta never had a birth certificate until 1985, when she wanted to visit her daughter in Germany, where Christine Sims was married to the heavyweight boxing champion of the U.S. Air Force and had a newborn son. Alberta couldn't get a passport. She could have been born in Oklahoma, Arkansas, Texas, or New Mexico. But a local congressman helped: she received a birth certificate listing Calexico, California.)

Also living with Daisy in 1940: her aunt Annie Tillman, widowed, forty-seven years old, and the terror of the Eastside, where she is still known as Aint Dear.

———

It's hard to reconcile the stories of Aint Dear, and the single photo I have of her scowling face under a church hat, with a vibrant girl who made a living in clubs. But those hard years must have been the reason Aint Dear turned so strict and fearful after she got to California.

Daisy was working days at a munitions warehouse in nearby Mira Loma, as a defense worker; at night, she and other women cleaned a meat-packing plant. Aint Dear was in charge of the four girls. She was so controlling that she'd timed the route they took to get home from school—two streets and one alley—and if they deviated for anything, which was always assumed to be boys, they were beaten. Ironing cords, those old ones that were woven thread wrapped around open wire. Wooden clothes hangers. Branches. Hands.

Aint Dear's view of the world was clear—every molecule of air was pervaded by danger, every daytime sidewalk and evening avenue, and every boy or man was a threat to Daisy's daughters. But there is a photograph of Alberta that we all love: She is a California girl, standing on the steps of Irving Elementary School, her grin wide, her hair in braids, and next to her are the friends she kept for her entire life: Susan Strickland, Oscar Medina. It is 1936. Every day, I drive to work past those exact steps where she stood, and every day I glance toward the historic wooden façade of the building where Alberta smiled with open joy. Of all four daughters, hers is the face and wide grin and expressive eyebrows that most resemble Daisy.

Daisy's girls were renowned for their looks, and countless men fell in love with them. I've talked to eighty-year-old men who recall seeing the daughters, and who re-created for me the stunned stumble in their walk, as if they would actually tumble. To escape the ministrations of Aint Dear, the first three daughters married as teenagers.

By June 1952, Alberta had just graduated from Riverside

Poly High School. In this snapshot, taken the next day, she is headed off to be married to General Roscoe Conklin Sims II. She looks down shyly, but you can still see her wide smile. Standing beside her is Fine's youngest granddaughter, Loretta Sims, watching sidelong in admiration. It is the joining of the two families.

Loretta Casandra Sims and Alberta Marie Morris, at Daisy Carter's house, Riverside, California, June 1952

That day by the fire, Alberta and I were sitting in Daisy's leather chairs. She was so proud of the house she finally bought in the 1950s that she took formal photographs of her living room, with these chairs. Daisy died in 1982, the year before I married her grandson.

Daisy Carter: Sunflower County, Mississippi, to unknown, Arkansas, to Wewoka, Oklahoma, to San Antonio, Texas, to Las Cruces, New Mexico, to Calexico and Riverside, California. Astonishing: 2,303 miles.

9

Driveway #1—The First Love Letter

Riverside, California,
May 1976

The driveway at 4289 Michael Street was the heartbeat of life for hundreds of southern Californians who made their way into the family of General and Alberta Sims. The first time I walked across the sidewalk, with their son Dwayne, I had no idea this thirty-foot stretch of concrete lined with car engines, a barber chair, folding tables, and ice chests was the apotheosis of the American dream, a corridor of American history, proof of loyalty and love that would not be denied.

I was full of apprehension, wearing a halter dress that I'd bought with money saved from mowing lawns, cleaning houses, and babysitting. It was Memorial Day, 1976, the year of America's Bicentennial, which we'd been hearing about all year in school, seeing giant flags painted everywhere. A hot May afternoon, and instead of casually stopping by one evening after school to meet Dwayne's parents and maybe some of his brothers and sisters, he was bringing me to Memorial Day. I didn't know until we pulled up to the driveway that any Sims holiday meant about a hundred people. Uncles and aunts, cousins, neighbors, and friends. People were holding Miller High Life or Coors tall cans. From a stereo set up under the carport, Richard Pryor's *Bicentennial Nigger* was playing, his inimitable voice mixed with roaring laughter from Dwayne's brothers and cousins. General Sims II shouted for them to turn it off because he was going to play Earl Grant, his favorite obscure jazz organist, and everyone protested. Then they noticed me.

I had taken off my glasses, so everyone was a little blurry until I got within about ten feet. But I knew what they saw: a way-too-short, way-too-thin white girl with my best attempt at Farrah Fawcett wings of hair (I had bought a blow-dryer). Platform shoes I'd borrowed from a friend, shoes so old that the tiny nails all around the edges of the leather, which kept the insoles and wood together, kept coming out under my heels. Dwayne had seen me at school between classes, crouched over trying to hammer the little black nailheads with the cap of my Bonne Bell lipgloss. He had knocked the nails back in with a pocketknife. He took my arm now and began to say my name to the assembled.

The assembled were the descendants of Fine and her daughter Callie. The descendants of Mary and her daughter Daisy.

To get to this driveway, in a predominantly black and Mexican-American community formed back in 1880, to have arrived this far west in America and then finally rested, those women had survived white people whose inexorable violence was like Charybdis, the deadly whirlpool that pulled in the ship of Odysseus, and Scylla, the six-headed monster that plucked men off the deck—one for each head to swallow. They had fled black men like the Cyclops in his cave, who had to be fooled in order for his captive to leave, and ignored male Sirens whose songs told them to leap into the sea.

By 1976, Daisy lived around the corner from Alberta, on Eleventh Street and Kansas Avenue. Callie lived on Tenth Street, near Park Avenue, a few blocks away. Their beloved grandson was bringing home a white girl.

I knew none of the stories yet. Dwayne and I had been "going out," meaning we had been meeting at parks and parties and riding around in other people's vehicles, for months, but we had talked mostly about how I had to clean the laundromats, and one had just burned down, which was hard on my dad. How he and his brothers had to trim branches for their father, who was a gardener, and because his father was too cheap to buy tarpaulins to cover the load on the way to the city dump, the boys had to lie strategically spread-eagled on top of the heap of leaves and fronds so the cops wouldn't give General a ticket. We talked a lot about basketball and tennis, and teachers, and our friends. Our friends could get drunk and high on Friday nights, but both of us had to be up at dawn on Saturday mornings—me for chores at the junkyard, him to trim trees and head to the dump. That was our bond.

But we were a couple now. At school, to recent public queries by cool athletes, "Oh, man, is that *you*, Sims?" Dwayne had raised his chin in the affirmative.

I knew nothing of Sunflower County or Tulsa. He knew nothing of the Swiss Alps or the Colorado Rockies.

In the driveway, he guided me first toward his uncles and the elderly neighbors. Some of the older relatives had watched black Tulsa burn in 1921 from fires set by white mobs after a young black man was accused of accosting a white woman in an elevator. Some of the older neighbors had lain as children under beds while the Klan wrecked their living rooms in Louisiana, looking for their fathers to drag outside. Two of Dwayne's brothers, along with many other young black men, had been hauled to the police station and kept there for hours after two white policemen had been shot and killed near the park at the end of Michael Street, in 1971.

I wore no glasses. All faces were blurred. But men shook my hand. Or they nodded. They smiled. They lifted their chins one inch, reserved.

Just before we got to the front door, I stopped to look up at the porch light, a Spanish-style lantern with amber glass. Dwayne's sister Christine Sims, granddaughter of Callie, and his cousin Margaret Chandler, great-niece of Daisy, both stood there, glaring. I put out my hand and Margaret said, "Oh, hell, no." Christine was wearing a dashiki. She rolled her eyes and turned away.

But Alberta opened the screen door and said, "Here she is! Come on inside and get you a plate."

At the long table in front of the mirrored dining room wall, Alberta made me a plate of food. Then, holding the plate, I met a whole circle of women in the living room, who sat near a huge fireplace with custom shelves on either side of the mantel, filled with black history books and Louis L'Amour paperbacks, and black cowboy portraits hung above. Maybe twenty women: Alberta's sisters and their daughters, General's sisters and their daughters, and his brother's wives and their daughters, along with godmothers and neighbors. But I really couldn't see the details of faces or hair or dress. I felt the stares of amusement, protective suspicion, and sidelong glances, and heard the murmurs of surprise. There were four generations of women inside that room.

Dwayne took me back outside to sit near the sidewalk with his brothers, who knew me from school and basketball games. They teased me for a time. I looked at the massive chimney at the head of the driveway. There was no garage, in this style of house. A carport, under which General II and the uncles and older men held court just on the other side of the distinctive gold-toned bricks from the women inside. General II and his friend Oscar Medina had built that chimney and the block walls surrounding the house, where he'd lined pots of orchids. From the huge ash tree, chains dangled to lift engines out of trucks and cars. By 1976, General II and his best friend, Jesse Lee Collins, from Muskogee, Oklahoma, had stopped working at the local Air Force base and become landscapers. Lawnmowers were lined up near the walls. But the most fantastical things were the odd trees plucked into comically Dr. Seuss–style shapes, growing in pots along the wrought-iron fence.

"My greens trees!" General II shouted. "Look at this young lady checking out my greens trees!" He led me over to the pots—the plants were collard greens that he trained into bonsai form, so people could easily harvest the leaves.

I heard laughter, music, shouted stories—circles of men, circles of women, kids our age sitting in truck beds or throwing footballs in the street. This was the exact opposite of my own grandparents' gatherings, at their mobile home in Hemet, with the tiny platform of porch off the wrought-iron screen door under their pleated metal carport, the rectangle of wood covered with bright green artificial turf, only a few folding chairs that held my mother and stepfather, my two uncles and their wives. I was the eldest of Rosa Leu's nine grandchildren—none from her own daughter. Every move we made annoyed my grandmother, so she invariably said, "Children are to be seen and not heard. Go now and play." We'd cross the yard of gravel painted solid green to resemble lawn, presided over by a cement roadrunner, and head straight into the alfalfa fields. I never heard a single story under that carport.

But Rosa had Swiss chard plants—like greens trees, after she cut the outside leaves with a knife, leaving the white stalks with amputated arms. In the driveway, General's perimeter garden was exactly like Rosa's, the five-foot strip of earth around her trailer, the trellised grapevines and tomatoes and the Swiss chard. Memorial Day, I was holding the plate of food—and if you asked me what it was, I'd guess it was what we still eat in the driveway even now: ribs, potato salad, macaroni and cheese, fried chicken, and collard greens. I remember this: I wanted these women to like me. I was eating greens, and someone said, "I bet you never had greens before."

I said, "They're like my grandmother's greens. But better."

They looked at me like I was crazy. How could I explain Switzerland? Explain a leafy vegetable named chard no one had ever heard of, and why my grandmother, the meanest woman I'd ever met, didn't even like the green part but ate the thick white stems, boiled until soft? No. These collard greens had been cooked with ham and salt; they were ribbons of flavor in my mouth.

I had been trained for this. I could not panic. I stood up and walked toward the front door, and went directly to the kitchen, where Alberta was checking pots on the stove. The Formica counter was exactly like ours at home, except we had pink and gray lines like cake sprinkles in the white, and Alberta had gold flecks and sparkles in the white. I began to wash the dishes. She said, "Now, aren't you sweet?" and as I had been trained by rigorous implacable Swiss women, I dried the dishes as well and cleaned the area around the faucet and then wiped down the counters. Alberta stood beside me, putting foil over the numerous plates I would later learn she prepared for everyone, the hundreds and hundreds of plates of food my mother-in-law sent home with people so they would not be hungry on a Monday, and then she began to talk as if we'd known each other forever. "You know, you have to make enough food for everyone," she said. "Even the stranger that might stop by. You never know who's gonna be hungry." The foil in her hands rippled like a silver sail and made that shimmery sound before she settled it over the meat.

Alberta changed my life in ways immeasurable. She was the center of every constellation of people gathered in her yard and house, every afternoon, every weekend. She was lovely as a Supreme, with her sisters. But Alberta had a different charisma from her sisters. It was as if her face could not hold somberness. Her mouth curved upward even as she spoke, and she would nod with the exact slant of encouragement or sympathy at whoever she was listening to—whether an elderly visitor or a small child, or me—and say, "That's right."

I knew no one in my neighborhood who wore sequined formal gowns and dazzling dresses, with high heels and hats, and went to dances. But Alberta did—with her social club, with General and other couples out at March Air Force Base. Her eyebrows arched and flew, her lipstick was magenta, and she was so tall.

In the living room, on New Year's Eve, she and General and their close friends Jesse Lee and Clarice Collins would dance. Cha-cha and mamba and hustle. They played cards, and music swung through the house.

But in the daytime, the house belonged to the women. Every afternoon when I was there, the soap operas playing were only choral background for the endless news and eternal weaving of family history and today's gossip that made Alberta's house, and General's driveway, the center of the neighborhood.

And from the first moment she took my hand and led me to the kitchen, she taught me to cook in a way completely different from my own home. I had been cooking dinner since I was ten and my mother went back to school—but that was hot dog casserole and enchilada casserole and tuna casserole. My mother cooked well, but only for our family—seven of us, seven pork chops or seven pieces of chicken. There were no strangers.

Alberta cooked for the whole community. Huge pots of black-eyed peas with neck bones, fried chicken in massive cast-iron pans, smothered steak with gravy, and entire hams. I was good at cleaning, and watching. And if someone came into the kitchen and saw me, a short white girl, and was surprised, Alberta just laughed and said, "Look at her! You wouldn't think somebody so little could lift a pot! She and Dwayne are so cute together. She knows how to clean greens!"

I had never known someone who had a line of credit at a department store, but Alberta did. Cocktail dresses, cocktail rings—I didn't even know what a cocktail was, and she taught me the fashion. She took Dwayne shopping for me, and chose a jade pendant in gold filigree. It was the nicest piece of jewelry I had ever had. I still wear it.

One thing Dwayne and I laughed about: On Thursdays, the day liver was on sale at the local market, our mothers were the same. "You walk in the house and you smell onions and it's the best smell in the world—and then you see it's liver in the pan. Damn," he'd say. "And your mom, too."

II

10

Castas

There are paintings of the sixteen racial classifications Spanish colonizers "invented" in Latin America during the fifteenth century. Soldiers and other men arrived from the Iberian Peninsula, Spain and Portugal, to a new continent, and immediately fathered children with women who were indigenous and then with women who were enslaved Africans.

Ironically, the painter chose very particular clothing and stylized family arrangements to display the fathers, mothers, and children for whom the Spanish gave an imaginary *casta*—a breed, a lineage, bizarre designations for each human.

Español con India: Mestizo. Mestizo con Española: Castizo. Castizo con Española: Español Criollo. A human could "work his way" back up to what was considered white Spanish within two generations, but of course that depended on melanin, facial features, and hair, and none of those characteristics were predictable.

Español con Moro: Mulato. Mulato con Española: Morisco.

Morisco con Española: Chino—from *cochino*, the Spanish word for pig. *Pelo chino*—curly hair, like that of a sheep or pig.

Mulato was dreamed up from mules. It gets worse. *Moro con India: Zambo. Negro con India: Lobo.* Wolf. The men who spent their days categorizing humans according to animalistic, completely non-science-based categories referred to themselves as *penínsulars*.

Love. Melanin. Hair. One category says everything: *torna atrás*, which means, literally, "turn back." This is a child of one-sixteenth black ancestry, born with dark skin and curly hair, to seemingly white parents.

The Spanish went to the Philippines, too. There, there were *torna atrás*, children who did not look like their parents. The Spanish, on those islands, came up with *indio* and *india* again, but there were Chinese people, whom they called *sangley*. A *mestiza de sangley* was a woman part Spanish, indigenous, and Chinese.

In America, the racial classifications set down in Haiti by the French and then brought to Louisiana employed more terms made up in random, dehumanizing fashion, and much more obsessed with mathematics: *noir* was a human thought to be "100%" African; *sacatra* was ⅞ *noir* and ⅛ *blanc*; *griffe* was ¾ *noir*; *marabou* ⅝ *noir*; *mulatre* ½ *noir*; *quadroon* ¼; *octoroon* ⅛; *mameloque* 1/16; *quarteronne* 1/32; and someone who was 1/64 black was called *sang mele*, which means "mixed blood."

In our part of southern California, not near the ocean, not anything the rest of America would have recognized as "California dreaming," we were the descendants of the love resulting from combat, military movement, and chance. As in other nations around the world, we were the result of war. The Civil War, which brought men from every state in the union, including Buffalo soldiers, Mormon soldiers, Mexican and Swiss and Apache mercenaries, and Italians who wanted to grow grapes;

the Mexican Revolution, which brought men from Mexico and New Mexico and Arizona and Texas; World War II, which took men to Germany, France, Britain, the Philippines, Japan, Guam, from which places they came back with brides; the wars in Korea and Vietnam took men to Korea, China, Japan, Vietnam, Cambodia, Laos, the Philippines, and Thailand, from which places they came back with brides. Here from the beginning of time: indigenous Cahuilla and Chemehuevi people who numbered in the thousands around inland southern California. A descendant of Hine Thomas married a member of the Torres-Martinez tribe, near Mecca.

Growing up here, if anyone had tried to use weird animal or math-related terms, a serious beating would be the result. People weren't necessarily polite, but before grilling someone about heritage, they tried to figure others out by looking at their parents, siblings, vehicles, houses, clothes, and second languages. The word most often used: *half.* She's half. He's half. You had to be capable of nuance and observation: Here for generations had been indigenous families, many Mexican-American families like the Trujillos, who had arrived in 1842, and pioneer African-American families whose ancestors had arrived in the 1870s. But many mothers were from somewhere else. Fathers were from every state in the nation, black men who'd decided never to go back to the rural poverty and racism of Louisiana, Florida, Alabama, Georgia, Oklahoma, Mississippi, South Carolina, or Texas, white men who'd decided never to go back to the snow and cold of South Dakota, Minnesota, or in the case of my stepfather, Canada.

We, their children, just wanted to figure out who had a car, money for tacos or burritos or pizza, money for alcohol or drugs, and a yard or field where we could party. We cared about transportation, clothes, shoes, hair, and who could dance. You had to be able to play music at deafening volume, and to dance. We only cared about which human might possibly come to love us.

II

Mulato

Riverside and Los Angeles,
California, 1979

To our daughters:

There is no way the Spanish or French colonials could have handled this place. They would have lain on the sidewalk in front of our houses and cried, while we laughed and stepped over them on our way to school or work.

In junior high, we were Lobos, the word those penínsulars assigned to people who were indio and moro. We were everything, in the orange groves where smudge pots still stood like one-armed soldiers, remnants of the winter freezes when kerosene was lit to send sooty smoke over the fruit to keep it warm. We were lobo and chino and pardo and cholo and zambo and mestizo and mulato; we were the Filipino version, sangley and mestiza, and the American versions. I was Swiss and French and the only person in my family with the last name Straight, as opposed to my parents, brothers, and foster siblings. People asked whether I was adopted. They asked why I had such a stupid name to go with the severe limitations of my wardrobe and body. I was not someone a Tony would call.

You couldn't tell anything about a guy from his name—because most boys had names that were variations on Catholic saints. Were girls named for saints? Wait—we were. Barbara and Teresa and Rita. Girls in the 1970s, in a place like this, were supposed to get ready for marriage; our classes were Home Economics, Sewing, Typing. There was a class called Mock Wedding, wherein an entire semester was devoted to the etiquette and practicalities of that day. Seriously, your dad and I have shown you the pictures in the yearbook.

In junior high, a boy would call and say to us, "Do you want to go with Tony?" (I'm using *Tony* because in our neighborhood there were multiples of Tony, Tommy, Michael, Johnny, Ronnie, Ricky, Billy, Wayne, Dwayne, Eddie, and Larry. In my neighborhood there was a Tony whose mother was Salvadoran and father Polish, a short black Tony nicknamed Cricket, for the chirping he made to drive our history teacher crazy, and a Mexican-American Tony. So if a girl said that Tony asked her to go with him, we'd have to ascertain which Tony, by his last name, neighborhood, hairstyle, or sports affiliation—I married basketball Dwayne Sims, not track Duane Sims.)

The caller would not be Tony. He would be Tony's friend. We would answer yes. Then we would be "going with" Tony until the next afternoon, when his friend would call and say, "Tony's breaking up with you." Then we'd be broken up, in all probability without ever having actually spoken to Tony, who might then write months later in our school yearbook something like "Big titty girl." (I got this lovely ironic missive in my junior high yearbook from a blond drug-dealing kid who lived three streets from me. One of four Rickies in my neighborhood.)

Then we went to high school, where the gradations of possible love became "talking to Tony," "messing with Tony," and "Tony, is that *you*, homes?" The last would be the indication that you and Tony were actually seen, physically together, all the time, and Tony had acknowledged that you were a couple. No one had any money for dating. That was not a word I ever heard said aloud. That was a word I read in Nancy Drew novels.

If we couldn't afford clothes, we learned to sew in Mrs. Zella Marshall's sewing class. She was Navajo, with her black hair in a high bun, turquoise earrings, and a way of looking at us over her glasses when girls were taking out their own earrings ready to fight in the hallway.

No matter our race—we recognized one another in our handmade clothing cut from Butterick patterns and sewn on school machines. We recognized girls who had money—outfits bought from Contempo, Clothestime, and Wet Seal.

The boys had their own uniforms. Stoners wore clothing saturated with smoke. Nascent gangsters, no matter what race, wore Pendletons, khakis, hairnets. Kids with money had Levi's. (The biggest night burglaries in Riverside were at the Levi's store, where men stole stacks of new denim to sell on the street.)

But athletes mattered most, and they wore letterman jackets. That's where we really looked different from the rest of America. The names scripted on the backs of young men whose parents had come from the South, brown-skinned guys who flattened people in football: Dr. Doom, Penguin, Bonedell; white guys whose fathers came from the South, or Ohio, or Montana: Blue, Dawson, Bobby; Chicano guys whose parents had been in California forever: Roberto, Camacho, Snake. Japanese-American guys whose parents had survived incarceration camps during World War II: Shige and Kumi. We had a black future comedian: Buddah.

If your father had the money, his letterman jacket would have said Feets, for his size 13s. But we had no money. Your father owned two pairs of pants—one pair of burgundy corduroys, and Dickies before Dickies were cool. I had two pairs of pants, which I'd purchased at a swap meet in an asphalt lot. We were the kind of kids who had to switch items up every day and pretend we weren't wearing the exact same thing. I borrowed clothes from friends, and I sewed blouses and skirts.

Your father, and you know this because he still does it, identified everyone by vehicle. "Your friend," he says even now. "The one drove the Duster." We went out in his sister's Pinto, which occasioned a lot of laughter at field parties. (The Batmobile had died.) My next-door neighbor Eddie Rose, whose mother was from England, was always "the dude with the Mustang."

Senior year, I sewed my prom dress, which cost $13 worth of pink satin. We borrowed cars from our parents. People would joke with us, "You ridin' in the Monarch or the Granada?"

Our parents had identical cars, silver sedans, one a Ford and one a Lincoln, with burgundy interiors. It was hilarious.

If I'd had money, or the ability to get a letterman jacket, mine would have said what the guys called me: Itsy-Bits. Really impressive. I sat close to the blackboard, squinting in my blindness. I had my books, my job at the movie theater, and your father.

In 1978, the Sims family did a formal portrait, in front of the golden fireplace. Everybody wore leisure suits with printed Qiana shirts, wide pointy collars. These are the photos you have seen since you were born. Humans of every race had gotten together and here were six Sims kids—all of whom looked different. Light skin, freckles, dark skin, rosy cheeks, wide noses, and prominent noses like those of Sioux warriors. Not one person looks the same. Christine gets mistaken for Asian, Derrick is very light-skinned with freckles, and your dad looks exactly like his mother, Alberta.

Those freaky damn colonials would have given each child a different casta, and the Sims reaction would have been swift, if anyone tried to say lobo or morisco or chino. The driveway would have been littered with ass-kicked penínsulars.

We loved showing you our high school yearbook, filled with people I see every week. JW North High School Huskies, varsity basketball teams 1976–78: Georgie Smith, only five feet seven, and famous for his ability to dunk. His father born in Texas, and his mother, Yoshiko, born in Kyoto, Japan, the seamstress who made our junior high pompon uniforms, a small, precise-featured woman who spoke Japanese and black English, who measured us with nudging fingers and cloth tape. We grew up with kids named Toshio and Mariko and Rishi, whose hair was braided down into cornrows for football and basketball practice, and blown out into epic proportions for dances.

But the star of our team was Richard Box. He was six feet six, bowlegged, pale as damp sand with hair that combed down straight. His jump shot was perfect. He was chosen for All-State. His mother was German, his father black; he lived one street over from me. His letterman jacket had stitched on the back in flowing cursive: *Mulato.* The Spanish version of the word. His girlfriend at the time was Mexican-American.

No one ever used that word. He used it with precise irony. We knew what people from other high schools, which were predominantly white or black or Latino, called us: mutts, mongrels, breeds. They're from way out there. The Inland Empire. Dirt people.

So when Richard Box dunked, that was something; when your father dunked, that was something; but when Georgie Smith, shortest guy on the court, with his bow-legged run and supercilious stone-face, his huge natural like a cirrus cloud of black, rose up in the air and dunked, and gave the bleacher crowd the most evil look anyone could imagine, since they'd been chanting "Kung Fu Fighting" or "Bruce Lee," everyone else could shut up.

When we graduated, your father went to play basketball at a junior college in Monterey, and I visited him to obsess over the landscape of John Steinbeck novels. (We walked eight miles to Cannery Row, carrying the boombox, so I could see the pier I'd read about.) Then I went home, and my parents dropped me off in the yellow pickup truck, in Los Angeles, where I had a scholarship to the University of Southern California. My task: to become a sportswriter so that my mother could one day meet Vin Scully. I had small goals. I also still had braces, a faint limp, and no decent clothes. Dwayne's and my best friend, Penguin, whose parents were from rural Florida, played football at a junior college in rural San Jacinto, along with five guys actually born in Florida. They lived in a ragged farmhouse, shared a few pairs of shoes, and lived on powdered soup mix.

So one summer weekend, just before sophomore year, your dad and Penguin wanted to see the other L.A. We'd been to Los Angeles only for Sims family functions—to Crenshaw, Inglewood, South Central. They wanted to see Venice Beach and Westwood.

We drove my parents' silver Granada, the hood with paint

scoured from the sap dripping off our crape myrtle trees, with shabby tires and aging maroon seats. We went to Venice Beach. We rented skates and attempted to look cool on the boardwalk.

Then we sat on the car hood and ate home-packed food. I changed clothes in the back seat. At dusk, we went to Westwood. Throngs of people moved toward the movie theaters where we were headed. Michael Jackson hung above us on the brick walls, hundreds of huge posters of his just-released solo album *Off the Wall*. He wore a black tux, a big afro, brown skin, white socks, and that odd shy smile. It was August 1979.

Your father's afro was thicker than ever, blown out that day with a small handheld dryer with a comb attachment. He used it first, standing behind me at the mirror, him six feet four, me five feet four, my face floating at the center of his wide chest. He'd been lifting weights for basketball. He wore new clothes—a black tank undershirt, khaki pants, and a cream-colored cowboy hat. Everyone was wearing cowboy hats that summer. I wore a white cotton blouse tucked into a white gauzy skirt, with a brown belt I'd gotten at a thrift store. I was copying a summer outfit far more expensive I'd seen in a magazine. When he was done with the dryer, I used it on my hair, which I always wore loose, but as I'd learned back in freshman year from my friend Vicky in typing class, I French-braided the sections around my forehead to keep my hair out of my eyes when I read. I tied off the braid dangling near my ear with a rubber band from my brother's newspaper delivery supply.

We thought we were ready for L.A. We thought we looked good.

Then two patrol cars swerved onto the Westwood curb beside us, and four officers leaped out and shoved us against the brick wall, just under Michael Jackson.

I remember how it smelled. The bricks. The exhaust. They

Dwayne Sims and Susan Straight, Venice, California, 1979

were shouting so loudly we couldn't understand what they wanted. We were on foot. We had parked two blocks away. They separated us.

It was your father they wanted. The power forward they love on the court. The human they hate off the court. His arms wide as crucifixion on the wall. His shoulderblades wide dark wings. His left cheek pushed into the red brick. One officer held the barrel of his shotgun against his skull, pushing it farther and farther into his hair until it seemed inside his ear.

They were shouting at all three of us: *Where you from? Where you from? A black man with a shotgun and a cowboy hat was seen threatening people near UCLA.*

I was taken from the brick and turned around. *Give me your license. You're from Riverside? Why'd you come all the way from Riverside to L.A.? Where's your car? Whose car is it? Does your mother know you're with two niggers?*

I said, *She gave me the car.*

You sure it's not stolen? Did you steal it?

My incredulity edged toward sarcasm. I said, *It's a '75 Granada.* But then the heat of fear returned. Penguin was talking back to the cops, refusing to give them his license. I thought they would shoot your father. Through his large ear. Even at that moment, I saw his ear, the one the nuns at Our Lady of Guadalupe had pulled so hard, the one he covered with that beautiful natural, which was smashed now by the cowboy hat they'd taken off.

He was breathing. He fit the description. He matched the suspect. He had not put down his hands to get his wallet out of his back pocket.

I said to Penguin, *Please. Please, just give him your license.*

I thought, Or Dwayne's going to die.

The black man. All black men. This black man. The width of his brown shoulders in the tank top as his arms were spread.

His wingspan, the coaches called it. He's got a hell of a wing-span. Great hands.

And your father would say, My dad's hands are even bigger. All that work, he always says. He's got the biggest hands of anybody.

Your father's hands like starfish clinging to the bricks. *Don't move.*

One officer went to examine the Granada, parked at a me-ter. He asked again whether my mother knew who was in the car with me.

My short Swiss mother, who loved sports above all else, who hated television and soap operas and didn't really like women, who said when I brought your father home, "Well, we can use some height in the family," who later told me, "Well, all the white boys around here are drug dealers," who came to your father's high school basketball games and sat in the bleachers actually knitting, while General Sims II sat on the top row with his friends, six-pack hidden in his coat, hollering "Fall, ball!" every time his son shot—she already liked your father more than me. She'd never come to a single one of my tennis matches, on the courts just across from the gym.

I said, *Yes.*

The throngs of people had stared at us and then moved around the scene and now thinned out because the police cars blocked the way. The officers said something to your father. The barrel of the shotgun was withdrawn from his temple and the stock cradled in the elbow of the man wearing the uniform.

How would you classify him in a fake Latinate imaginary word?

Descendant of mulatto and negro and colored, all the ways Fine and Daisy were identified, and white slaveowner and Irish overseer and Cherokee and unknown.

Your father was every black man we saw with a gun held to his head or body or in the hovering air just between two humans. Your father was Tom Robinson, in *To Kill a Mockingbird*, shot in the back by police in a field in the night—Wait, people say, Atticus Finch saved Tom Robinson!—and I always say, Did you not read the end? They killed him anyway. Your father was Jim in *Huckleberry Finn*; in the original version that man was called Nigger Jim. Your father was killed in countless novels and movies, so often and early that when we went to the theater he and all our friends would place bets on the single black man in the cast: "How long till the brother dies? Five minutes? You think he's gonna get ten? Nah. They gon' kill him off in five."

Your father was the source of fear for white Americans, when he stopped to offer assistance changing a tire, or held open an elevator door, or offered to carry a bag. Your father was the source of fear for his own father, who had seen his sons pulled over while walking, stopped on the street, booked into jail for questioning after someone was killed, suspects because of their tennis shoes, their hair, their skin. Your father was the source of fear for me, because while we rode in the Granada or the Monarch, or the pathetic Pinto, we were always pulled over. I saw his hands tighten on the steering wheel, or dangle outside. The hands I loved. We were so so quiet.

Your father was the guy who, later, on his way to work as a correctional officer would stop for gas at dawn and the cashier would "accidentally" trigger the alarm and police cars would converge and guns would be pointed across the roof while he held up his hands. Your father and I already knew the names of so many young men who'd been shot by police, young men whose names no one says now because there are other names that entered the American consciousness in the last six years, but those names we knew, we always said in conjunction with a place, a street or city where we knew someone shot by police, and finally Lakeview Terrace, where Rodney King was beaten and the whole world saw it.

Your father was the boy whose family had gone to see the Jackson 5 at the Swing Auditorium in San Bernardino. I was the girl who'd learned my first dance in sixth grade from my classmates, the only white girl in our group to perform onstage, and too scared so I was in charge of the record player and dropped the needle precisely on the right song: "ABC," by the Jackson 5, my classmates moving in perfect synchronicity.

In Los Angeles that night, Michael Jackson was also on the brick wall, his face frozen forever brown-skinned, his natural the exact texture of curl as your father's. They were born the same year, your father and Michael Jackson. When people say bitterly, "Why did he turn himself white?" I always think of that terrible moment when I watched your father hold himself so very very still under the world-famous face with the private yet entreating smile.

Your father did not smile. His license was handed back to him.

The officers said to us: Go back to Riverside. We're gonna follow you and if we see you walking around here again tonight, we're gonna shoot you on sight. Don't come here again.

They stood and waited until we got into the Granada. We drove back to the Santa Monica Freeway, which left the wealthy Westside of Los Angeles, and drove through the neighborhoods where your father's ancestors had arrived in California: Inglewood, Watts, Crenshaw, and historic South Central, where stood the house of Jennie Stevenson, the eldest daughter of Fine, the little girl who held the bullet in her fingers.

It was Jennie Stevenson who had brought the whole Sims family to California.

We drove east for fifty-four miles until we were home. I pulled the Granada near the curb behind the Monarch, and we got out and stood there in the driveway, on the cement crowded with people because it was August and hot, and the men drinking beer stared at us quizzically, asking why we were back so soon.

12

The Second Bullet

Jennie Stevenson, Outside
Tulsa, Oklahoma, Early 1900s

I never hear the song John Lee Hooker recorded with ZZ Top, "La Grange," without shivering. You know this song: It plays constantly in America, on jukeboxes and television commercials and radios. "Rumors spreadin' 'round, in that Texas town, 'bout that shack outside La Grange. Just let me know, if you wanna go, to that home out on the range. (They got a lotta nice girls. Have mercy!)"

I see the women.

In folding chairs along the driveway, summer heat held stubborn in the concrete and swarming around our feet, the darkness pooling between the porch light, the streetlamps, and the glowing embers of coals in the oil-drum barbecue, two of the cousins said softly to me, "There was the big house in front, and that was for the white men. There was a little house in the back, down a path, and that was for the black men. But one night a drunk white man came busting into the back house, and he raped her. Jennie. She shot him dead, right there. After that she kept her little pistol hidden in her dress. In her bosom. Whenever we saw her, we knew it was there. Dancing, cooking, whatever. Aunt Jennie always had that gun."

She was maybe fifteen or sixteen or seventeen. It was maybe 1903 or 1904 or 1905. There are no records for this—as is common for the violence against women even now.

The man waited until she was alone, walked down the path to the smaller house, and shoved his way in the door. Did he want to break the rules? Had he seen her before? Was he drunk and angry? Was it a joke to him? Was he a total stranger? Was he doing what so many men say—"teaching her a lesson?"

It doesn't matter.

Did she keep her gun in a different place, before that? Near the fireplace? Near the door? Near the bed? Had she already been attacked, and kept the pistol on her body?

She shot him in the forehead.

Now there was a dead white man on the floor. The reason didn't matter, in 1905. (It rarely matters today.) Jennie would hang. She ran up the path to the bigger house, to the white woman who ran the brothel, and told her what had happened. Everyone else must have been gone. For whatever reason, whether the woman didn't like this man, or liked Jennie, whether they were good financial partners or whether she felt pity for someone so young, the white woman went back with Jennie and together they dragged the man's body up to the front house. Then she called an official in local law enforcement with whom she was very close. Often. She told the official that the man had tried to attack and rob her, and she'd been forced to shoot him. The official arrived and disposed of the body.

Jennie Stevenson, Tulsa, Oklahoma, undated

Jennie didn't hang.

She eventually married a man named Robert Stevenson. They ran house parties and clubs in the black neighborhood of Tulsa known as Greenwood. House parties with alcohol, gambling, and dancing. Hush-hush, they were called, and Jennie Stevenson collected the money, and danced with her pistol in the bosom of her dress. She wears a fur collar in a photograph taken around this time. She has inherited her mother Fine's lovely features, but her face is more brown, more velvet over the high cheekbones. Her gaze is imperious, interrogative, incapable of fear. She is a badass. She has been on her own in the world since she was about fourteen. Just like her mother, she had to survive, but she married a man who should have known better than to ever become violent. That kind of man—Fine's second husband, Zach Rollins—was the reason Jennie ran away and had to work in a brothel. As far as family knowledge, Jennie never gave birth herself. Or perhaps she did, but no one ever knew. Maybe she couldn't, after all the things that had happened to her body in her young life. Maybe there would have been a child, and she made that never happen. But she became the fiery heart of her family, decades later.

I heard the story of the little house outside Tulsa that night in the driveway, when I was about twenty. Jennie's granddaughters told me, and my imagination moved slowly past the wooden house, the man on the floor with blood on his face, his mouth and teeth, and the darkness of the path upon which Jennie ran, the trees and the night birds.

13

Fruitful

My mother told me once about Lake Ontario, near Oshawa, Canada, a vast sea of ice in winter. When she was fifteen and walked there, an older woman, an Eastern European refugee from World War II, told her that babies were suspended in the ice, drowned by mothers whose young daughters had become pregnant on the journey to Canada. All my mother's stories were scary, but the idea that women had thrown their own grandchildren into the water was the worst.

In the 1960s and '70s, every story I heard about babies was terrifying, and many of them were about rape or coercion. *Then she had to marry him. Because of the baby. Her life was over.*

I expected nothing but danger and death for girls. Babies and betrayal. Because I was so small and didn't run quickly, I imagined guns.

When we were twelve and thirteen, men pulled alongside us in cars, the doors open like batwings, their four fingers scooping the air a few feet from us: *Come on, get in, you don't have to walk*. We were always walking—to school, to practice, to the store, to football games.

When I was twelve, and my brother Jeff was nine, hiking in the foothills near our house looking for gold, a teenaged stranger came toward me and said what he was going to do to me. My brother threw rocks angrily and accurately at him, and we ran.

When I was thirteen, a teenaged girl from Canada came to babysit us while my parents went on vacation; she lay in their big bed, crying. Something was very wrong. She asked me for sanitary pads. She was bleeding, a terrifying amount. She cried and cried, her face slick and swollen. She'd been sent to California to have a baby, and it had been taken away. Her grief was immense and went inside me, while I stood beside the bed breathing in her sobs.

When we were fourteen and fifteen, several of my friends were raped, some by strangers, some by boys we knew and thought might love us.

I remember this: Women who had been raped were never referred to as "innocent victims," like women who had been murdered by strangers or bears or dogs. The girls and women I knew were constantly gauging danger.

These were the boys and men who attacked us: The ones who gave us rides. The ones who asked us to dance, to study, to come and look at a poster, to come and look at a rug, a couch, a movie, a dog. The ones we married. The ones we might still call on the phone. The ones who sat beside us in junior high and college. The ones who chanced upon us at a party where there were too many empty cars or empty corners.

I had been forced into cars, shoved into elevators, and caught on stairways, but I had not been raped. I had fought and run; I had acquiesced to the driver until I could open a car door and leave. (It was astonishing how much of my young life revolved around car doors, my hand on the handle, the heated metal, the door locks like flattened silver mushrooms, the heavy wide swing so different from car doors now.)

Once, when a friend got into the back seat of a car driven by two older men, and I followed her because I didn't want her to go alone, I thought the whole time about Sula. She and Nel were walking home and expecting confrontation by older boys; Sula had in preparation brought a knife, and cut off the tip of her own finger to show the boys what she was willing to do to herself, so they could imagine what she would do to them. I began to speak toward the window as if I were insane, talking about my dad the sheriff, the shotgun, the consequences if they continued to drive us toward the river, the inevitability of death for all of us. They circled around and dropped us off near the convenience store where they'd found us. My crazy had worked, and my dependence on story was only intensified.

When I was sixteen, and got my first job at the Fox Theater, the required uniform was a striped minidress; when we ran out of popcorn, which happened frequently, the manager sent me around the corner to the Pussycat Theater, which never sold out of popcorn because it was the X-rated cinema. I stood in the lobby hating my life, while men made me wait for the five-foot-long bag of stale popcorn, enjoying my discomfort while they checked me out. At my dinner break, I had to walk past the Greyhound bus station and the Circus Bar to get food, while pimps and drunks tried to recruit me for work or marriage.

I went to Planned Parenthood the week I turned sixteen because I was terrified almost every day of my life. I went to Planned Parenthood because I was poor and prey, and girls had told me where the building was because they, too, were afraid of the same thing: We were certain we'd be raped at some point, and we didn't want to have babies because of that. We didn't want to have to marry our rapists.

But I was a girlfriend by then. My boyfriend was a large man. No one who knew us would bother me. I was also endlessly distracted by story and curiosity, and would talk to anyone, at the movie theater, at basketball games, at parties. Our senior year, at a New Year's Eve party in 1977, in a house near the foothills, more than a hundred of us drinking and dancing inside and outside, I saw a young man maybe twenty-five stagger across the lawn, his shirt unbuttoned, his long black hair in Bee Gee waves around his face, holding a bleeding hand in front of him.

I took him inside, to the bathroom, before anyone else noticed. I went to the sink, ran water, and grabbed tissues to clean his palm, cut deeply. He locked the door and attacked me. He smeared blood from both hands onto my breasts, in my new white sweater with gold stripes, and the first thing I thought was, Shit, I paid $17 for this sweater! (It was the most expensive piece of clothing I'd ever owned.)

I saw myself in the vanity mirror—a beautiful bathroom in a beautiful house. The red handprints. Then he broke a perfume bottle on the counter and stood there holding jagged glass, between me at the sink, and him at the door. He said, "I'm gonna kill you."

Talking didn't help this time. I have no idea what I said. I had just turned seventeen. There was loud music in all the rooms around us, and through the small bathroom window outside. But then fists were pounding on the bathroom door, and guys were shouting, "Who locked the door? I gotta drain the lizard. I gotta pee! Open the fuckin' door! If it's girls in there, stop doin' your hair and open the fuckin' door!"

Baseball players. If they hadn't been so drunk, they wouldn't have shoved the door open with their shoulders. They did. They saw me, their eyes went straight to the bloody handprints on my breasts in the white sweater. They rushed in and knocked the guy down. The police were called, and he was taken away. Dwayne was angrier than I'd ever seen him. He yelled at me for always trying to help someone, for being naïve. Someone put a letterman jacket around my shoulders to cover the blood.

All I could think about the next day was that I could have gotten pregnant, by a violent stranger, on a bathroom floor, if I hadn't gone to Planned Parenthood.

In college, a male acquaintance, an athlete who weighed 220 pounds, said one night, "I could just rape you right now." I weighed 110 pounds. I agreed that I was clearly incapable of preventing anything, but added that in the morning my cousin would drive in from Riverside and the acquaintance could choose which testicle he'd like to keep and which my cousin would shoot off with his Uzi. The casual forearm was lifted from my throat. I walked shakily down the dark stairwell of the building and ran home.

I ran so many times.

And until writing these pages, I never realized why I was so good at floating into another world. Even as the bad things happened, I noticed that the boys and men concentrated intently and didn't appear to be capable of abstract thought; I was the opposite, paying no attention to what was happening while completely absent and in a fictional world. This was because of my weeks in the hospital, when strangers came all hours of the day and night into my room—men and women, nurses and doctors and other people—and observed my body as a thing that had to work according to what they wanted. If

I squirmed in pain, I was restrained with straps, and tape was torn quickly from my legs, if my attendant was the older nurse with the accent like my grandmother's. She was terrifying. She inserted instruments into many parts of my body. She seemed interested in what happened when I had pain but no painkillers. Physical therapy hurt. My bones hurt. My broken leg bled onto the sheets. My other leg twisted itself flat after weeks, and people twisted up the right foot roughly and told me to hold it that way. Eventually someone put blocks there. (But my foot naturally falls to the side even now, when I lie down. Walking, I am duck-footed to the point of hilarity.)

I was alone then.

So I always made myself alone until I could leave. I pictured scenes from novels and stories, in vivid detail, down to the color of the leaves and the movement of the grass.

14

The Toast

Riverside, California, 1983

Jennie Stevenson sent for the girls first, back in 1940. Her half-sister Callie's children, back in Tulsa, were starving, and so Jennie took them into her home in Los Angeles: Minerva Kathryn Sims (known to us as Aint Sister), and Loretta Sims, the baby, who was only two when she came to California. These two impressive women watched me in June 1983, at the wedding of General III, where I endured a puffy organza bridesmaid dress and Dwayne wore a creamy groomsman tux.

That night, Dwayne said, "We should just get married, too."

I said, "Okay." We had six weeks until I had to go to graduate school.

When she heard this, Aunt Loretta summoned me to her house. She looked like Lena Horne. In a portrait taken of Loretta in the 1950s, she has bright golden skin, long hair pulled into a ponytail, confident smile tossed over a soft bare shoulder. But because of the circumstances of her life, Loretta, granddaughter of Fine, was regal but hard. She loved to cuss. She held the formal tribunal at her immaculate stucco bungalow two blocks from Alberta's house. (It's funny that I sort of had to ask the women for Dwayne's hand.)

I'd met her many times, but Loretta was guarded, her eyes sharp and assessing. In the driveway or at the park, she always looked as if she'd just stopped by on her way to a much more gracious event: her long hair styled in curls or a high bun, and in her later years, a shimmering wig that looked so perfectly glamorous and suitable on her head that my daughters never knew this was not her hair. Her forehead was soft and clear, her vivid mobile mouth lipsticked and full, and her cheekbones the same imperious ledges of bone as seen on Fine and Jennie and Callie.

She and Aint Sister wanted to talk to the white girl Dwayne thought he was going to marry. Other cousins were there watching. In the elegant chairs sat Sister, quiet, tall, and a legendary cook. Dwayne and I sat on an ornate couch, and I was afraid to look at Loretta, movie star haughty.

"What we want to know is can you *cook*?" I'll never forget Loretta's voice rising. "White people think putting salt and pepper on a hamburger is spicy. Sister and I are worried about our nephew. We ain't never had a white person in the family. We just want to make sure you can cook. We don't want him starvin' away."

I have no idea what I said. I was scared. I couldn't get up and head to the kitchen. This house didn't work like that. All the women stared at me. Dwayne saved me. He said I made the best chocolate chip cookies he'd ever tasted, and that Alberta loved them. "Well, shit, y'all can't live on no damn *cookies*!" Loretta said. "She better learn to fry some chicken." Then she laughed and laughed.

Alberta taught me to season and flour and fry chicken in her kitchen, and then she gave me a cast-iron pan already broken in by years of use. I still have it today in my kitchen. But

Dwayne had more patience with chicken than I did, so I made enchiladas and pork chops and thousands of cookies.

My mother had taught me to make the best chocolate chip cookies. She did not summon me for a lecture about the wedding, because I lived with her that summer. She told me we should just go to Vegas because she hated weddings. She took me to a sandwich place and said, "When you get married, you give away fifty percent of your life." My mom, a bank teller by then. Always with the numbers. I said, "What about the other half?" My mother said, "When you have a baby, you give away the other half." She ate her coleslaw.

So much bitter math.

Our August wedding day reached 108 degrees, so when we walked out of Allen Chapel African Methodist Episcopal Church, everyone in their suits and dresses started sweating. Our reception was a block away, at the Riverside Women's Club, the oldest women's organization in the city. We were tired as hell. Dwayne and his brothers had been up until 2:00 a.m. setting out chairs and tables for 225 people. My maid of honor, Laureen Morita, my college roommate, and I had been up until 2:00 a.m. making huge pans of lasagna, and carving watermelon bowls for fruit salad.

Dwayne's groomsmen were his three brothers, General III, Carnell, and Derrick, my two brothers, Jeffrey and John, and Penguin, our childhood friend. I was sad that day to have no sisters—but my sister-in-law Lisa was beside me, and Laureen, who was my college sister, and four childhood friends. Our wedding portrait is like an ad for required diversity—African-American, Japanese-American, Irish- and German- and Oklahoma-American, Swiss.

My Swiss grandparents, Paul and Rosa Leu, and my aunt Stini Leu were there, so short that Dwayne's family stared and I heard *like elves* from one of the Sims cousins.

In the kitchen of the women's club, Aint Sister fried twenty chickens, and General Sims II's friend Principal, a short dark man from Tennessee who had been a navy cook, who always wore a porkpie hat and talked to me of horse racing, made hams and meat loaves that he set beside the lasagna. As people pinned dollar bills onto my lace-edged dress for the dollar dance, I saw my father, Richard, and stepmother, Ruth Catherine, leaving. I was in the middle of dancing with my father-in-law; I didn't see my father again for fourteen years, until the death of my stepmother, but never knew why until last year.

Apparently my mother and stepmother got into a territorial fight in the kitchen, watched by Sister and Principal. My stepmother is said to have entered the kitchen to tell people that the food was not sufficient, and my mother, who had been called white trash too many times to take this from a woman who had also been called white trash too many times, lit into her. These two women had never in their lives breathed the same air in an enclosed space.

But Dwayne and I noticed none of this. We were dancing. General II was dancing, and General IV, who was two years old and our ring bearer, was dancing, and then General III, the best man, hollered for everyone to gather around, lifted his champagne glass, and gave his toast, which was brief: "Like the Bible says, be fruitful and multiply, y'all."

But we did not. Not then.

We fell asleep at 7:00 p.m., tired from all the chair-moving and cooking. We went across the border to Mexico for two days and ate lobster and buttered fresh tortillas. On the third day, we packed up the tiny Honda Civic and drove until we got to Tulsa.

My dad had taken all of us kids in a station wagon to Yellowstone, the Colorado Rockies, and Grand Canyon, but I'd never been to the South. Dwayne's father had taken all his kids in a station wagon to Oklahoma when they were young, but Dwayne hadn't been back. General II wanted us to stay with his father's brother, Uncle Lanier Sims, and his wife, Mozelle, who were in their seventies.

Their brick house in north Tulsa was beautiful and quiet. They stared at me, narrow-eyed. I don't think they knew their great-nephew was bringing a blond wife. On the couch, showing us baby pictures in photo albums, they told me the story of one of America's worst racial conflicts, which had been kept secret for decades. The polite, composed elderly couple, with golden skin and hair combed back and held firmly in place, had nearly died because of a white woman.

In 1921, Greenwood, a square of businesses and homes extending several miles in the heart of Tulsa, was the wealthiest black community in America. Movie theaters, banks, barbershops, stores, restaurants, and churches, most of them imposing brick buildings. Black people had migrated to Tulsa from many places, but especially Texas and Mississippi. W. Stanford and Minerva Sims, parents of General and Lanier Sims, left Grenada, Mississippi, in 1900 for Oklahoma. Their son General was not yet a year old.

Stanford was one of eleven children of Cary and Henrietta Sims, born in 1849 and 1853, both formerly enslaved; Minerva was one of eleven children of Albert and Ella Hardiman, born in 1849 and 1852, both formerly enslaved. Back in Grenada, both husbands were sons of white overseers and enslaved women; both wives were daughters of African and indigenous-descended parents.

Stanford and Minerva first settled in Muskogee, where he was a teacher and she raised General and her second son, Lanier. But at some point, though Stanford was teaching in Muskogee, Minerva and the boys went to live twenty-five miles away in Tulsa. Here is where the family story gets murky; no one has ever found out the truth. Stanford finished teaching on a Friday, January 11, 1905, but was not allowed on the train to Tulsa. It is said that he walked for miles on the tracks but froze to death. It is also said that Minerva was unhappy with him and he was somehow poisoned. After his death, the two boys went for a time to an orphanage in Broken Bow, Indian Territory. Eventually, Minerva retrieved them.

In every photo of Minerva, she does not smile. Always judgmental and dissatisfied, her face thin and eyes half-lidded, her mouth turned down, she was especially hard on her eldest son, General. If the freakish Spaniards had conferred with her, General would have been classified as *torna atrás*, and that altered everything about his life. His brother Lanier was light-skinned, like his father. General was brown-skinned, darker than both his parents. Minerva was open with her favoritism, especially after Stanford died.

Lanier married Mozelle Sims, one of eleven children of parents who were Creek freedpeople, black men and women who had been enslaved by Creek Nation people before the Civil War, and forced along with their owners to walk the Trail of Tears from Creek land in Georgia to Oklahoma. After Emancipation, Creek freedmen and women were each deeded eighty acres of land; Mozelle and her sisters owned acreage outside Tulsa.

This matters because in January 1921, the black people of Tulsa were independent, powerful, often landowners, survivors already of war and conflict on many fronts, and then the men returned from World War I with their brown uniforms and their military weapons, and their pride. Greenwood swelled with prosperity, in full view of white downtown, and white Tulsa didn't like black pride.

Dick Rowland, a young black man working downtown, entered an elevator, and a white woman, Nancy Pettis, claimed he had assaulted her (maybe he stepped on her foot, caught off guard when the elevator moved). He was arrested, and that night, a white Tulsa mob went to the jail intent on hanging him. He was seventeen.

The mob was met by a wall of black men, many in uniform with their service weapons. The night was described by Lanier and other relatives as open warfare—hundreds of armed men shooting one another. Then truckloads of white Tulsans and white men from outlying areas entered Greenwood, shooting men, women, children, systematically torching houses and churches and businesses. I have seen the postcards made from photographs taken by white people. These show the burned bodies of black men, hands curled into frozen fight or surrender, feet unrecognizable, and the slanted handwriting below: *Dead nigers in Tulsa, Oklahoma January 10, 1921*. There are many versions of this postcard, with different scenes.

Black Tulsans killed many white men, too. The National Guard was called, and then the unthinkable happened: Federal aircraft, piloted by National Guardsmen, dropped gasoline bombs onto Greenwood. Tanks entered the area. Black homes and churches were looted, and black residents were herded into the Tulsa Fairgrounds. Black bodies and white bodies were said to have been thrown into the river. These men were friends and neighbors of the Sims family. No one knows how many people died.

One baby was born, that first night. Mozelle Sims was seventeen, married for ten months, and alone. Her husband, Lanier, at work downtown, had been told to leave the city right away by his employer, so he wouldn't be killed. Mozelle knew none of this. Mobs were shooting people, throwing kerosene into homes and then torches, and Mozelle went into labor. She didn't know how to drive, but she got into Lanier's car, stepped on the gas, and drove as far from the city as she could. She made it to an area where other black people had gathered, in the countryside. There, she had her son, among strangers.

When she and Lanier found each other days later, they were taken to the fairgrounds, where thousands of people were held by armed National Guard, given badges and tags. Mozelle and her newborn slept in a stable. She and Lanier had planned to name him Stanford, after his grandfather. But there was no way to record his birth or his name for six days, and by the end of their imprisonment, they decided to name him Charles Wesley.

I try to imagine now what Mozelle thought, telling this to a twenty-two-year-old white girl from California. I flash back to the countless American histories of violence and murder built around those terrible moments: a white girl or woman, a woman who looked like me, a story so often not true, an idea that became a rasp and origin spark, like the click of a lighter held by an arsonist.

Their kindness to me was astonishing.

In the morning, we went out to Rentie Grove, a historic black community founded in 1880 by the Rentie and Walker familes, Creek freedpeople, where Mozelle had eighty acres. Dwayne had stayed here when he was eight, and the land was still farmed by relatives, including Mozelle's sister Georgia, who kept a pistol in her apron pocket.

We touched the headstone of General Sims, Dwayne's grandfather, who died when Dwayne's father, General II, was only seven. Then we touched the marker for Beloved Grandmother, Finey Kemp, 1874–1952.

Dwayne stood in the long dry grass, near a snakeskin like a sinuous ghost, and said to me, "Grandma Fine saved them all. That's what Daddy always said. He said they were starving out here and their other grandma, Minnie, came and took them to the orphanage. But Fine went and got them all back and then she went to Minnie's house and pulled a gun and told Minnie to never take her grandkids again."

Fine, the little girl who'd survived the world completely alone; Fine, whose daughter Callie had married Minerva's son General, knew Minerva as a woman who'd always had two parents, back in Mississippi, and eleven brothers and sisters, and a house.

Before she rested there, in Tulsa, Fine had survived alone in Tennessee, and then she had survived her second husband in Texas.

In 1902, Fine had married the older man who invited her and her three children into his house in Denton, Texas. Zach Rollins was thirty years older than Fine. He was the son of a white slave-owner and an enslaved woman, born in Grenada, Mississippi, in 1848, and brought to the countryside near Denton as a slave by his own father, in 1863. He was only fifteen. Freed after the Civil War, he registered to vote in 1867, had a daughter named Mollie that year, but didn't marry. By 1876, he had worked so hard and was so ambitious that he and another former slave purchased eighty acres of homestead land for $400. He married in 1880, was a widower soon after, raising his daughter alone. He married again in 1884, and was again a widower soon after. Either his wives were very unlucky in their illnesses, or he was a difficult man to survive. I wonder often what Fine knew, or guessed, after she and her children walked into his house the first time. But she made her calculations of existence.

By 1900, he had left his homestead and moved to Oakland Avenue, across from the Denton County Courthouse. He was "elected" the courthouse custodian. In 1902, he married "Fin Hofford," and after that she was known as "Vinie Rollins." Their son James was born in 1903, and Callie was born in 1906. But Fine's daughter Jennie had fled when she was about fourteen, and her brother Mack was dead by the time he was ten or eleven.

According to what Fine told her grandchildren, Zach Rollins was immediately violent and brutally abusive to his stepchildren. Jennie ran away to Tulsa; Mack, who was frail and disabled, was beaten often. He died in 1909. By the 1910 federal census, the household still contained Floyd, Fine's second son, born back in Tennessee, who was listed as fifteen years old, mulatto; James, seven, mulatto; and Callie, four, mulatto. In fact, the entire street, Oakland Avenue, is listed as having mulatto residents.

The house must have been a traumatic place to live. And by 1911, Zach Rollins was suddenly dead, at sixty-five. On his death certificate, the primary cause is chronic bronchitis, which had lasted only one month; the secondary cause is listed as somatic dissociation.

Today, somatic dissociation is defined as neurological symptoms related to memory or identity, not caused by disease but by past trauma or psychological stress. Zach Rollins had survived slavery, had been brought as a teen by his father, the man who owned him, to rough Texas land recently fought over by troops and indigenous Comanches. He had probably witnessed the same violent horrors, and different horrors, as had his wife, Fine.

Now she was thirty-three years old, living in a house that was not hers, with three children. Fine told her grandchildren that white relatives of the Rawlings family (spellings are varied), from the slaveowner Dan Rawlings's legal marriage, began to claim the property, taking farm equipment, livestock, and even furniture from the land. Fine believed that someone had poisoned her son James, whose body and mind deteriorated to the point of complete disability.

She wrote to her daughter Jennie, who was about twenty-three then. Fine and the children went to Tulsa, where Jennie gave them her room in the residential hotel where she lived. Jennie went to stay with a friend. Fine got work as a domestic and enrolled Callie in school. She was determined that her youngest child would graduate from high school and go to college.

By the time Dwayne and I left Tulsa, and drove through West Virginia and Pennsylvania and then up to Massachusetts, my head was full of history and family and American landscape. I had written four short stories, with young characters fleeing violence and poverty. That year, other writers, and professors, in my graduate program at Amherst questioned my work: "You can't use words like this. Not standard English." "Aren't you from California? Why don't you write about surfing?" "Why do you keep writing about all these working-class people?" This last term I had never heard, and the sneer in the voice of the graduate student, a woman from Smith College, confused me so much that I had no reply.

That night, after Dwayne went to work night shift at the juvenile correctional facility in a small Massachusetts town twenty miles away, I thought: What the hell is working class? Work or welfare—those two were the only conditions of life back home. *You got a paycheck job!* Kaiser Steel, Toro lawnmowers, Rockwell aircraft, Alcan aluminum, Goodyear tires. *You under the table, man?* That meant cash-only economy, for everyone else—housepainting, yard work, construction, shade-tree mechanic, and drug dealing. The only other category was welfare.

Two of my professors refused to call on me in class, and gave me failing grades, one claiming that a research paper was plagiarized because the last page was more yellowed than the rest; I had a job cleaning houses, had worked all day, finished the paper at 2:00 a.m. and had to find a random sheet in an old folder on the windowsill, because Dwayne was gone with the car to work. The professor said derisively that he'd seen me walking with a tall black man, and I said that was my husband. The professor said that Amherst was not California. Dwayne was so furious that he actually walked me to class, as if we were in high school; he stood in the doorway, glaring at the professor and the rest of the students. Then they were afraid of me.

We had James Baldwin. His class and friendship were life-saving. But after workshop, he held court in a local bar, where everyone tried to get close to him. Dwayne and I went once to the bar; the bouncer refused to let us in. He said California licenses were not valid in his eyes. His glare said we were black and white. He folded his arms. I thought Dwayne would punch him. We never went back.

But Dwayne punched a different guy, who taunted him and poked him in the eye during a YMCA basketball league. Dwayne was the only black player. He quit the league. Then ice shrouded the apartment complex where we lived. I cooked huge pots of refried beans to make us feel at home, and Dwayne turned up the heat and wore shorts. I had worked as a house-cleaner, as a parking lot attendant, and delivered newspapers to hundreds of rural road boxes before dawn. But I could write about nothing else but home, even if I'd never sell anything.

On our honeymoon in Rosarito, Mexico, while Dwayne slept, I'd gone down to the beach to write in my notebook a story called "Buddah," about a teenager who keeps himself alive by stealing food and cars. Now I began a story called "Training," based on two things that haunted me: A friend had killed himself by standing in front of the train that rolled above my neighborhood, and a nephew stopped speaking and was put into "educationally handicapped" classrooms.

Other professors saved me—Margo Culley introduced me to the novels of women such as Leslie Marmon Silko and Harriet Arnow, who wrote of home. I was given Flannery O'Connor and endless encouragement by Jay Neugeboren, and advice by Julius Lester, who kept saying, "Why are there so many damn helicopters and guns in your stories? Do you live in Saigon?"

And then, one afternoon at his home, while Dwayne played basketball in the driveway with Skip and Rico, James Baldwin spoke to me gently about my story of a young woman robbed at gunpoint on a Los Angeles bus. He told me the entire story hinged on the moments she spent at work with a man named Leonard. "It is always the secondary characters who save us," he said. Then he smiled, the way his whole face broke open. "You must continue to write. It is imperative."

I loved that word. *Imperative.*

Dwayne thought winter was a joke. I'd driven hundreds of careful miles delivering those newspapers. Dwayne drove at night to his job. When people warned him, he kept laughing. "Black ice? I'm a black man. Black ice don't want to hurt *me.*"

He spun into a chestnut tree hundreds of years old, on a rural road, with a juvenile prisoner in the passenger seat, transporting the boy from a police station. The Honda was totaled. The kid hurt his knee. Dwayne had a burn all along his chest and shoulder from the force of the seat belt, and a severe concussion. Someone dropped him off that night, at our tiny apartment.

He was in shock. He lay in bed shivering violently. The snow fell all night, and the temperature dropped to minus 24.

He threw up so many times into my only large cooking pot that nothing was left but bile and I didn't know what bile was. I called my mother, three thousand miles away on Christmas Eve, and she said, "Give him water. Nothing else." She sounded as dispassionate as my grandmother Rosa Leu, but possibly she was worried and didn't want me to lose my mind.

I gave Dwayne 7 Up. He vomited. I gave him milk. He vomited. I called her again, and now she sounded exasperated. "Did you give him water?" Water had seemed perfunctory. Uncaring. But I did. A spoonful, like a child. He didn't vomit. Every hour, I gave him another spoonful. The snow piled outside our window, behind my typewriter and the boombox, and he finally slept.

I lay beside him in the dark and wrote an entire short story in a notebook. An eighty-year-old woman and her husband, a former miner who has black lung disease. In my mind, I saw his great-aunt Mozelle, though this night had nothing to do with her. I just saw her face, her calm equanimity, her ministrations, and I heard her voice.

We bought a used red Renault from an Algerian guy, for $500. We left before the graduation ceremony, because there was no one to watch me, and we wanted to go home. The car broke down on many days. Through upstate New York, I told Dwayne the stories of Joyce Carol Oates. Through Pennsylvania, I told him the novels of Pete Dexter and David Bradley. In Ohio, I made him drive around Lorain, and told him every novel by Toni Morrison. That week, he was reading *Dune*, by Frank Herbert. Finally, we went through Las Vegas, and then the state line of California, the Renault barely shuddering.

Dwayne parked it in front of my parents' house, and it never again moved of its own volition until we sold it for $200 to two of my first students here in California: Hmong teenagers from the highlands of Laos, whose fathers had worked for the CIA during the Vietnam War. The boys were car mechanics to whom I taught English as a Second Language.

15

Fruitful #2

No one asked why we came home. Everyone we knew came home, unless they'd joined the military, and then they came home once a year. Everyone asked me why I still hadn't had a baby. *You sterile? That what they call it? What y'all waitin' for? You ain't figured it out yet?*

I was twenty-three. Friends and relatives had two and three and four babies already. James Baldwin had invited us to St. Paul de Vence, where he lived in France; I dreamed of going there, and then to New York, where we'd have an apartment with a fire escape. Above a restaurant, so I wouldn't have to cook.

But we lived in a one-bedroom apartment my stepfather, John Watson, had built in the 1950s. I wrote in our closet on the trunk that Daisy Carter had brought to California from Mississippi, back in 1936. I must have had memories of the Swiss clock, the oatmeal, my baby brother screaming in rage and dust; I told Dwayne I didn't want to have a baby until we had a house, with a bedroom for the baby, and a yard with grass.

We moved to a small duplex, and then I was twenty-four, and twenty-five. People said to Dwayne, "Damn, Sims, what's the problem? We want to see what these babies are gonna look like!"

Aside from the genetic lottery that was always a fun game in our family, he was hesitant, too. He was fine to wait until we had a little money, because a lot of our friends were in trouble. It was the beginning of the crack years, and already deep into the speed years, and we couldn't keep bicycles and hoses and trash cans and rakes from being stolen out of our yard. We never knew who we'd see on the street with dark haloes around their eyes, or teeth missing, asking us for a few dollars.

When I was nineteen, in my second year of college, I came home for summer to work at a gas station. One of my closest friends was pregnant, and decided not to return to college. She asked me to help her make a nursery for the baby.

She was living a few miles outside the city, in a beautiful old Spanish-style apartment building falling apart now, in a dusty clearing in the foothills. It was a hundred degrees that day in August, and her boyfriend was gone, so we were going to remove forty of his marijuana plants from the closet where he'd rigged up a heat and light system (this was 1980). She was eight months pregnant. We laughed and played the radio while we moved all the pots, sweating and damp, to the hallway. She kept looking nervously at the dirt driveway. So did I. Her boyfriend was six feet two and had a temper. We swept out the potting soil and spiders and fertilizer from the closet, which was large. We washed the plaster walls.

Then we painted the closet yellow. We penciled in a rainbow on the back wall, painted the arch in five colors, and inside we painted in delicate script the name she had chosen for her daughter. My friend was third-generation Mexican-American, and her boyfriend was L.A. African-American and Oklahoma Cherokee. We talked about what their daughter's hair and eyes would look like. We talked about what my future babies would look like. Then she said, "You better go now. Before he comes back."

I went to work at the gas station, where men drove away with stolen gas and my manager leaped onto the hood of one car and smashed the windshield with his baseball bat and demanded the driver's wallet, where men lingered in the tiny store where I stood behind the case of heated cashews and peanuts, and in front of the copies of *Hustler* and *Playboy*, the men who talked to me forever while waiting for there to be no other customers.

I wore my Mobil uniform shirt, with the embroidered Pegasus and my name below it. I did not yet want a baby. I knew where the baseball bat was behind the counter, but mostly I learned to look at men's hands and eyes and throats, trying to judge whether they were dangerous. The day after I quit, the girl who worked nights was robbed at gunpoint.

Five years later, in 1985, when we were back from Amherst, and Dwayne was working as a night custodian and I was teaching Southeast Asian refugee students at Job Corps how to pass their GED exams, when I was writing stories on the little blue Smith Corona by the light of a tiny lamp on Daisy's trunk, we were lonely.

On weekends, we went to my friend's apartment. She had two small daughters now, and her boyfriend had a thriving business. We barbecued outside, in the dusty clearing under the pepper trees, but the long-haired white neighbors were so high on Tuinals and tequila that they often fell face-first in the dirt and stopped moving. My friend brought us inside. We watched TV from the couch in the living room, her toddler moving around our feet, until someone knocked hard on the front door.

Her boyfriend gestured, and she went upstairs with their daughter. Then he reached under the couch and pulled out a semiautomatic rifle, aimed it at the door, and yelled for a name. Under the couch was cocaine. We thought we were sitting on weed.

The name yelled back was that of another childhood friend. When he came inside and saw us, his face was abashed, desperate, and haunted.

Driving home, Dwayne and I were devastated. He said we could never go back. "When the cops come bustin' in, they don't care we've been to college. We're goin' to jail. Or we're dead. Just like everybody else in there."

Two years later, I was teaching English as a Second Language to refugees and English to city college students, Dwayne was working at a juvenile correctional facility, and we had saved enough money to look for a house. We drove this neighborhood, the grid of narrow historic streets and old homes that seemed quiet. We saw a small shingled white house partly covered with wisteria, a bungalow I'd always loved, and a FOR SALE sign. This street was five minutes from Dwayne's neighborhood, and ten minutes from my parents'.

These sidewalks were shaded by old oak and carob trees, and houses had porches. Our house was built in 1910, on the corner of what had been an orange grove. Across the street had been a walnut grove. The first man who owned the bungalow was a farmer and then car salesman; when he was ninety-five, he sold it to the second man, a mechanic who was now ninety-five, a widower, his four kids gone to northern California. His old silver toaster was still in the breakfast nook. The windows had been nailed shut and paint applied thickly into the gaps around the windowsills to keep out heat and street noise. He sold it to the third man, Dwayne, who was twenty-eight, and me.

We couldn't yet live in the house, but it seemed safe to think about a baby. I was worried pregnancy might take a long time, that I'd blown it by waiting until I was twenty-seven. We began tearing out stained carpet, pulling vines from the windows, and in the back bedroom, which would belong to any baby who might show up, tried to sand the oil stains from the hardwood floor. The owner had rebuilt engines in that bedroom. My brother, Jeff, moved into that room, and he, Dwayne and I stripped paint from the windowsills and cabinets all night, after work. We put mattresses on the floor, and got ready to leave our old duplex.

My sister-in-law Margrett, married to Dwayne's youngest brother, Derrick, came to help me clean the duplex for the deposit. It was June. We had packed everything. We had both worked all day, she at the hospital where she did patient intake, me in the classroom. We scrubbed the kitchen: Easy-Off, Ajax, Windex, bleach. Margrett was at the sink, making fun of all the Sims brothers, and suddenly I knelt hard on the linoleum, dizzy. She had two teenagers; she was seven years older than me. She bent down and looked at my eyes, and said, "Girl, get your damn head out that oven—you're pregnant."

I went to the doctor a week later. Almost three months. And the next day, at the city college, standing in front of my class, I began to lose the baby. After the students left, I went to an office and called Dwayne. He had our only car; I had walked to work. But there was no phone in our house. I tried to call my mother, but she was at work. So I walked from the quadrangle where Dwayne's mother, Alberta, had gone to high school, when this historic building had been the only high school, down the ravine and toward the same hospital where I'd been born. The pain was intense. I walked up past the baseball field, and into the parking lot, and then I went nearly to my knees, leaning against a car.

Three older black women taking a lunch break from housekeeping saw me—one was Penguin's mother. She helped me inside, whispering, "Baby girl, baby girl, you shouldn't have worked so hard. Margrett was right." She took me inside, down a hallway, and then to a gurney, wheeled to the place where the baby was removed.

When I came out of anesthesia, Dwayne and my dad were there. Penguin's mother had called Alberta, and they sent someone to find Dwayne, who'd been sanding paint off the wooden sliding doors a few feet from where I sit right now. (Every time I touch those doors I think of that baby. I do.)

I slept one night at my mother's house; in the morning, she told me to go to work, because things like that happened to women all the time, and it was best to forget about them right away. But she went back to knitting baby booties and a tiny infant jacket.

Alberta told me quietly as well that it happened to women all the time. James, the son she had before Dwayne, had died at five months old, and she thought about him every day. At the fireplace, she put her hand on my knee and said, "The next one will be your girl. They're watching from heaven right now to see what she looks like. My mother dreamed about your baby. That's right."

I thought it would take forever to get pregnant again. In the fall, General II delivered to us a load of eucalyptus trunks from a tree he'd cut. It was hot, and I was grading papers on the porch while Dwayne cut the wood with my brother's chain saw.

The roar and spray of silvery woodchips. Inexplicably, I fell asleep so close to the roaring that when I woke, my clothes were covered with fragrant menthol sawdust. I was two months pregnant.

Dwayne was of course worried all the time that I'd lose this baby, too. He came home one winter morning looking mildly deranged, something very off-kilter in his face. He hung his jacket on our bedroom door, and stood beside the bed. I was getting up for work. He was going to sleep.

I asked him what was wrong, and he said nothing. I was six months pregnant. I went off to work, and that evening, while he was sleeping again, I read the newspaper. A juvenile offender at the correctional facility had escaped; an officer had been attacked. Dwayne's sheepskin-lined cloth jacket had black rings of burn on the chest. An elaborate plot: The juvenile, whose father was a white gangster of some note, had displayed a smuggled bottle of pills; he claimed an overdose, Dwayne had to escort him across the street to the hospital, walking, the kid shackled hand and foot. Old school. From the bushes, a man rose up and shot Dwayne with a Taser, in the chest. Dwayne glanced down, unaffected because of his size and the jacket, and punched the man in the face hard enough to knock him out. The kid was hobbling toward a van parked at the curb. Dwayne caught him there, and the door opened. A .45 was pointed at Dwayne's face, and he backed away. The gun remained trained upon his forehead until the kid was pulled into the van and the vehicle sped away.

"Why didn't you tell me!?" I said, waking him up.

He opened one eye. "I didn't want to scare you and you'd lose the baby."

The next day, in the driveway on Michael Street, all the women laughed at that. "If bein' scared by somethin' would make a baby come, by the time every woman was eight months pregnant she'd be *payin'* somebody to shoot her husband with a damn Taser! If gettin' on a plane would make you go into labor, the sky would be *fulla* planes just flyin' pregnant women around! I'da paid for that plane ride! A *baby* plane! We can make big money on that!"

In May 1989, a few weeks before I had the baby, I sat on the porch steps with Margaret Chandler, great-niece of Daisy, who was pregnant, and Nygia Preston, granddaughter of Callie, who was pregnant. Margaret named her son Marcus, Nygia named her daughter Porscha; I'd thought for weeks about making both grandmothers—Gabrielle Gertrude Leu Straight Watson, and Alberta Marie Morris Sims—feel honored. I had two choices, Albertagail, which would have been unfair even in 1900, or the name I loved and so did they: Gaila. I had saved Terry McMillan's book *Mama*, refusing to read past the first page until I was in labor. During the fifth hour, I asked Dwayne to read it to me. There is a moment when a mosquito roams a bedroom, and the mother exposes her own body to keep the insect from taking the blood of her baby. He read me the whole book. He brought me contraband M&Ms, which I could hold one by one in my mouth. It took forever to have this baby.

From the moment we saw Gaila, we knew she held the best of all the worlds in her tiny body.

I was pregnant five times in seven years. I had waited for five years to make sure Dwayne didn't leave, to make sure my kids would have a bedroom and a yard and a tree in which to read books. I had three daughters, and lost two babies, and sometimes I truly wonder if those were the sons. If boys had been born, everything about our lives would have been dramatically different. As it was, we were a nation of girls and women in this shingled house, north end covered with purple wisteria blossoms that tangled into the two fig trees. Towers of books in each corner, Barbies I stacked like firewood at night, wild animals that roamed the yard, flowers everywhere, and endless bowls of ice cream, for which we would walk one mile to the drugstore. As it was, we were four females whose view of the world began on that front porch, went out to the sidewalk, then two miles to the driveway on Michael Street, and from there into the world.

I hadn't realized how much my entire life was about fiction, the images and sentences and ideas of novels and stories, until I looked at my three small girls one night, all of them lying on the sheets I'd spread in the grass to escape the heat. I lay beside them, staring up at the branches of the carob tree and the police helicopter moving like a glittering wasp above us, my daughters murmuring their last questions of the night, and finally falling asleep. All of us facing the stars. I could smell the dew rising from the earth into the grass around us, the smell of silver. Into my head came one of my favorite lines from Toni Morrison's *Sula*, altered from the two best friends to how I felt about my children: "We were four throats and one eye and we had no price."

III

16

Run the World

Riverside, California, 1989

I never thought of my first daughter as anything but my companion. The companion of my dreams and books. It was summer. She rarely wanted to be inside the house, hated dim light, never wanted me to put her down. Every single adult I saw said either "Put a hat on that baby or she'll catch her death of cold!" (it was 95 degrees) or "Put that baby down or she'll get spoiled and be the death of you!" (Understandably—they had seen too much death.) So we walked the yard looking at branches and flowers while her eyes focused and went from night purple to clearest brown with rays of black inside.

I had the excuse now to read Little Golden Books and to buy more. I read to Gaila about puppies and kittens and skunks and possums and mice and moles and raccoons and elephants and horses and rabbits. Dwayne read his favorites: *Seven Chinese Brothers*, which the girls said later was oddly frightening, and *Love You Forever*, which featured toilet paper and was a hit.

Gaila never slept. She could hear the smallest sound that

made its way through the darkness into the gaps around the old wooden windowsills. Her father worked days then, and when we were sleeping, at 2:00 a.m. and 4:00 a.m. and 5:00 a.m., Gaila would stand in her crib and shout, "Train!" We lived about a mile from a rail crossing, and all night the engineers sounded their horns in distinctive songs to their wives and families as they passed through. She would shout, "Dog!" Night-barking dogs talked to one another through our neighborhood, and coyotes came up from the river to roam our streets.

"Input," Dwayne would say wearily, hanging towels and thick blankets around the windows. He loved this word. "She never stops wanting input."

But I was thrilled, in the daytime anyway, because Gaila was my buddy and I hated being inside, too. She never tired of each story I told her, and she gave the dogs names, and the trees, and the Band-Aid on the sidewalk, and the white stars inside the bougainvillea. Before she turned two, she required three books before considering her breakfast—no oatmeal!—and three books during her bath—no cheating! Dwayne was astonished that she knew when he skipped pages, and told him what should be happening to Mama Skunk or the Three Little Kittens.

We had taken Gaila to Ensenada, Mexico, when she was only six months old, her car seat wedged between us on the bench seat of the pickup truck; we camped on the beach. At the border crossing, a guard questioned me hard, asking why we were bringing a small Mexican boy back to California. I offered to nurse her, and he winced and let us through. When she was a year old, we took her camping in northern California and Oregon, to see elk crashing antlers in fall battles. She practiced her baseball throw with walnuts we found in a hot golden grove in the San Joaquin Valley.

She got valley fever from that agricultural dust. We messed up a lot.

I was told to play only Raffi. I had no idea who that was. I sang her "Angel Baby," from Art Laboe's *Killer Oldies* show, and Dwayne played her "Tear the Roof Off the Sucker" by Parliament.

I was told not to work. I liked being able to pay our mortgage and buy food. If she got a fever or a cold, I held her in front of my classes, rocking back and forth while I read aloud passages from *Sula* and Leslie Marmon Silko's *Ceremony*, from Larry Brown's *Samaritans* and James Welch's *Fools Crow*, which I taught to my students, most of whom were the first generation, like me, to attend college, so they could think about their homes and regions as those writers did, with love and tenderness. (Some of my first students back then were from Coachella, El Monte, La Puente, and Indio—they are the writers Rigoberto Gonzalez, Michael Jaime-Becerra, Alex Espinoza, and John Olivares Espinoza. All four write about home with loyal compassion.)

I was told to make homemade baby food. But Gaila spent her days with Alberta, and she ate with her grandmother—history and love in her mouth. Alberta chewed fried chicken or pork chops or smothered steak into softness and then pushed the meat into Gaila's mouth. She said, "You're never gonna starve. Now give me some sugar."

Gaila was Alberta's tenth grandchild, and she spent all day with her. Gaila slept in her arms. When she woke, Alberta let Gaila stamp on her thighs, and sang her songs. The endless succession of daily visitors to Alberta's living room held Gaila as well, telling stories that whispered past her eyes. I came home at lunch to nurse her, and we watched one soap opera—*General Hospital*. Alberta didn't cut her fingernails—Gaila would scream when I tried, with the tiny scissors—and cutting baby nails was said to make the child a thief. Alberta gently trimmed the soft nails with her teeth. Then Alberta bit her cheeks softly, leaving tiny marks like miniature staples, and said, "We're gonna raise you to run the world. That's right."

When Gaila got a fever, my mother came over at night, dipped cloth diapers in vinegar and rubbed Gaila's hot legs until the fever subsided. My mother's face would be drawn with worry—fevers took children to death back in the Swiss Alps.

I was trying to finish my first book, writing in the same notebooks I had used while sitting in our cars as Dwayne worked on the engines in our driveway. I had typed half of the book, sitting at a card table pushed against my side of the bed. The night James Baldwin passed away, I cried because I would never see him again. I would never forget anything he told me. *Imperative*, he said. I walked Gaila up and down the sidewalk near midnight, weeping at the disappearance of his kindness and his voice.

She never napped. I walked her for miles after work, the stroller bumping over tree roots cleaving the sidewalk. When she finally slept, I sat down on the curb wherever we were and took my notebook from the mesh storage pocket. I wrote for however long I had. But every time, passing cars stopped. People offered me money or a place to stay, figuring I was homeless, and their conversation woke up the baby.

I'm sure I looked tragically itinerant. I just wanted to finish my novel. When it won a prize, and was published, I went alone to accept the prize in a city full of writers. At an elegant lunch, two well-known women authors, not married, childless, told me that I'd never accomplish acclaim, because California had no true intellectuals besides Didion. They said my community would imprison me, and so would family. I said I didn't want to leave my home, and I could never take my baby from her two grandmothers.

That night, at the reception, I drank champagne and ate caviar for the first time in my life; at midnight I ate five pieces of roast lamb, which I'd also never had. Aha, I thought. Surprising cleavage in the cocktail dress I wore, that Alberta had lent me. Gold sequins, black silk fringe.

Already pregnant again, I realized, and had to laugh. I tease Delphine that this is the reason for her love of travel and fine food.

We were never alone, on this corner. Dwayne was now working night shift at the juvenile correctional facility, and that summer he probably slept three hours a day. We had an ancient fuse box that blew the power if we hung one string of Christmas lights or tried one minute of microwaving. I had Delphine in July 1991, so the girls and I spent all summer vacation outside while he tried to nap. But everyone had started to gather on our gravel driveway, where there was a pathway that according to our deed allowed us to "run our pigs along the easement all the way to the river." Our cousins and friends came to work on cars and hang out and listen to music Dwayne played in the garage. Kids played in the blue truckbed. We were the aunt and uncle who took all the nieces and nephews—ten at a time—to the beach or to Disneyland.

My mother's house, when I was a teenager, was quiet. I hadn't realized how much I wanted a house like Alberta's—but that open door meant constant company. Our neighbors all had small kids and babies, too. My sidewalk was crowded with Big Wheels and pails and buckets, kids playing in the flowerbeds and under the mulberry tree we planted. I left the branches low and untrimmed so children could climb up into the trunk more easily—and I climbed up there with them to read and hang sheets for pirate ships.

There was no privacy. People would drive by and holler, "You better put them kids to bed!" or "You got your hair cut?" Cars stopped and women asked if they could enroll their kids in my day care. I said I didn't run a day care. They raised their eyebrows at the multitude of toys, the plastic pool, and the Radio Flyer wagon. Dwayne sighed and hauled some of the toys up on the porch to hide them.

I had two small girls. Gaila was turning three, and went to day care at the house of Clarice Collins, Dwayne's godmother, five doors down from Alberta. Alberta was trying to keep Delphine on her lap, but it wasn't working. (Alberta watched babies until they could run down the hallway at full speed, which meant she'd miss major portions of the soaps. She always said, "I'm done chasing babies. Once they can run, they go to Clarice.")

Gaila had taken my Barbie, meaning my childhood doll, purchased for me in 1966, to day care; while the kids played in the backyard near Jesse Collins's truck—the one the men used to drive to the night shift at the Air Force base—a girl named Skeeter, who was six, threw Barbie into the alley, where she was mauled by Jesse's guard Doberman. When retrieved, Barbie had, in addition to the greenish discoloration on her thighs from mold, which resembled bruising, new lacerations to her head and teeth marks all over her body.

At home that night, sitting on our front porch steps, I tried to prevent Delphine, who walked at nine months and was consistently covered with real bruises, from falling on the cement. Gaila had gotten out the colored chalk. She kept telling me about Skeeter and Percy and Maisha. She told me about her cousin Holla, my brother Jeff's daughter, who was seven. These were the powerful people in her life.

I turned around, and she had written in block letters

SKEETER on one ancient cement step, and HOLLA on the other one.

In one of our favorite films, *My Mother's Castle*, Marcel Pagnol's father, a teacher, sees that his son, only three, visiting his father's classroom, can write. I was stunned. Gaila could read and write. She had taught herself. That moment, it felt as if I would be replicated in the world, even if I were to disappear at that moment.

But I couldn't disappear, because Delphine was careering like a baby Michelin Man toward the flowerbed, where she and Gaila had made a secret place inside the Shasta daisies and black-eyed Susans I'd planted after falling in love with them along the Oklahoma roadside.

From then on, our lives revolved around animals and books. The stack of children's books I read to my girls, every day, every night: *Tacky the Penguin, Owl Moon, The Snowy Day.* Soon Gaila could read Junie B. Jones and Amelia Bedelia, whose wordplay was her favorite: *Dress the chicken. Draw the drapes.*

I read to them the more dense texts of the vintage books of my childhood—which remain here in the house now: *Winnie the Pooh* (they loved hearing that their father had a close friend named Woozle!), *Heidi*, and *Little Women*.

We ate ice cream every night, walking the mile to 7-Eleven to get Creamsicles or Drumsticks. Dwayne did bath time, reading the books in the steamy room while the girls threw water at him and Gaila corrected any dubious sentence he tried to invent. Then he went to sleep, and they went to sleep, and I wrote until it was time to wake Dwayne up for work. If I wrote by hand, he'd say, "I thought you were gonna work?" and I'd say I had worked, and he'd say he hadn't heard the typewriter. He'd say he slept better when he could hear the typewriter because we'd make some money. Sometimes while he put on his shoes, I'd have him check something in a story—what kind of tires would someone put on a dually truck? What brand of .25-caliber cheap handgun often blew up in someone's hand?

My husband's life was like Narnia, I know. He went through the wardrobe door to the world where at midnight, he'd be processing young men who were increasingly violent. He asked one boy why he'd shot a woman in the face, and the kid shrugged and said, "I don't know." He had teenage drug dealers, gang members, and boys who'd been abandoned their entire lives. He broke up fights and stayed awake, and then came home at dawn to sleep for an hour before his daughters woke up.

He returned through our front door to a house of girls. The opposite world. Little girls and stuffed animals and Barbie high heels were everywhere. I was told by some white women who meant well, "I can't believe you let your daughters play with Barbie dolls. My daughter will never have something so brainless and clichéd." I replied, "All the other dolls are white. Or pink. Barbie is the only doll that comes in different races. These are actually Teresa, Kira, and Skipper."

Teresa had brown skin, Kira was meant to be Asian, I believe, but she looked multiracial, and I kept my old Skipper from childhood because she was skinny, flat-chested, and dismissable, hopeful and yearning—she was me. I did not believe those other mothers deserved this last information.

We washed and braided and styled a lot of Barbie hair. The girls always took the right leg off the Ken dolls, which also came in various races. But all of the men were right-legless. Eventually my girls told me it was because they wanted Kira and Teresa to drive the pink Barbie limousine someone gave us. Gaila and Delphine figured Ken was better powerless.

In the evenings, Dwayne wanted to watch the Lakers or the Dolphins, and the girls wanted to watch Fairy Tale Theater videos rented from the downtown library of my childhood. Sometimes he went out to the garage for sports and male company. On the tan pleather loveseat handed down by my mother, the girls loved *The Twelve Dancing Princesses*, *Rapunzel*, and *Rumpelstiltskin*.

Dwayne never had a single moment to himself. Our house was evolving into the classic style I'd seen growing up—women inside, men out in the garage and driveway. I was okay with it—I sent the girls out with pie plates full of food for him and his brothers and friends. On his days off, we went everywhere—to the beach, to the snow, to any zoo within one hundred miles, taking whatever cousins would fit in the truck.

I wrote every night. I published *Aquaboogie*, dedicated to James Baldwin. I published *I Been in Sorrow's Kitchen and Licked Out All the Pots*, whose main character was inspired by Big Ma, a woman who'd lived in Daisy Carter's house, who came by Alberta's driveway with a lit newspaper torch to smoke out the wasps underneath the eaves, to use the larvae to fish in the Salton Sea. I published *Blacker Than a Thousand Midnights*, inspired by my brother-in-law Derrick, the only black wildland firefighter in the California Department of Forestry. In the driveway, he'd told me stories of deer and snakes and coyotes racing toward him, ahead of towering flames.

That year, 1994, Alberta said to me, "You don't want one more? Just one?"

I did. I had always wanted three kids. But Dwayne had said in the hospital ten minutes after Delphine was born, "I'm headed down the hall to get cut. Two's enough."

He hadn't.

He and his brothers and his father would be in his father's driveway, with an engine dangling on a chain in the huge ash tree. We'd be inside, where we women watched the smaller grandkids play. I told Alberta that her son thought life was hard enough. (He had spent a couple of nights on her couch, as did all the brothers and cousins when someone had a disagreement. There was the day couch, and the night couch, I knew. But his mother had heard him and come from her bedroom to yell that she loved me and he'd better take his butt home. She wouldn't let him stay. I liked having her on my side.)

Now she said, "You ain't gotta ask him. You ain't gotta tell him you want one more. Just one."

Aint Sister nodded in agreement. I told them, "He says if I get pregnant again, he's getting a Harley. I take that for a death wish."

They laughed and said, "He can't ride a motorcycle away from those girls. Look at them!"

Alberta had told no one about how blinding her headaches had gotten. When she watched the girls, she returned to bed after we left. We'd come inside midmorning and she'd have gone back to sleep, her face swollen with pain. One February morning, in 1995, she had a small stroke in the living room. When Dwayne got to the hospital, a few hours later, she awakened and felt sick. He held on to her when she tried to get out of bed, and she had another stroke and collapsed in his arms.

She never regained consciousness. She was transferred to a convalescent facility a few blocks from our house, and we all went in shifts to sit beside her bed and talk to her, touch her face, hold her hand. We hadn't told her I was nearly three months pregnant, in case I lost the baby. By the sixth day, she looked like a different woman. Her bright brown skin was fading to pale gold, her hair turning silver so rapidly at the roots that we her daughters-in-law and nieces cried. Her breathing was ragged, the violent desperation of inhale that shakes the whole upper body. That night, Dwayne sat alone by her bed and whispered into her ear that I was going to have another baby; he read her his favorite book, *Love You Forever*, and cried. Then he kissed her, and left. Twenty minutes later, while I was driving there, she died.

I had never been with women who did their own ministrations of love to the deceased. Her daughters-in-law and nieces and neighbors painted Alberta's nails, dyed and straightened and styled her hair, chose her blue dress, and did her makeup. The third of Daisy Carter's daughters was gone. At her funeral, there were six hundred people, and though her lips were red, they were held too closely over her teeth, and we broke down and cried on our knees at the loss of her smile.

17

Wild Things

When I was pregnant with Delphine, the possum showed up. The week after we bought the house, three years earlier, my brother Jeff and Dwayne had gone into the basement and crawled under the pipes to remove asbestos. They found a skeleton—the biggest possum they could imagine. Perhaps she was the mother or grandmother of this large female possum, with gray fur and a dark ruff around her shoulders and cream-colored face looking impassively past me as if I were not there when I saw her in the backyard, rooting around the apricot tree, clawing at the loose screens that led to the basement, and then rustling to the area underneath my bedroom to prepare her home.

When I was pregnant with Rosette, I felt a renewed fear of hospitals that I didn't even understand until I began to write this book and remembered my broken femur. Alberta's time in the hospital had been torturous. Two months later, her sister-in-law Minerva passed away. It was a spring of mourning.

By August, it was over 100 degrees for ten days in a row,

and at night, when Dwayne was gone to work, the girls and I slept on blankets laid on the cool cement of the porch. The air would shift, the leaves of the old carob tree would fall like a few random coins, and finally the night would cool.

But the night before I had Rosette, the second to last day of August, it had been 108 degrees. I walked up and down the sidewalk at midnight, then went inside to check on the sleeping girls. I walked at one. Two. At three, I sat on the porch steps, drinking iced tea, panting. A coyote floated down the middle of the street, upright and intent as coyotes always run, and I'll say it was a she. She moved as if parting water, directly down the yellow divider, and looked over at me. Her head cocked, she slowed for an instant, and then seemed to raise her chin. A cool coyote. Native to here. Maybe it was a male coyote. Like the cool guys used to say in high school: *What it is?* Girls would reply, *What it ain't.* And the guys would say, *What it shall be.*

I went into labor just after that, pacing, pacing, and three hours later Dwayne came home from work. I told him we should go to the hospital right then. He thought I was messing around, because I never wanted to go to the hospital. I called my mother to come stay with the girls, and when she arrived, she yelled at him to start the car. (She says she slapped him, but I don't know if she could reach that high.)

I had Rosette seventeen minutes after we got inside the hospital. I wasn't tethered to an IV or even hooked up to a monitor. I was still wearing my sunflower-printed maternity dress.

She was the incarnation of her grandmother Alberta. Her eyebrows, her dimple, her smile, her legs. Rosette was the third girl, like Alberta. Watchful, listening. She had small, perfect black beauty marks on her cheek, chest, and wrist, like the ones Frenchwomen in Marie Antoinette's time painted on themselves.

My childhood freckles disappeared, but I have several of those brown beauty marks, in almost exactly the same places on my cheek, chest, and wrist. When I held her, I sometimes saw the tiny constellations of melanin on our faces pressed together as if we were marking each other.

The small bedroom now held two beds and a crib, and the floor was reduced to a walkway between sleeping daughters. Every night, they knew to pile up the dolls, books, toys, and shoes into the baskets I bought so we could survive.

But Rosette had an early evening restless cry, every evening, and someone had to walk her up and down the sidewalk. My neighbors, my friends—we all rocked her on the porch, twirled her around the sunflowers in the yard. By the time the girls and then Dwayne went to sleep, she was still awake. Dwayne got no rest. When he left for work, I brought her into the bed with me.

He didn't buy a Harley. He got a Kawasaki motorcycle, which he rode to work. He spent more time in the garage, making shotgun cartridges and bullets with a machine he'd bought, watching the tiny red television we'd taken to Amherst so long ago. We were a house of women and a driveway of men, a division that functioned for so many older couples we knew. It might have sufficed for us, if we had lived in an earlier time, but we both worked long hours, our house was aged and needed repair, the yard and living room full of children not even our own. Three daughters who were so curious and smart and demanding meant the days stretched very long, and the nights, too. Sometimes he just wanted to ride the motorcycle all weekend, by himself—another American dream.

18

Pig

Rubidoux and Riverside,
California, 1997
(South Carolina, Oklahoma,
Florida, Georgia)

That October, just before we were divorced, Dwayne and I walked down a dirt lane into the spangled cottonwood and sycamore trees near the Santa Ana River, where we both had grown up catching crayfish, where our daughters now looked for crayfish. The Santa Ana is the longest wild river in southern California—concrete-channeled in Orange County, but here in Riverside and San Bernardino counties, flowing from the mountains and through the wide riverbed that begins at the arroyo below our dead-end street.

I had just gotten home from work, and the girls would be with my mother for another hour. After we returned from the walk, Dwayne would take his nap and then head out for the night shift, after the girls were in bed. They didn't even know he was going to leave. I did. It was near my birthday—pretty soon I would be thirty-six, divorced, with three kids.

But we'd been walking here forever. I was going to miss walking with this man, who had walked all the way to the playground to meet me for the first time, who'd walked with me up the Swiss Alps, around tiny Italian villages where everyone thought he was Magic Johnson, around New York City when we took the bus there from Amherst to see the beginnings of wild-style dancing and hip-hop music on the sidewalks, and down the boardwalk in Venice, Italy, and Venice, California.

We headed toward the river, on a narrower trail near a thick tangle of wild grapevines, and heard a huge shuddering in the arundo cane nearby. "Damn," my husband whispered. Yes. He whispered. We both froze. "Must weigh four hundred pounds."

The cane shook. A strange deep noise came from the dry stalks. An inquiry. It was the vespertine hour. Pink and gold light before sunset.

The wild pig had heard us. It stopped moving, and the cane quivered. Dwayne pulled a black 9-millimeter handgun from the back waistband of his jeans. I couldn't believe it. I knew he was getting more paranoid because of the juvenile criminals, because of worry about protecting his daughters, but I didn't know he was carrying.

"Go," he whispered to me, and I backed away, and he backed away, aiming at the canestalks. The pig must have stomped or smacked its head against the cane, and then it thundered off, crashing in the direction of the river.

"What the hell are you doing with that?" I whispered fiercely when we got back to the main path. We were passing a homeless encampment, with clothing in orange crates, a blackened fire circle, a bamboo chair suspended from a tree.

"I brought it for people or dogs," he said. "Not one of Floyd's escapees." And as we walked in silence, I felt a visceral stab of sadness—because we had known each other since we were fourteen and fifteen, we had our own language, and who else would ever know all our people and our vocabulary, know immediately what he meant?

Floyd Walker was like family. He was a longtime friend of General II, since his mother-in-law and Daisy Carter had been very close. Floyd had retired from the military, and he loved pigs. He loved pigs so much that he was famous for driving down the alleys behind restaurants, his huge truck with the flatbed enclosed by wooden pallets, filled to the top with discarded produce he collected every day for his pigs. About thirty of them, living in corrals made also of salvaged plywood and pallets, across the river in Rubidoux. We'd fed Floyd's pigs for years. Rarely did any leave alive.

But pigs had escaped from other nearby farms for a century. Colonies of feral pigs had terrorized the river since we were children. Those pigs had tusks. They confronted people walking, people on horses, and they weighed up to five hundred pounds.

I knew Dwayne had his father's old hunting rifle, and he'd bought a shotgun. I had no idea he was keeping a handgun in his car, and carrying it with him. The 9-millimeter Ruger was a favorite with law enforcement, solid and black and menacing, and he held it with affection. "Well, if you shot it in the head, we were in trouble," I said. "People say bullets bounce off their heads. The pig would have just been pissed off, and he wouldn't go for you! He'd have tried to kill me, except I would have climbed a tree."

He'd put the gun back under his shirt. He was a bigger man by then—three hundred pounds. When we did get divorced, my mother was angry with me, saying I had not been a good enough wife, and I should have cooked more, and kept the house cleaner. Very Swiss. My house was perfectly acceptable, though Barbies were strewn everywhere and Dwayne had hopped through the hallway sometimes with a Barbie high heel embedded in his own heel. Pretty sure he'd always had enough to eat.

My husband had become a mystery to me. He wanted more freedom to spend with his brothers and friends; he'd bought the Kawasaki, and a Ford Ranchero, which seemed another message as the bench seat clearly couldn't hold three girls, the baby in a car seat. His mother was gone. She could not chase him home from the couch on Michael Street.

We had gotten married too young, he said; he wanted to learn to be independent, he said. Every time I heard that word, I imagined Herbie, the elf who wanted to be a dentist, in *Rudolph the Red-Nosed Reindeer*. I couldn't help it. I heard the word in four syllables—*in-de-pen-dent*—in Herbie's nasal pronunciation, and had to keep myself from laughing. "You gonna be a dentist?" I'd say, and Dwayne would shake his head.

That day at the river, the gun wasn't funny. But he grinned and said, "Yeah, but if I killed him, think of the old days, how happy somebody woulda been to get that meat. That streakalean."

How could I hate him? We spoke a secret dialect no one else would know.

Floyd prepared a few of his pigs for slaughter when the weather cooled in November, separating them from the others, feeding them only corn. He'd get orders from families like ours; we'd put in $50, along with Alberta and General. One man would shoot the chosen in the head, and other men hung the bodies from chains in the trees and butchered them expertly.

We took part of the bacon and fresh pork loin chops. Others took ribs, feet, head cheese, and fresh ham—everyone wanted some part of the pig.

Then there were the chitlins. Joe Killer, a family friend, taught me how to clean chitlins on Alberta's Formica counter. Alberta said she'd done enough chitlins to last her a lifetime, and soon, I saw why. Scraping with a short paring knife, scraping the foul mess of digestion from the waxy white tubes, I listened to Joe Killer's stories of all the places he'd cleaned chitlins.

But Alberta taught me how to fry the fresh bacon, to sprinkle it with a bit of brown sugar. "Streakalean," she called it, laughing. Streak of fat, streak of lean.

Each night, while Dwayne was at work and the girls were asleep, I sat here at my old mahogany desk, bought for $10 from an elderly woman down the street who had been an accountant. I thought about the gun, and the wild pig, and how hungry our ancestors had been. The first year we lived in this house, we'd trapped a smaller possum in the yard and Daisy, a neighbor born in Kentucky, came by and told me, "I can show you how to cook that up right." I remembered Alberta chewing a piece of pork chop from one of Floyd's pigs, sliding the softened bits into Gaila's mouth, and then Delphine's. Rosette is still sad, to this day, that she was never held in Alberta's arms, like her sisters.

When we were teenagers, I told Dwayne the story of my dad's junkyard dog, which once bit my brother. He countered with his Rubidoux cousins' junkyard, where cars were kept for parts to sell. One cousin had a fierce hungry guard pig. "A junkyard dog might bite you, but it probably wouldn't kill you," Dwayne said, laughing. "That pig? She weighed four hundred pounds. She'd kill you, stomp you into pieces, and eat your sorry ass. Bones and all. No one would even know you tried to steal something."

That junkyard was just across the river, near Floyd's leased land, which was adjacent to a long narrow one-third acre owned by General II. When Gaila and Delphine were small, we'd collect excess apricots from the old tree in our yard, and shovel heaps of fallen carob pods from the city tree at our sidewalk, and take trash barrels full to Floyd and his pigs. We'd lean on the plywood fences, the girls holding tight while the pigs gleefully rooted into the soft rotting apricots, crunching the pits. They crushed the carob pods with their hooves, sweet brown powder the pigs licked up like tinted dust from Pixy Stix. Floyd threw overripe avocados into the mud, and he laughed and pointed to one very large male pig, alone in a big pen. He said, "Watch that one—he spit out the pits like a natural man."

Floyd spent every day out there with his pigs because he loved them; they were his piece of South Carolina under the California sun. No pines or oaks, but pepper trees, with their feathery branches and red berries, and eucalyptus windbreaks with bark shedding under our feet.

But at night I thought, *Those pigs would kill us if they could.* I remembered my father, Richard, talking about the ranch near Purcell, Colorado, on the prairie where they lived when he was only two. He fell into the pig enclosure and the animals tried to kill him, but his sister Beverly rescued him, though one pig broke her arm. She was nine.

Of course, I'd read *Charlotte's Web* to my daughters. But they heard scary real-life fables, too. Mr. Gainer, father of our childhood friend Penguin, put on our new roof. After the tar and shingles were done, he'd sit on the porch with iced tea. My girls were terrified of him. His turquoise eyes seemed unearthly in the sunburned brown of his face, and he had no teeth, because he'd fallen from a roof onto his face some years earlier and refused to wear his dentures.

He would say: "My daddy worked that teppentime. North Florida. He died before I was born. Worked in that pine forest, gettin' teppentime, and he was ridin' on a cart. Cartwheel fell in a hole in the road. Them barrels crushed him. I was in my mama's belly. Never known him."

"I was so hungry, all the time. All the time. My brothers and sisters wouldn't do nothin'. My mama was hungry. I was seven. Took me a hammer and walked in the woods where I knew this man had pigs, and I hit one them pigs in the head with the hammer till he died. Squealin' and squealin'. Then I dragged him home. I told my mama come out there, and she seen the pig, and I told her, 'Cook me some meat.' And I ate me some meat. My mama had meat."

My girls were required to come out and greet him, to sit for a few minutes. This was an obligation of our extended family of kin, and they performed it gracefully. He would tap them roughly, examine their faces, say, "You scared of a old man like me?" It was his eyes—the intensity, the supernatural beauty of blue-green. It was his words. "You eat you some ham for Christmas?" He'd lean forward. "I can smell it in your house."

Alberta taught me to make a fifteen-pound bone-in ham, basting with honey and mustard and cloves. The streakalean was sweet and dark. That was 1992—long before gourmet America talked about pork belly or home-cured ham. At book events in New York and Boston and Chicago, talking about Floyd's pigs and the butchering, other writers were appalled that I lived in a place where people killed pigs and grew marijuana and were routinely shot at by police, gang members, and criminals, and that I expressed no desire to leave home. I went home to write about a cynical assassin dumped into a junkyard, his body disappeared by pigs.

My husband and I had been hungry, but never as hungry as our parents in their desperate childhoods, and our daughters had never been hungry at all. We had been poor—finding our furniture on the street, walking when we had no car, eating beans or ramen for days. But not until I had children, and I got divorced, did I understand the fierce desire to fill their mouths with meat.

So of course they all three became vegetarians.

19

The Santa Ana River

I have walked along the same river trail for thirty-five years now, since we returned from Amherst. I walk it nearly every day. I climb the steep foothill called Mount Rubidoux that overlooks the Santa Ana riverbed and think about what I told my daughters: No matter race or wealth or religion or desire, there are people who leave and people who stay. I had to stay. If we'd left, my girls wouldn't have had the safety and tether and history of our families. Dwayne wouldn't have had them. Since we stayed, I'd make sure we went around the world, like Alberta had said, so my daughters would know how big it was, in order to run it.

They had to spend days in the driveway, or at the city park, or in the car with my mother, to know their history. They had to have a father, especially one like theirs. And I needed the country of women to help raise them. They had to watch their aunts and cousins and me serve the food and listen to Marvin Gaye and the Bar-Kays and be sentimental; they had to watch their father and their uncles go crazy over a lowered 1964

Chevy Impala, those men always ready to defend the girls if they were scared.

Also there was this little house I couldn't leave behind, because it was the museum of children. (Once a neighbor counted the children on our long dead-end block—fifty-four kids.) There were children under the old maple table, with sheets draped over, kids sleeping on blankets and eating fruit snacks and Teddy Grahams. There were children in the tree, with sheets draped on branches, spying on people moving along the sidewalk. There were children in the driveway, shooting baskets on the gravel that messed up their dribbles. These children were truly the heritage of our defiance of casta—school friends who were Mexican-Scottish, Hawaiian-Filipino, Ecuadorean-Irish, Chinese-American, and all the cousins who were everything.

My two older girls rode their Big Wheels, with baby Rosette at the handles, until Dwayne bought the most beloved vehicle on the block: a comically tall red-and-yellow plastic car he found at the swap meet, which Rosette pedaled like a mad queen. She never had her grandmother Alberta, not for one hour, and I'd never had Ruby or Frieda, so I wanted to make sure she had everyone else. What had those women passed down to her, and to me, that we'd never be able to show them?

20

A Secondhand Lonely

Riverside, California, 1998

There's no need to lie. I barely survived. The first Christmas Eve, when the girls kissed me somberly and went to their father's house, I lay on the cold maple floorboards and cried like I've never cried before or since. I lay near the spruce tree we'd bought as always at the tree farm, hung with the decorations of my childhood and theirs, and cried until I couldn't see. Christmas Eve tradition was that Dwayne went to work, and the girls and I watched *Little Women*. I turned on the movie and cried for another hour. But Susan Sarandon's Marmee is raising her daughters without a husband—by the time Mr. March comes home, he just mopes around in the library. My girls had memorized the story—they were three sisters, and they already recited our own traditions matched to the story's lines. We took cakes and cookies around our streets, to neighbors and to homeless people, as had the March sisters. Also, the Sims sisters wanted epic lives. A collapsed mother wouldn't help. So I got up and went to bed.

———

At dawn I turned to my books. I read *Sula* for what must have been the thirty-third time. Sula and Nel were childhood friends, the kind you find only once. But years later, Sula took Nel's husband away, and then rejected him. Nel raised her three children alone. When Sula is dying, and Nel finally visits, Sula says that no man is worth keeping. She tells Nel:

> "Me, I'm going down like one of those red-woods. I sure did live in this world."
>
> "Really? What have you got to show for it?"
>
> "Show? To who? Girl, I got my mind. And what goes on in it. Which is to say, I got me."
>
> "Lonely, ain't it?"
>
> "Yes. But my lonely is *mine*. Now your lonely is someone else's. Made by somebody else and handed to you. Ain't that something? A second-hand lonely."

I had read this many times, but now I would live it. I would keep my own mind, and my own lonely. No man would hand me anything. I would never hand my girls that secondhand lonely, either.

Then I opened a novel I'd found in the library in 1987, *Lovers of the African Night*, by William Duggan, a writer I'd never heard of before. This book was a totem for me as well. A girl raised by her single mother in a South African village, where the women cook for visiting men, remembers looking at the world upside down near her mother's cooking pot, her mother who is strong and comic and independent, who whispers to her child, "You work so hard . . . Mothers dream of daughters like you."

A secondhand lonely had been given to me by my husband; and I had never heard my own mother say that to me. Her only daughter. But my mother-in-law said many times to me, "You're the best wife my son could ever have."

I regretted not one moment with her son. Later in Duggan's novel, the young woman has fallen in love with a young man who reminded me so much of Dwayne—and even though later he abandons her, and her life is difficult, she recalls always the first time her new love had a bath, and his knees rose like islands in the soapy water, and he grinned. The tenderness with which some images stay with us cannot be lost. No matter what. That is what the novel taught me. There is nothing wrong with still loving the past, the way it looked and felt and smelled and sounded. The way someone looked at you. That cannot be secondhand.

21

Dew Point—A Pack of Four

When it was so hot in the summer that the fig beetles died flying in the air, falling onto the grass beside us, shining iridescent green as tiny Christmas ornaments, my girls held that beauty in their small palms. It was so hot, butterflies landed on our arms for sweat. Yellow finches flew with their beaks open, panting. Golden baby lizards slipped under the screen door to sleep in shoes deep inside our closets.

Just as when I had Rosette, it would be 108, 109, 112 for days in August. My old house still had no air-conditioning, and three girls were sleeping in one small stifling bedroom near those fig trees, beetles crashing into the window screens like drunken bombers. The girls trooped into my bedroom.

I put two sheets outside on the grass around 11:00 p.m., and we lay in the yard, staring at the sky, the impossible night blue. My first years at this house, I'd planted a seed packet of Italian sunflowers—all colors, from white to lemon yellow to buttery gold to deepest red. Now the sunflowers had all hybridized and came up from new seeds every year, growing to twenty feet tall around the fences. At night, the yellow finches that hung upside down on the seedheads were still so hot their sad chirps fell like mournful commas around us where we lay.

We talked about the night blue. All the different blues, in the art and nature books we'd read, the paintings they'd seen at museums, the varying skies. Humans love blue. Winter sky faded pale, summer electric turquoise, Pacific Ocean blue as new denim, so we talked about Nîmes, France, where the material for Levi's was first made. Lapis lazuli on a street vendor's necklace. The lakes in Switzerland vivid as Windex.

When they finally fell asleep, one by one—and I never knew which one would stay awake the longest, ask the last question about a cousin or whether the rustling in the branches was a possum—I would lie there and wait for that moment when the earth changed each night. When the earth below us, under the thin sheet and tired grass, would release the coolness of dew, and the moisture would rise up around us, and the girls' breathing would deepen into what I imagined as magical sleep. I could smell the invisible drops gathering on the blades of grass near my face. Then along the sidewalk would come a drunk man or homeless guy on a bike or sometimes a woman who liked to stand on my corner and wait for men in passing cars to notice her—she would break off my yellow roses and put them in her hair.

I'd pray no one would shout and wake up the girls. Sometimes the people spoke to me; sometimes they moved along. I'd wait until we were alone again, realize it must be 1:00 or 2:00 a.m., and I would pick up each girl and take her quickly inside.

Then of course I was awake for a long time.

We survived the heat of summer inside museums, which were blissfully air-conditioned. My girls fell instantly in love from the time they were small with the order and quiet and careful display of museums, in exactly the same way I had fallen in love with the public library and then the bookmobile and then every museum I'd ever entered. I had such tenderness for the library, the quiet, and especially the rotating metal numbers and ink of the due-date stamp, which appeared magical. My girls loved each museum entry ticket, each painting or sculpture, each café with trays and elegant "museum food."

Those buildings were how we kept the chaos of our lives at bay.

I went to my first art museum when I was thirteen, just before freshman year of high school, when the "mentally gifted minor" group of students in our city, designated by kindergarten IQ tests, was taken on a bus to the Huntington Library near Pasadena. As things were back in the day, we were allowed to wander for hours through the art galleries in the former mansion home of the oil baron Henry Huntington and the historic gardens designed by his wife, Arabella. I was obsessed by their dour faces and black clothing in stiff portraits. I walked near the arched bridge of the Japanese garden and through the formal aisles of roses, and imagined the garden I would have.

But the landscape that changed my life hung on a wall inside the gallery: a massive six-by-nine-foot painting of the Stour River, by John Constable, which I didn't understand fully then. I stand before this painting every year and still thrill to find tiny details anew. The Stour is a small river, with children playing in the reeds and men pulling horse-drawn carts along a dirt road, not an idyllic river but a messy one, like my own Santa Ana. These English trees and woods are not my own. That is why I love them.

I took my girls to this museum more than any other, from the time they could walk and for all their childhoods, and every year now. I couldn't afford the admission and to buy lunch, so we four sat on the steps outside, sharing two sandwiches from Subway and one large drink, and then my daughters were immersed for entire days in art and cool air and gardens.

Delphine remembers the children's museum that opened in downtown Riverside, where a mist fountain outside kept them happy in summer, and inside, the girls played in the actual ambulance stocked with stethoscopes and bandages and a gurney. (I told them with selected detail about my ambulance ride from Boo Boo Lane.) They sat atop a police motorcycle. They drew pictures of themselves, and put on plays with other kids, while I sat on the floor near the air-conditioning vents and graded student papers.

We went to every natural history museum in every city we visited, every art museum, even to the historic Mission Inn Hotel, where their father and I had spent our wedding night. We sat in the huge chair built for President Taft's visit to Riverside, touched the gilded altar from Mexico. In this way, museums shaped so much about the lives of my children.

But we still had to sleep at night. In fall and winter, at 3:00 a.m., the Santa Ana winds gathered in the desert and swirled screaming down the pass and directly at the girls' bedroom facing north, hitting their windows. The old metal weather strips would hum like a god playing a terrifying harmonica of our house, and my daughters came into my room to sleep. Four to my queen-size bed, sweating saltier than tears into my eyes.

Another summer, another heat wave, I'd taken them outside again to sleep in the yard, and I sat near midnight on the porch steps, crying. It had been hot for ten days. I didn't think I could do this. A white truck with contractor's toolbox and metal rails rattled slowly past my house. Someone looked at me.

At dawn, before we were even dressed for summer camp

and work, there were two men at the door. Gaila came to the kitchen and said, "It's Mike."

My neighbor down the street, who'd bought his old house the year before we bought ours, who'd become a contractor, stood on the porch. Behind him were wide silvery tubes of metal ducting and an air-conditioning unit. Mike's father was from Chihuahua, and his mother an American student who'd gone to Mexico. The girls loved his dry one-liners and impassive gaze. He had a two-bedroom house like mine, and two small sons, and was remaking his attic into a loft for them. He said now, "I saw you crying on the porch. I'm putting in AC. You can pay me later."

How could I ever leave a place that loved us like that? We were a pack. Rosette in my arms, then holding my hand, then running past me to follow her sisters and the neighbor kids and her cousins and kindergarten friends. We did swimming lessons at the city college pool together, they all got summer pneumonia together, and that was another year. The girls went to nature camp at the river, and rec league basketball. I drove to preschool, elementary school, and practice, and another year was gone.

Women saved me. My friend Holly, who called every day, who had been divorced with two children, said, "You were with the same man for twenty years! Other people we know are just getting married now, and they're forty! You're ahead!"

My friend Elizabeth who came over to help me trim the mulberry tree, who had been divorced with four children, said, "It's like a hundred leaky faucets in a house. Everything you feel. You just turn off one faucet at a time. Drip by drip. It takes forever. But one day you'll wake up and hear quiet."

One morning when I was frosting still-warm cupcakes in the back of my van, in the elementary school parking lot, for

Gaila's classroom birthday party, Gaila stood beside me and said, "You're the best mom anybody could have." Everything felt backward, and I was dizzy for a moment, but then I recovered and remembered she'd asked for sprinkles, too.

At night in the old laundry room, which was a screened porch facing east, the full moon rose each month as Delphine sat on the dryer waiting for the last of the thick cotton athletic socks to dry. I folded shirts. Rosette didn't even have a bed, as she likes to remind us—she had a tiny green fold-out couch printed with zoo animals, and her feet dangled off the edge of the sad not-mattress.

Perhaps the funniest part was when I reread Joan Didion one summer, still marveling at her tone and the precision of her sentences, the way she wrote about the wind and the earth, and I had a revelation: Many of the women I was closest to had been married three times. They weren't the divorcees of "Some Dreamers of the Golden Dream," with aspirations to kill a husband for money. They just kept surviving each husband, having more kids, and making a sisterhood of single mothers.

There was my friend Terri, with freckles and auburn hair, who ran her own landscaping business. Her trailer bore my favorite sticker:

GROW YOUR OWN DOPE
PLANT A MAN

Terri kept telling me, "Just find a contractor and sleep with him for a couple years till you get your house in shape. You can dump him then. Come on—you need a new roof and paint and your floor redone." Her third husband had a tattoo of a woodpecker on his calf; he gave her a ruby ring after a drunken spree, but it turned out he'd stolen it from Sears, and she laughed when she told me he called her from jail. She eventually took her three sons and moved to another city. (I didn't take her advice on love with repairs.)

I couldn't cut the grass because when we divorced, Dwayne, the son of a gardener, took the lawnmower. Within weeks I met Inez, a woman born in Mexico City, whose third husband, born in Guatemala, ran a landscaping business. She and I have known each other fifteen years now. Her first husband brought her and two daughters across the border, and then he died. Her second husband, with whom she had a son, left. She became a citizen ten years ago. She divorced the husband from Guatemala and bought her own house, but they still work together one day a week. She and I share plants and seeds and raising our chickens; she keeps the ancient sprinklers working.

In the house across the street was Maria, born in the rural forests of the Philippines, who was married to her third American military husband. With the first husband, who was Mexican-American, she had two children; with the second, who was African-American, she had one son; with the current husband, who was European American, she had two teenagers. Maria loved trading my fresh eggs and cherry tomatoes for her chicken adobo and lumpia. On my porch, she told stories of how back home in her village, women turned into black dogs and black birds at night, and you never knew the true incarnation of who you met in the dark.

At night, the girls and I had visitations from the animals. It was so hot, and the three big windows in their bedroom opened inward, so the visitors were not startled, as they couldn't see our faces in the screen, watching the characters we knew from books.

Mother possums wore bonnets and kept babies in tree hollows. Mama bunnies scolded their naughty sons. Templeton the rat was sporadically heroic in *Charlotte's Web*. Raccoons were guys, because of the bandit face, eternal sunglasses, and ringed tail. Stellaluna the bat and hundreds of her siblings flitted erratically through the dusk above the carob trees. And Mama Skunk took her babies for evening strolls with their tails waving jauntily, like flags.

The animals had a primeval homing instinct for our neighborhood of former citrus and walnut groves, and a nesting impulse for my house and yard, which had been theirs long before I showed up. Those pregnant mothers had their own Homeric journeys, which ended in my basement. Especially the largest possum, a marsupial descended from the dinosaurs, ancient in lineage. Every night, at exactly the same time—11:09—my possum of many springs clawed frantically at the crawl space screens, banged against the foundation of the house just below my bedroom window. Maybe her six-times-great-grandmother was born there, underneath my wood floor. Maybe she was the tenth generation of her possum family. I lost count. When I was first divorced, and too tired to reinforce the battlements, she nested there beneath my bedroom, spending the midnight hours chomping happily, noisily, on snails and apricot pits and other loudly crackable delicacies.

We named her Daisy Mae. A single mother like me. But she got so obnoxious and smelly that we had to get out the old humane trap my elderly neighbor had made for Dwayne and me when we first bought the house. A long, wide trap with a metal ramp that tripped the wire, so the girls and I slid a can of tuna carefully all the way to the end, with a mulberry branch. We watched from the bedroom window. On the sixth day, she finally went inside.

My girls cheered, Daisy Mae bared needlelike dental work,

and Dwayne came to put us all in his truck. We drove her across the river to the other side, near the nature preserve. But in the rippling movement of her creamy underside, the girls saw seven hairless, thumbsized babies. She banged her nose against the metal cage until she bled.

"Hurry, Daddy," they said. We parked, he picked up the trap, and we walked partway into the jungle of grapevines. "Happy trails to you," he sang loudly, the old Roy Rogers song. This is why we still loved him, even though he didn't live with us. "Happy trails to you," he always sang even more loudly when he used to descend into the basement or ascend to the attic, "un-til we meet a-gain." He'd turn to us and whisper, "Just to let any critters know I'm here. I don't want surprises."

The possum scuttled off into the brush near the river. She was back within a week. She swam across the river and walked about five miles. To get to my yard.

For three years, she returned to have her babies, and for three years we trapped her. She didn't care. This was her ancestral home as much as ours. The last time, her scarred nose white and thickened, she moved through our backyard slowly as an ocean liner, stately and pregnant, searching for apricots and her condo. She had eleven babies under my bedroom. Ironic, since I'd been divorced for several years by then.

But it took weeks to catch her this time. By the night she entered the trap, the babies were half-grown, the size of small rats themselves. Some of my neighbors killed baby possums with baseball bats or shovels or guns, when they got into a house, because they looked worse than rats. These babies swarmed over the trap, confused as to why they couldn't touch their mom, and her nose was bloody again. My girls cried.

So I spent an hour cleaning out a gray plastic trash can, propping it up with bricks, setting up a ramp with a piece of plywood, and sliding a can of tuna into the bottom. We watched from the girls' bedroom window, standing on Gaila's bed. Ten times I went back outside, as each baby slid down into the slick plastic. (The eleventh baby eluded us, and lived in the mock-orange hedge by our porch for about a year.)

We called Dwayne again. He laughed. But he brought the truck. We rode across the river. He sang the song.

My mother said I should keep the yard cleaner. Then again, her favorite hiking trail was patrolled one year by a mountain lion. That didn't scare her at all. She refused to stop walking there alone and defiantly showed us her arsenal: a cartridge of pepper spray, a hockey stick, and a Swiss Army knife. We applauded the America-Canada-Switzerland vibe, but asked whether the mountain lion would wait while she decided whether to use the corkscrew or the nail file on the Swiss Army knife. I actually got out a children's science book to show her the speed and length of the mountain lion's leap from a rock. My mother remained secure in her weapons and heritage, and took my daughters down the trail, so of course I had to follow.

One fall, we had a posse of raccoons. An especially aggressive raccoon was working his way through the unshelled pecans we laid out on the porch to cure in the sun, pecans Rosette and I had spent hours gathering from the trees near the river. Each night, the raccoon found them. Rosette was upset because pecans were her favorite.

The third night, I confronted him, yelling and waving my arms. He studied me quizzically, and then he charged. I ran inside and slammed the screen door. I opened it to throw a handy brown paper trash bag at him; with the humanlike fingers we admired in our books, he opened the bag, withdrew stale cookies, and had dessert.

It was a matter of honor then. My daughters were appalled at my inability to take back the porch turf. The raccoon came to the door, actually clawed the screen in my face, like, *Yeah, I desire fresher cookies now. From the kitchen.*

Obviously, humans didn't intimidate him. Next to the front door was an inflated Shamu the Killer Whale, the one Rosette used in the city pool. I hadn't wanted to blow it up again in the morning. Shamu was about four feet long. I put him in front of my body and charged out the screen door, making eerie high-pitched screeching noises (my best version of killer-whale anger). The raccoon leaped four feet into the air, flew off the porch, and raced across the street to the hollow in the pepper tree. He never came back.

My girls were stunned. Weirded out. But maybe proud.

That fall, my neighbor Mike said, "We have to secure the basement. And I can build two bedrooms and a bathroom, if you take out the wisteria and the two fig trees. You can pay me later."

I sold a book and gave him all the money. He excavated part of the backyard. I couldn't breathe—I was not leaving, we were not leaving, I was gambling on my house and yard and street and Dwayne and my family and my community.

When the small bulldozer left, there were hills of clay piled in the place where the wisteria had once twined over a rotted lattice gate, the vines that once tendriled inside the bedroom windows. But my daughters weren't sentimental. They were excited—Delphine held aloft Mike's pickax, and he said she could use it for the weekend to dig a mine in the dirt. I had once dragged a pickax into the foothills to mine gold with my brothers, so I smiled and went inside.

Then there were screams, and Rosette came running inside, holding her fingers, which dripped blood, and of course she'd kept putting her fingers in the way of Delphine's pickax, and of course she didn't pull them back the one time, and Delphine was crying harder than Rosette, and I smacked Delphine on the shoulder and said "How could you?" and her eyes went obsidian and Rosette fanned open her hand and one finger had just a flap of skin missing. All fingers were still attached.

That night, I apologized to Delphine and told her that I had once done the same—to my own finger, which made me an idiot. Before she got into her not-bed, Rosette sat on the bathroom counter and said jauntily, "Tighten up the bandage for me, Mommy. I want to take my finger to show-and-tell tomorrow." Then she studied me critically, my haggard face, two curlers in my hair, and said, "Mommy. Did your pajamas come with the wallpaper? I mean, did you *plan* that?" Her tone was not admiring.

I was stunned. Dwayne and I had papered the hallway in pink rose-garland stripes, popular in 1990. Now I was stripping off the cheesy vinyl-based pattern to get ready for the new part of the house, not a master suite but a daughter suite, the bathroom with two sinks. My threadbare flannel pajamas were pink striped with sad roses washed to blur.

"Just saying, Mommy," Rosette said, hopping down off the bathroom counter. "It looks pretty funny."

Mike thoughtfully built a narrow laundry room that became my refuge—cool black and white tile, the place where I made phone calls because no one wanted to come in there while I folded socks. My brother, Jeff, and his friends painted the bedrooms (one for Gaila, one shared by Delphine and Rosette) in three shades of lavender and three shades of yellow. My brother told them he made the ceilings lighter so it would look like the sky when they lay in their beds at night.

22

Love Strands

Riverside, California, 2000

To my daughters:

I knew my responsibilities. I was serious about your hair from day one.

All three of you remember Friday nights. When the other mothers from school or sports mentioned their evening plans—dinner, movies, concerts—I had an unwavering commitment that sounded like an excuse for refusal to date. Mine was not "I have to wash my hair." It was "I have to do my girls' hair."

The cracked pleather loveseat, the three of you, damp heads springing with waist-length freshly conditioned spiral curls, or in summer, the front porch with wooden chairs.

In winter, we watched Disney movies. The mothers were all dead. The fathers all raised daughters. We discussed the dead mothers of Belle, Aurora, Snow White, and Sleeping Beauty. We talked about Grimm's fairy tales and other folklore of Europe translated to Disney, and my own mother's haunted forests in Switzerland, her mother dead, Heidi's mother dead, Snow

White's evil stepmother and the woodsman who was meant to bring back a girl's bloody heart.

I sprayed homemade detangler and combed through every section of hair, separating them with clips. Then I parted carefully and braided each head for the weekend, because we always had basketball and family events, when everyone would watch you three. "Here they come! The girls! Look at them! The Sims girls."

In our family, and in black communities at large like ours, the care and maintenance of your hair meant more than just barrettes and ponytails; your hair reflected our pride and care and love. Neglected heads displayed for the public a serious lack of all three. We could pick out a child whose mother knew nothing about her hair, or didn't care to learn, within a few seconds. Especially for mixed-race girls. It was everything.

Given my childhood, I was grateful for conditioner, an item my mother didn't know existed. But it was expensive, and we used so much that I made my own mixture and shook it in a bottle: Frizz Ease and leave-in spray, almond oil and chamomile tea, and a base of Suave cherry-scented conditioner. That I could afford.

The years passed so quickly. We watched *Sabrina, the Teenage Witch* and *Family Matters*. We moved on to Jane Austen films, *She's All That*, *Gilmore Girls*, and *Girlfriends*. We saw every evocation of sisterhood available on noncable television. (We had no cable because the massive avocado tree next door blocked the power pole, and the drug dealers who lived there didn't trim the branches. That lasted for ten years.)

Gaila, you were always first, as you were the oldest and your hair was the longest, dark brown waves that hung all the way to the base of your spine, lightened to copper at the ends in summer. Delphine, your hair true black, a dense cloud of ponytail that with moisturizing turned into, as you put it, a million slinkys. You wanted it tamed for basketball, combed flat and shiny at your forehead and braided tightly. Rosette, you were three, in the bathtub with your sisters, impatient to have hair as long as theirs, and I looked up and you were seven, and suddenly your hair was down your back, a shoal of dense curls that acquired shots of gold and bronze from the sun.

After long days of swim lessons and sports, I had to carefully tease out tangles of hair in the kitchen.

Most white women didn't know about this kitchen, the dense hair prone to snarls at the nape of the neck. Most white women I knew expressed shock that I spent that many hours on your hair. My friend Holly used to laugh, "I don't even think I technically washed my kids' hair until they were four." Her children had wispy blond feathers that she just rubbed with a damp washcloth. "Mine won't let me touch her head," someone said on the playground, and I studied her daughter's straight red hair tousled into nests that actually looked as if birds could live there. "I just run my fingers through and stick a barrette on there," another told me, her daughter's thin brown strands pasted flat with water. "What a waste of time for you."

It was never a waste of time. It was the truest part of my existence as a mother. I believed women who didn't get to do this missed out on hours of touching and talking and closeness. Lots of women had much better hairstyles than mine, meaning they had actual hairstyles, because once I was done with three beauty queens of curl, all I ever did with my own hair was stick my wet head out the window of the Mercury Villager van on the way to work—seven miles of blow-drying. Sometimes my hair dried while I walked Rosette to preschool. I'd use the curling iron for five minutes, and my hair looked, inexplicably, exactly as it had when I was a high school junior.

Motherhood was my excuse, because I believed it dangerous to care too much about my own hair and clothes. We had seen the stepfathers of some other daughters. We'd seen destruction and dissembling of family, we'd seen shouting and violence and another divorce. Your father and I were friends again after the first terrible year. My inattention to style was practical, but also purposeful and avoidant. I wanted no man to disrupt our *Little Women*, our *Sense and Sensibility*, our *Gilmore Girls*, though you three girls had much more impressive hair than anyone in those stories.

On schoolday mornings while we styled—buns, ponytails, braids—we went over spelling words, talked strategies for playground bullies, and chose something for preschool share day. Those were hours I would never trade with other mothers.

There had been serious code in Alberta's living room about my first coming child, in the place where I'd spent years watching women braid hair and apply Jheri curl lotion and make lemon cake and talk forever. They used to tease me about the perm I'd gotten in the 1980s. Margaret Chandler said, "One thing I hate in this world is a white woman who won't learn to do her kids' hair. With the combination of Dwayne's and yours, girl, they're gonna have a lot. Don't let it get all nappy, and don't let it get all dry, and don't ever think it doesn't matter. 'Cause it does."

Twenty-two years ago, when I was pregnant with Rosette, I won an award for a novel and went to a ceremony in Washington, D.C., wearing a batik dress with an empire waist. (I can't believe you wear that dress now, Rosette.) I met a woman there whose mother was German and father was black. Her mother had refused to style her hair at all, and a black female relative finally rescued the girl and took her to a salon. This woman, at fifty, told me about the hours required to remove the knots and tangles, the anger of the black relatives and the stylist. Her voice was still raw with hurt and rejection.

———

I never regretted our Friday nights. Your friends had their own bedrooms; you three had one small room. Your friends had their own televisions; we had the one twenty-five-inch set in the living room. They had separate lives and we did everything together.

We talked about Steve Urkel, watched figure skating, *My Fair Lady*, and all the bride movies. We talked about marriage and divorce and rich and poor and black and white and all the things in between all those things. We talked a lot about navigating the middle of everything, while I was parting down the middle and then dividing the strands and securing the ends with glittery elastic.

The whole of America did your hair. By high school, my friend Nicole came to straighten Delphine's curls, heating the metal comb on the stove burner while we talked in code and laughed. (She's from the Bronx, so sarcastically hilarious that I laughed until I cried; you three were as fascinated as when Sula makes Nel laugh until she has to go to the bathroom. I couldn't have survived without that laughter.)

But the day I remember best was outside, in summer. Gaila, you were eleven, Delphine was nine, and Rosette, you were five. You all had swim classes at the city college pool. Summer always kicked my ass. None of you wanted to wear the ugly swim caps which, stuffed with the loose masses of your hair, you felt resembled alien heads from a sci-fi movie. (You caustically described white girls who did not wear swim caps, but tossed their hair in the water and then tossed the water around the pool.) I braided each head, tucked two thick braids secured with bobby pins inside the caps, and prayed.

That afternoon Gaila came home from a weekend birthday party where she would have been the only one with a cap. She swam for hours, let her hair dry, and swam again. For two days. By the time she got back home, she was crying. Her waist-length hair was barely touching her shoulders. She had dreaded up big-time.

I wanted to cry, too, examining the mass of fused hair. But I tried to joke around. "Okay," I said, "so I like dreadlocks, and if you ever decide to dread up, that's cool. But most people have multiple dreads, sweetie. We've just got one here. A ten-inch-wide, horizontal one."

Delphine, you actually ran across the street for help. Emergency. Juli, your fairy godmother for seven years when she lived in the house with the river-rock porch pillars, ran back with you. You idolized Juli, five feet ten, her wild red-brown curls to her waist, an environmental geologist trained in the military, a woman who loved to sew for you and comb your hair but who also said frequently to guys whose behavior was unacceptable, "In the army I learned how to kill a man with my bare hands. Do you want me to demonstrate?"

She spent many evenings with us. She had also been, in high school, the only white girl on her native Texas track team. In the bus and on the sidelines, she learned to comb and braid extremely well. She loved you all, and my porch, with passion.

It took us two hours to work almond oil/chamomile tea/creamy conditioner mix into Gaila's freshly washed, damp hair, then separate the curls with a rattail comb. Gaila teared up at the process and the pulling of the tender skin at her kitchen. Delphine held her hand, and Rosette sang her songs. The whole time, even after Juli's wrists got tired and she fetched iced tea and I combed, we talked and you three listened. Juli and I discussed the ethics of her workmate Tiffany, who had dumped another guy but kept his multicarat engagement ring. Then Juli, who had just finished reading a history of Henry VIII and his six wives, told you girls tales of the nuptials, their true political

Susan, Delphine, Rosette, and Gaila, in Washington, D.C., 1999

(Photograph courtesy of Tod Masinter, Westways)

and social and romantic intentions, and some murderous ends. We had time to cover it all, instructive female history, contemporary and medieval. You were spellbound. I pulled yet another section of hair loose and combed it through, and Juli began to braid Gaila's hair from the other side, adding gold fasteners she'd bought especially for an occasion like this. Delphine said thoughtfully, "So if you were a woman back then, you were sick, pregnant, dead, or in a tower. Right?"

"I'm sure glad I'm alive now," Gaila said, wincing.

Rosette said, "But I love princesses!"

I can see it now. Juli took another drink of iced tea. Rosette's hand was on my leg, Gaila's shoulders companionable against my knees, and Delphine's breath on my neck. My fingers wove and wove, and I knew what was braided into each minute we spent there.

23

Crosses and Missions

California, 1998, 2000, 2004

Three dusty California missions sat near my desk for years. One has corrugated cardboard for a roof, one has sturdy plywood painted red, and one had magenta-tinted lasagna tiles until the rats in the garage got to them. That mission is gone now.

For three springs, we roamed the state, learning about life and darkness and hidden history. It was not expected. It changed me as much as it changed my daughters.

Every fourth-grade child in a California public elementary school must construct a mission. I'm talking about our famous California missions, strung as if on a flung rosary chain throughout much of the state. During that spring, students take field trips to missions, study the California history they were given, and then replicate a mission of their choice. The week that they stagger through the playground carrying their buildings used to be one of my favorites.

I made a mission with my dad, John Watson, in 1969. In our garage, he mixed plaster of Paris with me for the whitewashed adobe walls, and then helped me fashion a vineyard with twigs. I went to the foothills to find lichen and moss to place on the plywood base, sprinkling with water from the 7 Up bottle we used for ironing. But it was the field trip to San Gabriel Arcángel that began my desire to drive the state every year, to touch history and feel its grandeur and poverty and injustices.

As a single mother, I turned the mission project into something that lasted for months. Each child picked three missions to visit, so she could decide on the one with the architecture and landscaping she wanted to build, and the history she wanted to report. Getting out the map of California was the first thrill. Gaila chose San Juan Bautista, San Borromeo Carmel, and La Purisima.

During spring break of 1998, we loaded up the van and headed north on 101. The April rain-fed grasses were lush, the oaks looked like dark green parachutes landing on the distant hills. (Our constant soundtrack was the Spice Girls, if you need a timeline.)

San Juan Bautista was a lovely small town, and the mission was beautifully preserved. The square form appealed to Gaila. She took notes, drew sketches, and we admired the garden. Then we wandered to the rear of the property and saw the faint remains of the original Camino Real.

The four of us found a dirt path and we walked on that trail. We imagined how hard the journeys must have been, even with the beauty of wild mustard in clouds of yellow all around us. Entering the mission grounds again, we saw the cemetery. The headstones carried only the names of the Spanish. No indigenous people were there.

We spent the night near Hollister. The girls were quiet. And the next day, we walked a dirt road in an agricultural area, where women picked blackberries in a field, the vines stretching forever down wire supports; at the field's edge, in the shade of huge cottonwoods, were small children and a few babies on blankets. They were alone.

Gaila had seen this before, when she was very small, camping with her father and me. She had said then, "Those kids are brown. Like me."

Now she bit her lips. The girls had seen people in fields of strawberries, lettuce, and peppers, all along the highway north. They had many classmates born in Mexico, or whose parents had come from Mexico or Guatemala or El Salvador. We talked about how Americans ignored where their food came from, and who harvested it, about the Spanish words all around us and the ironies of anti-immigration politics.

Two days later, outside Lompoc, north of Santa Barbara, we saw La Purisima. That mission was more isolated, standing not in a pretty town like Carmel or San Juan Capistrano, or in a city like San Diego or San Francisco. The buildings were isolated on a windswept plain. The walls were rosy buff, and the chapel stark, with a wooden altar and cross. In the soldiers' quarters were small rope beds. We halted at the infirmary, where many native people had died of smallpox in that dark cube of a room. There were iron bars on the windows, and a guide told us offhandedly that on many nights, indigenous girls had to sleep in the infirmary to keep them safe from harm. From soldiers, we knew. We shivered.

Walking just outside the mission boundaries, Delphine saw small crosses in a barren field. Simple wooden crosses. No names. Indigenous people had been buried there—not inside the cemetery. All their work and death, all in the name of religion, and their bodies not honored on the land taken away from them.

Delphine's face changed. She said, "This is where I would be buried."

She knew the history of Fine, of her grandfather and his family. Cherokee, African, Irish, English. She was right.

The romance of bougainvillea shading plaster walls, gilt decorations in ornate chapels, the red tile roofs and celebrated mission culture, faded as we stood there. We got back into the van changed. We talked about our family heritage as immigrants, enslaved people, military veterans and female survivors. From then on, we saw our landscapes—the walls of tumbleweeds lining chain-link fences in winter near Glen Avon, where people had been Dust Bowl migrants; Floyd's pigs and why he loved them; the street near our house called Wong Way after the original neighborhood of Chinese men who owned laundries and shops—shaded with a patina of history.

Our California past was being erased quickly and thoroughly by housing development and freeways and shopping malls. But I was lucky enough to have three kids who loved to drive and stop to look around with me, to find beach glass and iridescent fig beetles and even a fossil now and then.

Gaila constructed her San Juan Bautista with the help of my dad, John Watson, and my neighbor Juli's husband, Jason. They sawed a plywood roof, Gaila mixed plaster of Paris, and then she painstakingly collected gravel from my garden paths to glue together stone walls. Two years later, Juli helped us make Delphine's San Juan Capistrano (with accessories found at a wedding shop—tiny white doves perched on the lasagna roof tiles to represent the famed swallows). But we talked all the time about the thousands of people who had died in these places.

Last year, California finally acknowledged the truth that one of my favorite poets, Deborah Miranda, whose father was Ohlone-Chumash-Esselen and mother was Jewish, wrote in her memoir *Bad Indians*: To glorify the missions of California— built with enslaved labor, the cause of disease and death and rape and murder—and to ask children to construct their own missions, without teaching the true history and cost of those compounds that influenced California architecture and design more than any other buildings, would be akin to asking children to build scale models of plantations in the southern states or concentration camps in Europe without teaching the true history and cost of those places. Most children had begun to build missions from kits sold at craft stores. The California state legislature rescinded the education requirement in 2018.

When it was Rosette's turn, she was a much more thoughtful, less innocent fourth grader. She knew I'd gone to Mission San Luis Rey, near Escondido, with a friend from the Pala reservation. He and I had lingered at the large outdoor lavanderia where his great-great-grandmother and ancestors had washed the laundry of soldiers and padres on stone steps around a pool. The women had been taken from their homelands in the Palomar mountains.

Rosette chose the mission that seemed the least glorified and most original—San Miguel Arcángel, tucked into a hollow off the 101 freeway between Paso Robles and King City. Women from the small community had been praying in that chapel when we stopped briefly years earlier.

The older girls grumbled. They were thirteen and fifteen; they had basketball and friends, high school and junior high importances during spring break. But I prevailed, stubborn and already afraid of the slipping away of our travels and our own history. We got into the same van; Rosette's musical choice was S Club 7.

Headed north to San Miguel, they were all old enough now to hear my freeway stories: how when I was a student at USC, and their dad was a basketball star at Monterey Peninsula

College and then at a state university, we drove back and forth, or rode the bus, on this long highway to see each other. How we went to many small towns like San Miguel, tucked off the highway, for games and tournaments, and met farming kids who saw sports as a ticket to a bigger life. How their father and other players took pig corn from nearby fields to survive some weekends, how he worked the almond harvest and spiders fell from the trees into his afro.

At San Miguel, heavy winter rains and damage had left the mission closed. Large patches of whitewashed plaster had exposed adobe bricks to the elements. We paced around the chain-link fence, wondering where the parishioners worshipped.

Rosette was crushed. She did that third-kid-nothing's-ever-as-good-for-me stomp for a brief time. It was late afternoon, though, and we needed a place to sleep, so I decided to cut across the hills to Cambria.

The winding two-lane highway passed through the old landscape once wandered by the indigenous people of this area, the trappers and hunters, and the padres who wanted to enclose them in adobe walls to pray. We saw a flock of wild turkeys moving through high grass, and then deer, with two spotted fawns studying us from the trees. We pulled off the road to study them back, in silence.

That is the moment my daughters still talk about. We were never afraid to be the pack, moving through the world, stopping to listen, to tremble at small wooden crosses half-hidden in yellow grass.

24

Coach—Driveway #2

Riverside, California, 2004

To Delphine,

Do you remember our driveway as it was in the beginning? The place where you spent most of your childhood?

When your father and I bought this house, I fell in love with the driveway. It was gravel and dirt, lined with the original cement curbs from 1910. The roses alongside were choked by crabgrass tangled like old wigs. But I cleaned out the flower-beds and planted Swiss chard and delphiniums, the tall blue flowers for which I named you; your dad lined up his tools on the curbing. It was our first driveway, and nothing is more important to the Sims family than a driveway. You know this. We have held wedding receptions and funeral repasts in the driveways of your childhood.

Your father finally had a place to hold court—in the old barber chair—while his friends and brothers worked on engines. The oil soaked into the gravel, the pebbles mixed with screws and bolts. Near dusk, we brought out plates of hot food and listened to the men talk smack. You heard them talk about bringing down starlings with a slingshot and roasting the birds in the field. You heard jokes about Pinto doors stolen by Midnight Auto Supply, guys who lifted car parts on order.

He put up the homemade plywood backboard and iron hoop before you were born. After your dad left, the driveway became not suddenly but steadily a girl place, with skates and scooters and bikes replacing the engines and stacks of spare tires. But you were a serious baller by the time you were ten. You needed a new hoop.

You told me you were going to play on the boys' varsity team in high school.

I took down the old backboard that summer. Your uncle Jeff and our neighbor Mike put up a new one with a breakaway net, which your father bought. Mike poured a concrete driveway so you could practice. I nearly cried to see the forgiving gravel gone. I had raked for years, a zenlike practice, sifting out lug nuts and rose hips and cigarette butts.

Then I was the one out there shooting free throws with you, guarding you with stunning inefficiency while you brought the ball down the long driveway, aiming for the chalk marks where your father said you should take off for layups. I tried to trim the nodding English roses, but their long thorny branches forced you into a sweet head fake.

"Fifty layups!" your father used to shout, when he dropped you off in the truck. "Then put your right hand in your pocket and dribble past your mom left-handed."

"Anytime you want to step in here," I used to shout back—do you remember?—but he would grin and gun the engine and drive off to the house he'd bought, three miles away.

We were in the driveway almost every day after school, your sisters and me chasing you while you fended us off and launched your jump shot. I remember one evening after your first Park and Rec games, with mostly boys, the fingers on your right hand swollen and purple. You'd deftly stolen the ball from a boy, and he'd knocked you down and stomped on your hand, saying he'd kick your ass. You'd held up your hand, given him an evil glare, said, "And that's gonna start *when?*" You dribbled with your left hand, as your father had taught you.

But at home, you said to me, "They don't want me playing 'cause I'm a girl." I felt a jagged pull in the muscles between my hipbones, the one I get when someone messes with my kids. I knew I had only ten seconds to decide—comfort you, or arm you.

"It's always gonna be like this," I said. You turned your head so I wouldn't see the gleam of tears. "You have two choices. Get sad and be a victim, or get mad and kick their butts." The driveway was where I listened, and tried to figure out what to say.

I remember this. You took the ball and shouldered past me for an aggressive layup, then started shooting free throws with angry precision. With my toe, I nudged the big V-shaped dent in the old curbing, the mark of a missed hammer years ago when someone tried to fix a U joint. Then you went down the driveway, out the gate, and up into the neighbor's driveway, shooting from the three-point line, which meant over the roses and the concrete-block wall.

You needed your dad. I waited until you all went to bed, and then I made my phone call from where I always made serious phone calls, the ones that mattered, to my friends Nicole and Tanya and Kari, the other single moms, and to your dad. None of you girls would ever enter the laundry room accidentally, or you might be asked to fold something, so I banged the dryer door shut twice to ensure that you'd stay away. Banging the dryer door was my code for *I've had it, it is hella late and I am in here waiting for your damn athletic socks to dry and they are the thickness of things designed for snowbanks.*

I called your dad and told him that if he didn't coach you, these boys would continue to talk shit, and one of their dads would coach you, and he might talk shit, and I wasn't having that. I told him he had to be your Park and Rec coach.

The next year, he coached you with his friend Don Reynoso, also a bear of a man. Two huge plush former ballers, one black and one Mexican-American, and they took their teams to championships with what I always thought was the best fatherhood skill ever: Pass the damn ball, because if every single player scores, we take the whole team to Dairy Queen.

We spent years sitting in that parking lot eating ice cream sundaes.

By 2003, we'd bought him his own shirt. In embroidered letters on the right side of the chest, it read COACH DWAYNE SIMS. Do you remember when you were finished with high school basketball, and your team, with all those girls he'd known since they were ten and twelve years old, had dismantled after making it to the second round of the playoffs? It was almost time for the last high school banquet. You had a letterman jacket, something neither of us ever did. Embroidered on the back: SIMS. The ultimate tribute.

Your father was melancholy—it was ending. He was everyone's favorite coach. Hearing him shout his simple rules—"Look up! Get back! Watch the trap! Box out!"—to girls who'd never played until that team formed, we could see how much they loved him. When they apologized for fouling, he said, "You ain't foulin', you ain't playin'." Both you and Gaila came up to me in a kind of sullen wonder, at different times, and said, "You know, Daddy's a really good coach. It's so weird."

When you were a freshman and Gaila a junior, he coached your high school team in the spring league. From the sidelines,

I again heard his mantra: *Look up! Get back!* His two basic tenets for victory: Look up when you get the rebound or begin to dribble, because someone is probably already under the basket, and you'll have an easy layup. Cherry picking, he loves to point out, is not something to be ashamed of. Get back on defense, because there has to be one person who races down after a shot so the other basket is never left completely unguarded.

He transformed into a man with no name. As with many men who look the part completely, he was now Coach. He will be that forever, to a certain generation of girls we see at the park or the mall. Coach! they call happily. Coach Sims!

He was forty-nine years old then, three hundred pounds in that coach shirt. He had been afraid that his size and appearance would make girls and parents fear him, but instead, because he was so intimidating, he rarely had to raise his voice. "Y'all know what to do," he'd say. "I'm just sittin' here." His advice was simple and doable. For point guards, "When you pass the last defender, cross over so she can't come behind you and poke the ball." For posts, "Stay at the free-throw line on the inbounds and look like you're tying your shoe, and then jump up and snatch the pass. Free layup."

Not innovative, but it worked. That's what the team wanted, someone who didn't scream at them and take them out for the smallest infraction. Someone so low-key he didn't learn their names for a long time. "D, tell the one with the grandma drive the Escalade to go in for Al's daughter," he'd say to our kids, who had to translate. Of course. He knew cars and ancestors. "G, tell little Rubidoux to watch back door." (The father of that girl had ancestors in the historic community along the Santa Ana River.)

I used to hear your dad's words in my head, when I drove to work and to Target and took you all to practice and games. *Look up.* We hardly ever do. We look at the road ahead, the driver we think is too slow, the train stopping our progress, the back seat where you all argued or ignored me or ate hurried snacks.

I started to look up on the way to the high school. The road I had driven hundreds of times skirted an arroyo, where fog lingered like dragon breath inside the canyon. I saw the palm trees washed clean by recent rains and sparkling like giant toothbrushes bent sideways by the wind. The huge boulders on the foothills where I played as a child, like rock sugar sprinkled on the crest.

Get back, I said to myself. Even if nothing I did seemed to work—the possum in the basement, the new novel, my college freshmen who hated commas, PTA meetings I always missed because they were scheduled during work, the stack of bills on the table—I had to race back and be ready for the next onslaught. Or I might as well give up.

After you left for college, he was bereft without basketball. Rosette played tennis in high school. She hated basketball, understandable since she spent her entire childhood in the metal bleachers doing her homework, and then helped me and Tanya, who worked for the IRS, run the food stand. Your father had hated tennis when I played in high school: He found it boring, and inexplicably, in a weird white classist tradition, the audience had to be silent. What the hell was that? he always said.

During Rosette's tennis matches, sitting on the benches, I said to him, "You should just go home and get some sleep," because he'd worked graveyard shift. But Rosette was good. She played number one doubles and went twice to the regional playoffs. That wasn't his proudest moment, though. The year-end banquet was held at the city's oldest country club, where his father had been allowed to trim and mow the grounds, but never enter the club. Remember? Your father made Rosette put her feet into the pool, and he looked up at the sky and told his father that Sims had put some black in the pool.

I am telling you now that in all the years of driving and tournaments and bleachers and snacks, maybe fifteen years of my life, his words meant the world to me: If you think I was ever resentful, know that even now when I'm walking the dog, or driving to work, I hear *Look up!* and I see redheaded woodpeckers navigating the palm trunks, and the pale golden spray of new dates, and then I feel capable of *Get back!* in order to survive.

25

The Batmobile

Riverside, California, 2005

We bought the first car for our daughters together. Gaila was sixteen. A red Honda Civic, circa 1995, with only three dents. She and I were impressed by the chrome rims, but when we brought it home, our neighbor corrected us with a laugh. They were hubcaps. Cheap ones.

Dwayne helped out physically and financially. We checked out the car together, where it was parked in a dirt backyard not far from where we grew up. After we examined the dents, we both glanced at the pepper trees and then squinted at each other. Even though we had by then been divorced for seven years, we knew the other's thoughts: Wait, didn't we party in this yard, during high school? Didn't we party hearty in this big field?

Yeah. We did.

I thought about that day for a long time. My mother still hated my father with an undiminished intensity, forty years after their divorce. She wouldn't say his name. The hate seemed as insoluble as the granite boulders on the Jurupa hills above that tiny house where we'd lived—rocks so hard that a single massive boulder is famous as an exhibit at the Los Angeles County Museum of Art. Once a month, when my father drove me back to Riverside from his house near Pomona, he would show me a hunk of granite the size of an Airstream trailer, perched near the freeway, and tell me that was my rock. But he never mentioned my mother's name either.

I never wanted to be divorced like that. I was happy to remember that we partied, and to stand there in the field considering the red Honda together.

Southern California—cars figured in nearly every memory of our lives together. Our daughters and I are the kind of women who know vehicles—the Super Sport, Ranchero versus El Camino, the Crown Victoria as retired police vehicle. Classic Mustang.

I learned to drive with my father, Richard Straight, on deserted vineyard roads in Cucamonga and Ontario. He'd built and raced cars as a teen, told me stories of using a sewer pipe for a muffler to amplify sound. I practiced in his 1970 Mustang, and when I swerved on a dirt road to avoid a ground squirrel, he shouted viciously at me for the first time in my life. "Who's gonna live—you or the damn squirrel?! Never choose an animal over yourself!"

Dwayne learned on dirt roads, too, near junkyards. But we didn't have a date, in a vehicle, for a year, until the debut of the Batmobile. "You went out in the Batmobile last night?" his friends teased me at school the next day, in 1976.

"You let me go out in the Batmobile?" I said to my mother the other night, in 2018.

"What did I know?" she laughed. "I didn't watch you leave."

We never had much money growing up, but when we tell

our girls our best stories, they all involve cars. (Except for the Country Squire. That was a Stephen King–worthy car.) My stepfather, John Watson, bought a vintage 1965 Mustang from a barn; the convertible top was gone, while a hay bale filled out the missing back seat. During high school, no one wanted a ride home from me. He restored and sold that and bought a 1959 Thunderbird, which I raced against our friend Bonedell in a Pontiac named Maybelle. Where the road narrowed to a bridge, he chickened out. I did not.

We cruised with eight bodies packed into Penguin's Dodge Dart, and when the Bar-Kays sang "Your Love Is Like the Holy Ghost," we all moved in unison so that the car leaped up and down without the aid of hydraulics.

We brought the red Honda home for Gaila. The car drove fine, but it didn't have a radio. I offered to have one put in, but Dwayne said he wanted to take care of it.

He bought an inexpensive CD player at his favorite shopping venue: the Rubidoux Drive-In, where we watched all our movies, which held swap meets on Sunday. When I came home from work, Gaila had her first car story.

"I was doing my homework and Daddy kept calling me with his cell phone."

"Where was he?"

"In front of the house installing the stereo," she said, rolling her eyes. "First he said, 'G, bring me a lighter.' We didn't have one, so I gave him some matches. Then he called again. 'G, bring me some tape.' I brought the wrong kind twice. The silver tape and the white tape. He wanted that black one."

"Electrical tape," I said.

"Yeah. Then he said, 'G, bring me some water.'"

I laughed. "You're slow," I said. "Didn't you realize what your dad wanted?"

She shook her head.

Oh, our early days of marriage, our old broken-down cars—the Fiat, the Toyota truck, the Bronco—each of which required hours of Dwayne's time under the hood. In the gravel driveway, in the driver seat trying to write a novel in a notebook, every few minutes he would ask me to do something. "Start it up. Rev the engine. Push down on the brake pedal. Okay."

Really, he wanted my company. I used to grade papers on the steering wheel, too.

"He just wanted you to sit out there with him," I said.

She sighed. "Well, I had homework. Then he called me again and said, 'G, listen.' He turned the music up real loud and I heard Kanye."

When he came by the next afternoon, I said, "Thanks for the stereo." He handed me a small silver figure with a clip. It was an angel holding a scroll that read, "Drive safely, Daughter."

"I got this at the swap meet too," he said. "Put it on the visor, okay?"

"I will," I said. "You know she named the car. Thelma."

"What? Thelma? For *Thelma and Louise*?"

"Maybe," I said.

When he left, he hesitated by the red Honda for a moment, and nodded his head.

We had Thelma until Delphine one night drove a boyfriend home, and while they were inside talking to his mother someone stole the old Honda. It was found in San Bernardino days later, completely stripped. Dwayne and I went to the tow yard, and I drove Thelma back along the old highway below the Cajon Pass. The thieves had taken the entire interior, but not the engine. I was actually sitting on the bare metal floor of the car, with the freeway visible in the gaps between the missing door panels, the missing console, the missing windows allowing the winter rain to hit my face. Behind me were empty fast-food bags; the thieves had eaten dinner while removing the seats. I pulled slowly off the freeway and into the driveway, where Thelma stayed home for a few weeks. Then Dwayne went to Pick-a-Part, the massive automobile junkyard in a canyon just past the rock my father gave me, where people like us dig through piles of wrecked cars for what we need. He found the right seats, the right windows, and a center console, so Delphine could drive again.

26

The Yard Couch

Riverside, California, 2008

"She thinks she's all Pemberley," Gaila whispered to me, seeing a mother at our high school basketball game, and I smiled.

"But she's all about Lucas Lodge," I whispered back.

Even though we did not live in Jane Austen's England, and even though my daughters were not yet married (given that they were seventeen, fifteen, and eleven), and I did not spend my time searching for future husbands for them, or for me, and even though this was the land of huge SUVs inching down crowded freeways with cell-phone-wielding mothers glaring and toddlers watching in-seat DVD players, my girls and I maintained a complicated system of analysis and judgment for our rather broad society.

It was complex and ever-changing, far bigger than what most daughters and mothers could conceive because we had a massive black and mixed-race family wherein people knew everyone, and a quirky, deeply embedded white family wherein my brother and his friends had painted hundreds of houses, and he'd delivered his cannabis cash crop to many more. We knew our southern California cities as comprehensively and intimately as Edith Wharton knew her New York, and we'd read not only *The Age of Innocence* but memorized much of the movie version; we'd read *The House of Mirth* and *The Custom of the Country*. We knew our homeland as Louisa May Alcott knew Concord and environs. To tease poor Rosette when she talked about fads like MySpace, Gaila imitated Amy saying, "Limes are all the fashion, Jo!"

But Jane Austen was our favorite right then, because we had gone to Bath, and visited three of the houses where Austen wrote her novels; we'd learned the social hierarchies of money and class and what women were not allowed to believe about themselves in Britain then. We'd seen huge country estates like Pemberley, and smaller houses like Lucas Lodge; we'd walked along Hadrian's Wall and talked about the Romans and the Saxons.

When we came home, we watched all the movies made from Austen's novels. So though we said these things only to a few friends, we often made fun of people based on *Pride and Prejudice*, though elements of *Sense and Sensibility* and *Emma* featured now and then. We dined with more than four and twenty families, in a sense, given our involvement in Girl Scouts, high school basketball, French honor society, prom, and college recruitment.

We'd learned in Bath that it took only $10,000 back then to be considered a man of fortune. In California now, that wouldn't buy a garden shed or a Toyota Camry, the carriage of mothers like Mrs. Bennet.

Our bungalow would have been a cottage; we knew which girls lived as the Bennett sisters, and which mothers aspired to guys like Mr. Bingley and Mr. Darcy. We laughed at the pretensions of McMansions in new neighborhoods. A mean horrible mother who lived in Netherfield Park tried to go big-dog on our intellectual pursuits, our clothes, and my dusty green Mercury Villager with the magenta stripe. Some girls didn't like that my daughters played on the car stereo Chamillionaire and early Beyoncé, and some girls rolled their eyes when my daughters played Cake and Cold War Kids. We spent a lot of time talking about *noblesse oblige, nouveau riche,* and strange French terms that apply so aptly to American culture, especially *bourgeois,* which our Sims family had employed for decades when someone thought she was all that: *So damn boujee!*

In summer, we would heave the porch couch from its winter home near the front door, where the winter sun fell just right for naps, and onto its summer home, four pebbled paving stones set on the lawn under the Raywood ash tree. The couch, then ten years old, would remain there in state until the first rains of November.

The yard couch was dark blue with multicolored flowers that seemed mythical and not native to anywhere but fabric. I bought it when my girls were small, and dark colors seemed like a good idea in case of stains. But there were never any stains. They loved that soft couch with a passion, and countless children and teens slept on it. So when I bought a new cream-colored couch one June, actually to impress a few Lucas Lodge mothers who were holding a French club meeting at my house, my girls and their friends protested vehemently. When they said, "Can we just keep the old couch outside for a week? It's summer!" I gave in.

At first I was mildly embarrassed, even if the flowers kind of blended in with my garden. At least the couch wasn't plaid or nubby wool. But it was in the tradition of the driveway—where truck benches, black pleather couches, and Naugahyde love seats all had their time.

The summer before Gaila went to college, "the outdoor room" was the thing. Ads for upscale outdoor furniture were relentless, making me mildly resentful. It was not enough to have redwood tables, plastic-strap gliders, and metal chaise lounges with puffy oilcoth cushions, though that's what I grew up with. (No feeling like peeling your sweaty legs from oilcloth.) We saw elaborate curtained gazebos, wicker and teak furniture, coffee tables, rattan rugs, and actual outdoor chandeliers.

We had weathered wooden chairs sold to me by a Roma family that comes by every June bearing homemade unstained furniture in their pickup truck. Most houses on my block have these redwood chairs, in varying shades of gray, because this is the street of peasants who work for Pemberley, and we are too tired to paint and stain outside furniture. We have the redwood picnic table and benches my mother handed down to me twenty years ago. She bought them in 1958, for her first patio when she was a young married woman in Glen Avon.

My children find it hilarious that the picnic table is older than I am by two years.

My mother hates the fact that the couch is outside for the third year, and all that portends.

For Gaila's June birthday party, we bought a $9.99 cotton tablecloth for the ancient picnic table, two new cotton cushions ($4.99 each) for the grayed redwood chairs, and four strands of outdoor lights ($9 each) for the trees. It took about two hours total for the transformation.

It's not an outdoor room. It's our front yard.

We have about six yard parties every year, with more than a hundred people for the big ones. These are not Netherfield garden parties. I do have immense borders of perennial flowers and roses. But our parties—Easter potluck, three birthdays, Fourth of July, and Christmas open house—feature foosball and ping-pong. For Gaila's eighteenth birthday, an actual bounce house, as if for children, but standing guard outside with a cheap cigar was Mr. Sims, making sure no boys acted a fool. Sodas in an old green plastic turtle sandbox, now filled with ice, hilarious to Gaila's friends. A boombox on the porch. (Speakers? A decent stereo system? So much trouble . . .) And under the tree, the couch where five or six kids crowded on.

The week before, Gaila and Delphine had gone to a party at Netherfield. A brand-new custom home on a hill, where the elaborate landscaping included a copper firepit blazing on top of a fountain, which I found hard to visualize, surrounded by formal furniture and rugs, a manicured putting green, and a saltwater pool.

The next morning, she described the yard while I made pancakes. "All the work it would take to do that," I said. "And all the concrete and building materials from the old yard having to go to the landfill."

"We're so green," Rosette said, smug because we were eating eggs from our chickens and blackberries from our yard.

But I realized suddenly why our carbon footprint was so small. "That's because I'm way too lazy to renovate."

"We *are* incredible slackers," Gaila said.

I'd have to drive to a big store, walk around and look at stuff, and then buy it and get someone to drag it home— probably Dwayne in his truck, since he ate here in the yard so frequently. But he couldn't actually barbecue here, since we'd been divorced for ten years by then. That might be too weird for the Lucas Lodge people, kind of publicly odd if everyone saw him holding tongs and joking around. Then we'd have to assemble things, and find room for them, and clean them.

"Wait," Gaila said suddenly. "It's not just that we're lazy. We're like the Marches, in *Little Women*. We think this is okay, to not care. We think this is a good thing."

"I guess," I said, stirring. "I guess we're kind of transcendentalist."

"Wait," she said again. "It's not just that. We have absolutely no pride."

"What?" I said.

"Look at what I'm wearing." She was wearing a red checked sundress I'd seen all last year on her friend. They'd traded.

"Look at your bowl." The mixing bowl holding pancake batter was bought for me by my mother, when I was a newly married twenty-two. I wish it appeared heirloom-like, but the burnt-orange color, wheat motif, and Kmart origin made that impossible. I use it almost every day, even though I still don't like it.

"That's why we're green," Gaila said. "We just don't care enough."

Most things in our house, except those couches, were inherited: the dining room table, the small golden oak side table, with graceful curved legs, that Daisy Carter bought from the Sears catalog in the 1930s. Other things Dwayne had found on the street. Our ancestors survived Reconstruction and Depression, war, race riots, prejudice, and near starvation. We survived the 1970s with those parents. The girls had survived our thrift, college poverty, and an unwillingness to cease finding discarded treasure on a curb. The week before Gaila's birthday, Dwayne showed off three ladders and a 1970s casket-like deep freezer, and our girls rolled their eyes and said, "Oh, my God, Dad, please don't tell us where you found them." They're good metal ladders. He'll probably drop one off to me when the girls aren't here. I turned down the freezer.

Our eldest daughter was right. Ours was a strange California transcendentalism which never fit in with American upward mobility, or impressing anyone.

But this absence of pride was always tempered with my nostalgia, which I kept hidden. I loved that picnic table because my brothers and I used to eat there. My brother, Jeff, had recently died, and my half-brother John moved to another state fifteen years ago. I had never seen my five foster siblings again, but I could remember all of us at the redwood table with our cupcakes and hats. I remember their eyes and their teeth and their laughs. I loved that couch because of all those teenagers who slept on it, their faces for once at rest from the studying and arguing and worrying at which they excelled. I loved seeing them every summer, sprawled and laughing, their faces aglow from the new strand of lights that I affixed to the branches of the Raywood ash with leftover kite string I found in a drawer, wrapped around a popsicle stick by Dwayne ten years before when we used to fly kites with the girls, the string waiting for resurrection.

27

Grizzly

On her birthday and on Christmas, I left ham and homemade tiger butter candy at Alberta's grave. I felt the same pleasure as she had, when I bought and carried home a haunch of meat and spread it with spices and honey. You three girls liked to poke whole cloves into the skin. You helped me pull off the leathery brown collar around the bone. The smell of salted pork is probably inside the old lath-and-plaster walls, after all these years, even though I haven't cooked a ham in a long time.

You three became vegetarians, and even vegan for a time. On Memorial Day, August Family Reunion, and Labor Day, the uncles would say, "Ain't no such thing as a black vegetarian." They couldn't believe you didn't want ribs or hot links. And on the way home from the gatherings, Gaila said, "Seriously, Mom, everything we ate had meat in it. I thought there was gonna be meat in the fruit salad."

Your dad and Uncle Trent and Uncle Eddie bought more than a hundred pounds of chicken, hot links, hot dogs. Pork ribs like huge xylophones on the oil-drum grill. When they came off, Uncle Carnell's wife, Marcella, and I cut them apart with hatchets.

You know the side dishes by heart. You have eaten them since you could walk. Barbecued beans with ground beef, green beans with bacon and salt pork, black-eyed peas with neckbones and salt pork, collards with softened ham hock floating amid the tangled ribbons of green. My dirty yellow saffron rice with black beans and lots of hot red-pepper sausage.

There was no meat in the ambrosia or the potato salad, but you all were suspicious.

"Practically everyone in our family is worried about high blood pressure," Gaila said.

"So much pork," Rosette said.

You all knew what I'd say. "We have meat because no one had any in the old days."

Meat was our means of displaying survival, and prosperity, and pride. While everyone stripped the soft flesh from the ribs, holding the bones aloft like gleaming instruments, you girls had always listened to the elders.

I remember when I was not an elder.

Super Bowl Sunday, maybe 1981, before we were married. I was still an unknown quantity at Uncle Bobby's house in Inglewood, which your dad and I thought palatial, with the most beautiful bathroom of maroon and gray tile from the 1940s. Your dad still talks about that bathroom. Super Bowl had a fixed menu: Uncle Bobby and his wife, Lee Myrtle, made spaghetti with ground beef; pigs' feet; chicken wings; and side dishes.

All the Sims brothers were there: Stanford, who lived in Watts; John, who lived off Crenshaw in South Los Angeles;

and your grandfather General II. The men sat holding their plates, glancing at the football game, and someone said, "No, man, coon was the worst. You had to hang it up for two days, and then boil it with salt water. Those animals that eat meat themselves, that's the worst."

Someone else said, "Possum. Possum was the worst. It just looked nasty. You had to parboil that first with vinegar, before you roasted it. Then you had to put all those sweet potatoes around it just to make it seem like it was good."

"Rabbit. I hated rabbit. I hated hittin' them in the head. And they kicked you. Kicked you hard. Cut you up."

Your grandfather went last. He said, "The worst was squirrel. You had to shoot twenty of them suckers to make a meal. And all we ever got was the bones, anyway. Pickin' out those bones from every bite. You didn't get any meat for all that work."

I never forgot those voices, in the elegant living room with a bay window. Your grandfather said, "By the time we left Oklahoma, there were no animals left! We shot them all. We shot so many squirrels the snakes started showin' up hungry!"

I tell you this because I was a small white woman, the only white person in the house, and Uncle John saw me listening intently. He said, "She must think we're crazy, talking like this about killing."

I thought for a moment. Then I said, "My father told me the worst thing he ever ate was grizzly bear. He said it was fatty and greasy and full of worms and it made him sick."

These men, who had never made me feel unwelcome for a moment, stared at me in silence. Then someone said, "Damn, who eats a bear?"

I did not tell the rest of the story my father had told me. In the Rocky Mountains of Colorado, the bear that had been eating his father's sheep, the jaws of the terrible trap and the silvery grizzly hanging dead in the tree and my father being made to help cut it down and cut it up and haul the awful stinking worm-ridden flea-pocked flesh down the steep forest trail. He was nine.

I told them my father's family also ate the older sheep that starved to death during the Dust Bowl. The sheep had eaten cactus. Mutton, he called that meat.

"Yeah. Mutton," Uncle John nodded. "Terrible stuff."

The football game roared. Our plates were loaded with meat falling off the hooves of pigs, chicken wings with delicate bones. Then your grandfather said, "Well, that sounds about as bad as it gets. Who knew white people had it so hard?"

Your grandfather—General Sims II—and mine—Robert Bates Straight—were born some thirty years apart. But in photographs, they look like twins. They were lean brown men until they died.

When General II was nine, he was put to the plow with his brothers.

28

Nine

When you were nine, Gaila, we walked every day in the summer, to one of two places: Thrifty Drugstore, for their 99-cent ice cream cones, for which they are famous in southern California; or 7-Eleven, for various flavors of Slurpees. Depending on how hot it was, how much money I had, and who was walking with us, we did this for all of your childhood. A mile each way. Delphine was seven, and Rosette was three. She was still in the stroller. On a night when there were no cousins or friends, just we four, you held your cone of chocolate and said seriously to me, "I'm worried about my SATs. If I don't get a good score, I won't get into Kenyon. I want to go to Ohio."

I tried not to drop my cone. You were not joking. Not at all. You were already planning a life of books and history.

I said, seriously as well, because you deserved nothing less, "Well, you're the best reader of anyone I know, and that means you should be fine with all the weird word combinations. Your vocabulary will be great. Your comprehension will be fine."

"But my math."

"Yeah. I remember my math score. Terrible."

The four of us on Magnolia Avenue, where we had made our particular history of each block—the Band-Aid sidewalk, where someone had plastered a very large bandage that stayed for years; the letters and arrows in red and white and orange painted by city and cable crews on sidewalks that your grandmother Gabrielle had inventively told you were cryptic witch messages. All I could think was, My daughter is nine, and she's thinking about college. I brought her that Kenyon T-shirt when she was not yet two, after I did a reading there. She wore it as a nightgown for years, and then an actual shirt. Damn.

Holding our cones, we started talking about words that began with the same letters, the way the SAT tries to confuse you with synonyms and similarities: fervent, feverish, febrile, feral. I hoped that would be preparation for the time being.

My father, when he was nine, was put onto the outside running board of a Model A Ford, because his legs were too short to reach the gas and brake pedals if he were seated, and told to keep his foot on the gas and drive toward the cows scattered in the summer pasture of the Rockies. He helped round up the cattle with the car, hanging his body inside to steer. He was terrified by each turn the car took.

Then, he said, his father told him they had to trap the grizzly bear. The huge bear dangled from the trap like a monster, and he had to stand close and help the men cut down the body.

My mother was nine when her mother became ill with cancer. *Bedridden.* My mother darned socks and listened for bombs. The Germans had accidentally bombed some areas of Switzerland, one near their village in the Alps. But the Swiss military had built traps at the base of the mountains near the border, caves where tanks and spikes and bombs were hidden, ready to ambush the Germans if they were foolish enough to invade this tiny fierce nation. My mother said that even when she was nine, she knew her people were too crazy for Hitler.

When I was nine, I did nothing remarkable at all. The bookmobile was purchased in 1970, the summer I was nine. Every other week, I walked unaccompanied to the bookmobile, leaving our garden laced by silvery trails I was instructed to follow, to smash with a rock the snails eating the Swiss chard. The bookmobile was parked at the Alpha Beta market for two hours. I arrived at precisely the minute the doors on the converted bus opened and checked out my stack of young adult books. I spent the next hour and a half lying on the carpet, reading completely unsuitable novels by Dashiell Hammett and Agatha Christie and Ross Macdonald. I walked home thinking about all the ways there were to die, sliding my books carefully under a hole in the chain-link fence before I climbed over, and then crossed the railroad tracks, thinking those two silver lines shone like the marks left by the snails across the earth.

When you were nine, Delphine, you were already the fiercest kid I knew, and you scared the crap out of everyone. You wanted to be an entomologist and pro basketball player. You collected fig beetles and butterflies and moths, and all summer you wore a pale blue sleeveless jersey with the figure of Shaquille O'Neal and matching blue baller shorts that hit below your knees.

You were pissed when we went to France. No one to play ball with in Paris, where we did join you in making fun of the thin legs of French boys, calling them *baguettes* to cheer you up. We traveled with a filmmaker and her toddler daughter, and stayed out in the countryside of the Drôme, between Lyon and Avignon, in a stone house up in the hills near the villa of the filmmaker's parents, a painter and his wife.

It is the summer I remember with the most passionate affection of my life as a mother.

Gaila was eleven, and had brought music for us—Foo Fighters, Linkin Park, and 3 Doors Down. (She had begun to educate me about white music, which was funny—I still listened only to the music of my youth, Chaka Khan, Kool & the Gang, Tower of Power.) Rosette was five. She was amazingly cheerful at having to walk up the endless stairways of castles and medieval villages.

We were in the middle of nowhere. Our stone house was small and golden, with sheer white curtains that blew inside with the constant wind of southern France. We had a pool. We ate ice cream. We had watched *Knight's Tale*, with Heath Ledger, and the bad guy was French, Count Adhemar, a dude with protuberant eyes and a small mouth; so around the pool when huge biting flies came for us, we shouted *Count Adhemar!* and leaped into the water. We attracted three French girls your age who were staying half a mile away on their grandparents' farm. I had a house full of girls, playing Uno in both languages, eating dinner with us, long interludes of *chat y souris* (cat and mouse) in the foothills, which looked so much like home, chaparral and boulders and leathery sage.

But you were full of wonder, that month you turned nine, even though your birthday party was in the home of strangers—the painter and his wife, on a terrace overlooking the valley. I made butter cake with caramel icing. The sirocco wind came up, just like the Santa Anas at home, and your face transformed.

You were already feeling the traveling bones inside you. We walked for six and seven miles some days, all the way to the village, so you three could see Fatima, the Algerian-born young woman who worked at the café and brought you ice cream and exclaimed over your hair and smiles. She looked like you, and you adored her. Then we walked all the way back up the narrow lane into the hills.

And one day, you were determined, in your blue Shaq jersey, to have white cherries from the trees we'd been passing, and you climbed up and collected some. Then the branch broke and you almost fell. We kept walking, eating cherries, and Rosette found wild garlic, which she carried home like a rare treasure. Gaila and I talked about the plaque we had seen in the village, near the café—the names of the villagers shot in the Resistance. We talked about the films of Marcel Pagnol we had watched again and again—*My Mother's Castle* and *My Father's Glory*, set not far from where we were. We talked about the Palace of the Popes in Avignon, the hidden passageways we'd seen where queens were murdered by poisoned dresses.

There were cicadas in the Pagnol movies. Delphine, the entolomologist, you were determined to catch a cicada, so we went into a grove of trees to listen. And then, that afternoon I treasure even at this moment because I don't know how anything will ever be that way again, we saw an old man wearing tall black boots, carrying a burlap sack, and a dog snuffling along the earth among tree trunks.

We were in a grove of white oak trees. He told me in French that he was searching for truffles, that this was his farm. "A truffle farm," you said in wonder. We stood in the late sun, rays spangled through the oak leaves, the dry stems of grass around the bases of the trunks, and you said, "Someday I want to have a forest like this, and I would grow truffles."

I stood there with Rosette holding my hand, and I was in the orange groves of my childhood, the regimented rows of dark leaf and the water slipping like mercury down the irrigation furrows, over my bare feet. I was in the dark fairy-tale forests of my mother's childhood, and the forbidding snowy woods of my father's. We were in France. Gaila said, "I want to work on the truffle farm too!" and Rosette said, "I want to work on the truffle farm and I would take care of the dog!"

The sound of cicadas began to fill the air above us, and you looked up, narrowing your eyes at the bark of a tree.

When you were nine, Rosette, my beloved brother, your uncle Jeff, died. We inherited his favorite chicken: Coco the Mexican Fighting Hen, native of Chihuahua.

Your uncle had lived in a barn on twenty acres of citrus trees, between two ranchos: on one, Little Jose grew palm trees for landscapers, and on the other, Big Jose raised fighting roosters in a hundred tiny enclosures. You walked there with my brother. Fighting roosters are trained to be vicious, but they begin as baby chicks. Coco was matchless as a maternal source for countless fighters.

My brother ended up with Coco, along with some reject fighting roosters that he taught to sit on the couch beside him and eat Doritos while watching *Monday Night Football*. You remember she stayed in a long narrow wooden pen because of the wild animals that roamed my brother's grapefruit groves. When he died, his partner told us to come get Coco, so she could live with our other chickens, Butter and Smoke and Chili.

No one had ever caught or touched Coco. She was terrifying. We got her into a cage and brought her to her own coop, separate from all the others. She was small and brown-feathered. We let her out once, and she walked casually over to Butter as if in a movie like *Mean Girls* or *Never Been Kissed*, as if Butter were a golden plump cheerleader who said, "Oh, my God, are you the new girl? 'Cause you're, like, scrawny and brown and your feathers are tragic," and then Coco was like, "Yeah, and about that, I'm going to kill you now by first pecking out your stupid eyes."

She flew at Butter with fury like we'd never seen. I had the broom ready, but it was hard as hell to guide Coco back in her coop. I thought she might kill me, too. I'd worn boots and jeans and gloves. I gave her ripe bananas as my brother had. I looked like him. She didn't have to know I was a girl, too.

She was aloof in her coop. We didn't take away her eggs. One day I threw her some dandelions, which the other chickens liked. But in the morning, Coco was half-dead, having choked on a long slippery dandelion stem. It lay five inches out of her beak, and she lay limp in the dirt.

You always loved animals more than anyone, Rosette. You were brave enough to do what I asked: I picked up Coco, for the first time, held her against my chest, which was not the hard part, and you stood directly in front of that murderous beak and with your bare fingers pulled the long stem from her throat while she stared at you with those fighting hen eyes. It was petrifying. Then you said, "Oh, God, that's gross," and dropped the dandelion and Coco blinked twice and breathed. (She lived to be fourteen.)

Later that year, you told us you wanted to be a casting director. When you were eleven, you began the process of casting the pantheon of Greek mythology, from all the stories we had read for years—all the major gods and goddesses and also the muses and mortals because you wanted a large number of roles. You were casting only black actors and actresses. The summer you turned twelve, you spent hours here at my desk, looking at thousands of images and head shots and biographies. Faces and faces.

You were a loner. You had ideas. You had no trouble with Zeus—Idris Elba; Apollo: Michael Ealy; Aphrodite: Kerry Washington. But you struggled with Hera. Zoe Saldana was too thin. Halle Berry was too sweet. (You did not have Rihanna or Beyoncé in mind yet as actresses—they were still singers.) It had to be Tisha Martin-Campbell, who would talk shit to Zeus and call him out on his affairs with other women.

You knew this kind of audacious. It is in your blood. You had heard it from the woman laughing in the driveway.

29

Al Green—Driveway #1, The Second Love Letter

Riverside, California

The young girls—not just my own daughters, but all the nieces and great-nieces and cousins, maybe thirty girls—look at us like we're ghosts when Al Green comes on the stereo the men have set up in the driveway, just as the sun is going down and we're done putting up the rest of the ribs in foil-covered pans, when we who are now the ancestors are sitting in folding chairs with our feet out in front of us because we've been on them all day cooking.

Back when we were the young girls, the elders played Etta James and Charles Brown in the driveway. Today, during the afternoon, Nelly and Ciara and Usher blasted from the speakers of a nephew's car. But when the men want us to get forgiving and misty-eyed, right when we women start to clean up all that food, someone puts on Al Green.

Not electrified drums that shake our ribs, but the sparkly snare drum and organ riff that tap companionably at our sternums—the long bones that cover our hearts. We hear Al Green sing, "I'm Glad You're Mine."

Even though most of us are not theirs now, the men on the other side of the yard, we might as well be, because we're still here, remembering all those cars creeping down dirt roads out past the orange groves, remembering all those nights on the phone, all those house parties where the DJ played Al Green when it got to midnight and it was time to pair up and move more slowly, to have a hand planted on your backbone just where your spine ended.

We are the cartilage of women. Most of us are separated or divorced or widowed. Revia is no longer with Eddie, Shirley never was married to General III. Sitting beside me is Lisa, General III's first wife; she and I have been Sims family now for forty years; she is remarried, but always comes to gatherings. Teri is widowed, Tina and Christine and Sandra are divorced.

My daughters and the other girls glimpse our faces as Al Green sings about the only thing he sings about—that which transformed us when we were young like they are, when our feet didn't hurt and we were in darkened living rooms with record players spinning "Call Me" and "Let's Stay Together." The only things we cared about back then—"Love and Happiness" and "Let's Get Married."

Our faces get softer. Our eyes narrow to slits as we study the men gathered at the huge smoker and the card tables, drinking their Hennessey, slamming down dominoes and hollering. They hear Al Green, too, and they smile, because Al used to work for them.

"Girl," Sandra says to me, leaning back and folding her hands across her stomach. "Girl, this song used to kill me. Every time. It was this one summer. You know."

The eight beats—stark and sweet—and then the guitar plaintive and the organ rolling in to make it sacramental. "Love will make you do right, love will make you do wrong."

We think we did right. We think the men did wrong.

But here we all are, the dishes of macaroni and greens and rice behind us on the tables, our kids playing basketball in the street or bent over car hoods looking at something, the girls walking on the sidewalk with their tight jeans and little tees.

They think we look old. We're in our forties and early fifties. Like we're in Lutcher, Louisiana, or Grenada, Mississippi. Tulsa, Oklahoma. Or right here.

Nearly every one of us was born here in southern California. But our parents were born in the South or Mexico (except for me) and between the smells of smoked meat and the sound of Al Green's voice catching in his throat when he says, "We'll walk away with victory," it sounds like church and testifying and that kind of love and loss that the young girls are dubious about. That kind of love seems to come from a place with too many trees and not enough cars, of women sitting not in a fancy club or casino but in a driveway, on folding chairs, with faces melting a little.

It is like church, for us. Al Green wanted to love us and take care of us and take us to church in our own houses, in our living rooms, on our couches, which were not the couches we wanted. We wanted better couches, and less hard work, and the men to stay home and stay married to us, and we loved our children once they were the ones sitting near us on the couch, but when Al Green came on the radio, we still smiled.

I was twelve when "I'm Still in Love" played every hour on my tiny yellow transistor radio that my mother and I got with Green Stamps that summer before junior high. Then I met Dwayne, who slams down a domino now. We learned about the crucible of love at house parties and backyards where Al Green wafted through the pepper trees.

That was the year, 1974, when Al Green's former girlfriend broke into his house in Memphis and poured boiling grits on him while he was showering, inflicting second-degree burns before she killed herself in an adjacent bedroom with his gun. Older guys used his name as part of the lexicon of love and obsession: "You bet' not mess with that woman, fool—she look like she can cook some grits. You let her go, she do a Al Green on you, man."

But they've all let us go. When we hear him sing, "For the Good Times," we don't care. We had our times, and we would never trade them.

Our daughters stalk toward us and then away. One of them says, "You all look like—"

They don't know how we look, because they haven't looked like this yet. I wonder if they ever will—they don't have house parties and driveways and dances in the gym and in the park. They have cars rolling past, boys studying them, yes, but the voices are blaring X-rated instructions from huge car stereo speakers, rappers that sound to us like their love requires commands given by slightly bored field generals.

Back in our day, there was going to be a bed, or a couch, or a back seat. There was going to be possible disappointment. We revered the love we knew was to come, and even the hurt. Because being hurt was inevitable, we knew from watching our own parents.

Al Green testified to how powerful it could be. "Take me by the hand. Take me to the river—wash me down." Sandra closed her eyes next to me and moved her shoulders, danced just a little in the folding chair. The roll and trill of the organ like wavelets leaving ghostly foam arcs on the sand.

Will our girls, watching us, have this? Maybe not. Our driveway cannot exist everywhere. We might be thought of as too accommodating. Future women might never put up with the dominoes and our patience. There will be Facebook and Tinder, but we don't know that yet. We love our daughters, and we don't know if they'll ever feel how deeply these strings pull inside, the way love is all tangled up with this voice that means time gone past, but the memory of how we were once sanctified.

It is the companionable line of our knees in the folding chairs that comforts us. We have one another.

30

Travels with My Ex in the Time of Revenue

Orange County, California,
2009

Southern California in mid-July. Everyone in the world wants to be here, but in reality they want to be dropped directly from the plane onto the beach, not to have to drive on this freeway.

We've lived here all our lives, but Dwayne and I didn't want to be here. The foothills were not just dry but drought-parched and ugly, with burnt grass like the orangey tufts of hair on Jim Carrey's head back when he was the crazy fireman. We weren't going to Laguna. That's a beach we actually like. We were headed to Huntington because Delphine wanted her eighteenth birthday party at that beach.

I almost don't want to talk about this day. I don't want to remember it. The terror that scarred my lungs. My heart. *Probable cause. Put your hands out the window. Step out of the car.*

"I hate Huntington," I said that day. "My least favorite beach. It's always crowded. There's a reason we haven't been to Huntington in years."

"I didn't want to go either," Dwayne said. He was driving.

"That beach reminds me of J—. I'm always gonna hate it now, 'cause I might see him."

"We're not gonna see him," I said. J— had once been a basketball coach. We had gone to high school at the same time—Dwayne played against him. He was ambitious, having bought a house at that beach. But he was a capricious, moody, punitive man. He had deeply disrespected Dwayne.

"You know why his life was bad that year," I said. In 2006, the coach's brother had been shot and killed by police during a routine traffic stop. His other brother had been killed by sheriff's deputies in 1992 after being pulled over.

"Look at this traffic," I said. "This is why I hate going through Orange County."

The 91 freeway, multiple lanes, often the most congested in the nation. We were driving parallel to the Santa Ana River. The freeway winds from Riverside through Orange County, past Disneyland, Knotts Berry Farm, to the beaches. "Why couldn't they just go by themselves? I told her last night I wasn't going. She's eighteen. She's not even polite most of the time."

"You know you love her," Dwayne said. "And you know they want us to bring the coolers and chairs and pay for the parking."

This was a very strange feeling, to drive directly behind my own van, the dark green Mercury Villager I'd fired up every day for thirteen years. Delphine confessed to me once that she was comforted by the unique headlights; they looked like shark teeth grinning white through the darkness of the high school parking lot where she waited after practice.

It always felt a little funny to ride alone with my ex-husband in his white GMC truck, the battered metal toolbox attached to the truckbed.

You riding with your ex? People would laugh. But we know countless ex-couples like us. Whether it's because we can't afford to move away after we divorce, or we're too lazy to dislike each other efficiently and permanently, it seems to work.

Gaila would be a junior at Oberlin; Delphine would start USC in weeks, with nearly a full scholarship; Rosette had just won a DAR award for her history scholarship at middle school.

But that's why I was broke. Two kids in college. A California economy in shambles. My upcoming pay cut—10 percent. Dwayne's—14 percent from the county juvenile institution.

He still worked graveyard shift. That meant he'd slept for two hours, after spending the night monitoring the cells of two teenaged boys charged with a gruesome murder.

This was the first summer none of us had gone on vacation. Nowhere. The girls and I had been watching DVDs on the old TV Dwayne found in his garage after my more elderly TV finally gave out. I read classic vacation stories on the couch— John Steinbeck's *Travels with Charley*, Calvin Trillin's *Travels with Alice*, trying to figure out an ironic way to write about not traveling. When it got cool, the girls and I walked to Dairy Queen and then picked up movies from Blockbuster.

Today we'd have the beach. In the truckbed were buckets of KFC fried chicken, watermelon in the cooler, and homemade Funfetti cupcakes.

Ahead of us, my van was packed with teenagers. Driving was Gaila. Next to her, Delphine. In the back seat, Rosette, along with Bianca, one of our daughter's basketball teammates, and Delphine's boyfriend. We will call him Our Laurie.

My house had for years seen various successions of boys who tried to be the equivalent of Louisa May Alcott's Laurie, the young man allowed into the lives of the March sisters. My girls were quite strict about it. When Christian Bale comes out from hiding in the attic, holding his hands over his heart and pleading, "We'll share in the telling of our most appalling secrets," my daughters always said, "We want a Laurie!"

Gaila was our Jo, and according to her sisters, Rosette was sometimes as annoying and spoiled as Amy. Delphine, sensitive and secretive as Beth, has had scarlet fever not once, but twice; my mother and I sat vigil beside her bed, my mother trembling because her best friend died of scarlet fever when she was a child in Switzerland. (No one claimed to be Meg.)

The boy in the back seat of the van, Our Laurie, is willing to sit on the couch with all three Sims sisters and any attendant girls and watch *She's the Man* or *Fired Up*. A lefty quarterback, he throws the tennis ball accurately and untiringly for the dog. His thick eyebrows rise frequently on his mobile face, and when he's lying, he smiles only on the left side.

He makes everyone laugh except for my ex-husband, classic hater of young males, who still refuses to pronounce his name correctly. And his name is one syllable.

By 2:00 p.m., we'd gone only thirty miles in traffic that was now, unbelievably, stop and go. We were talking desultorily about how many police cars we'd seen that summer, how everyone we knew was getting tickets, how Delphine and Gaila had both gotten their first citations this year under dubious circumstances. "Revenue," Dwayne kept saying. "The state is broke. They have to make money, and it has to be on us."

A car suddenly exited the car-pool lane to our left by crossing the double yellow line, and then another guy tried to bail on the traffic by cutting across four lanes and heading for a toll road. A California Highway Patrol car went past us on the right, but did not pull either of those cars over. He pulled alongside the green van. "What's he doing?" I said. "Is he getting ready to run a traffic break? We'll get separated."

The cruiser slowed at the rear of my van's bumper, pulled quickly up to the side, and then hit the flashing lights.

"What the hell?" I said.

"He's pulling her over," Dwayne said, resigned. "Of course he is. Car full of black kids in the OC."

The patrolman was shouting at Gaila through the loud-speaker. She had to slide across four lanes in heavy traffic to reach the dirt shoulder.

"Driver, pull over to the side!" he was shouting.

Dwayne said, "I'm going too. He's not gonna pull any shit. I'm not having it." His voice was grim.

The feeling jolted me—every time we'd been pulled over by police, every time he'd had a gun pointed at his head, every time I thought he might die. He's the one who fits the description. The six feet four Black Man.

"D—," I said, the name of Delphine's boyfriend. I felt that nausea under my ribs. "He wants D—. He's gonna make D— get out of the car. And then something could happen."

My ex-husband was jerking the truck across the lanes, too, holding up his huge hand in the rear window to signal, following the cruiser that was herding my green van like a huge border col-lie, barking and slanting. "He better not mess with her," he said.

"It's D—," I said.

He's the six-feet-five Black Guy, the one with elaborate braids under his NY Yankees cap, the one wearing size 13 shoes and a South Carolina T-shirt because he'd gotten a scholarship offer from the Gamecocks, the one with brown skin almost exactly the same shade as my ex-husband, the one we tease our daughter about because she always said the last thing she wanted to do was replicate my life.

"He has a cell phone," I said. That could get him shot.

"Damn," Dwayne said, and pulled into the dirt cloud raised from the hot shoulder of the freeway by the California High-way Patrol car and Gaila, who'd driven the van into the de-serted weigh station where trucks were meant to stop.

Our Laurie was in the dark recesses of my van. He had a Sidekick and an iPod. Metallic rectangular objects that fit in a hand. I was so scared I was panting. The back windows were tinted. What did the highway patrolman want? Gaila had been going thirty-two miles an hour, between stops. She had always signaled. After all, it was a twenty-year-old's least favorite scenario for a summer day—driving your mother's ugly aged van, filled with your younger sisters and their friends, being followed by your hypercritical prison-guard father.

"The right taillight's going out again," Dwayne said.

"My seat belt is still broken," I said, my heart thudding all the way into my ears.

Dwayne fishtailed in the dirt of the shoulder, trying to pull ahead of the van and the cruiser. The patrolman shouted, "Ignore the white truck!"

"Pull behind him!" I shouted.

"No, then he'll get scared," Dwayne shouted.

If he got scared, he might shoot us.

We went around them and they went around us, and Gaila must have been completely panicked now. She stopped, and the cruiser stopped, and my ex-husband accelerated and went around one more time, a terrible dance which wasn't funny but it kind of was when the highway patrolman leaped out of his vehicle then, agitated, staring at us, holding both arms wide in the air, signaling, What the hell?

He had reddish-blond hair cut just longer than stubble. Big shoulders. Sunglasses. He didn't have a gun in the hands held to the sky.

He looked straight at me, and frowned. And that was good.

I was going to write an ironic piece about Dairy Queen. The high points of our previous summers had always been eating ice cream far from home. Gelato in Thun, my mother's hometown in Switzerland—*hazelnüsse*, caramel, chocolate. Fatima, at the local bistro in Valreas, France, serving us sundaes with little clown heads on wooden toothpicks. Three of those dusty little clowns still on my dresser. Maple ice cream on Prince Edward Island, at the *Anne of Green Gables* house.

Travels with Charley—Steinbeck, riding in his truck named Rocinante with a camper shell on the back, with his large French poodle named Charley, who is "bleu" when clean, which means black. When they hit New Orleans, a man leans in and says, "Man, oh man, I thought you had a nigger in there. Man, oh man, it's a dog. I see that big old black face and I think it's a big old nigger."

In 1986, Dwayne and I drove across the country in a different truck—the blue Toyota with a camper shell—and we spent an uneasy hot night in McClellanville, South Carolina. At dawn, he got up and took a walk beside the intracoastal waterway. While we slept, the campground had filled with hunters. I lay in the camper, and from the open window near my head, heard a man our age say to his young son, "See that big nigger? That's a big nigger, right there. When you get older, I'm gonna buy you a big nigger just like that."

I never told Dwayne exactly what the man had said. I just said there were scary people here and we should pack up and leave. We did. I shook and shook until we reached the next city.

Routine traffic stop. For us it's a Lite Brite. I picture a dark brain map with tiny bulbs going off. *Blink. Blink. Blink.* Routine traffic stop. Dead men.

The names and faces we've known all these years. The older generations had faces surrounded by rope and branches. They had Eddie Chandler I, in our family. Emmett Till. The men who died in Tulsa.

We grew up in the 1960s and '70s. We remember the Watts Riots, and the Los Angeles Riots, and yes, Rodney King. Alberta went to church with his mother.

We have our own names and faces from inland southern California. The coach's brothers, both of them shot. Tyisha Miller—shot eighteen times in her parked car at the gas station on my street. My brother Jeff's best friend, Bruno—shot nineteen times in his white truck as he maneuvered on the center divider of the freeway, having refused to pull over. He was on parole. Either hung up on the cement or trying to back up. No weapon. A toolbox. He'd just delivered a load of cut orangewood to my driveway.

He was blond.

"I ain't getting out," Dwayne said. He had his hands displayed on top of the steering wheel. As he always does when he's pulled over, or when the silent alarm is tripped.

"I know! I'm going," I said. I needed my wallet, but I didn't want to duck down for my bag on the floorboard.

"You go!"

"I'm going!" The dust was settling on us. I was scared. In the truck's side mirror, I could see the patrolman approaching the driver's window of the van.

Police officers have their own Lite Brite. We knew that. Dwayne was a correctional officer. Theirs is a completely different pattern and color. *Blink. Blink. Blink.* Ambush. Domestic disturbance. Routine traffic stop. Dead officer.

I had my pink leather tooled wallet. My job is to be the short blond mom. At basketball games, at parent-teacher conferences, in the principal's office when a boy has called Rosette a nigger and the male vice principal who hasn't done anything about it sees my ex-husband—Big Dog shirt, black sunglasses, folded arms the size of an NFL linebacker, and a scowl—and looks as if he'll faint.

My job is to smile and figure out what's going on.

The truck door was locked, then jammed. And that was good. By the time I got out, the patrolman was looking at me, and Gaila was pointing at me.

I felt faint, in the heat beating down. Would he pull his weapon on the five-feet-four blonde? I was wearing the right thing—khaki shorts, a white cotton shirt. Nothing but a mom. The traffic roared so close to us, twenty feet away from the silent weigh station. But no one to see us. I took my sunglasses off and felt my mouth smile.

"Why did you stop? What are you doing?" the officer said loudly at me.

"That's my mom and dad," Gaila said, aggrieved. She wasn't scared. She was pissed. Like Jo. Her default setting.

I smiled wider, trying to see Our Laurie behind her. "We're on our way to the beach for her birthday," I said, cheery and momlike. "Her dad and I didn't want to get separated, 'cause in this traffic we might never see each other again!"

My little women hate when I do this. They imitate me viciously afterward. They hate that I have to do it, that I am good at it. "What's the problem? Is it that darn seat belt?"

The officer squinted at me, then at the van. "One of the male passengers wasn't wearing his seat belt."

I was frozen. But then he said dryly, "He's wearing it now."

He stepped back. I breathed. Then he asked for license and registration and insurance. I leaned into the driver's window, between him and Gaila, making jokes about how deep in the glove compartment the registration might be. I pulled the insurance card from my wallet. He glared at me but carried them back to his patrol car.

Gaila began a low invective, and I leaned into the window

to say to Our Laurie, "You weren't wearing your seatbelt? You always wear your seatbelt!"

He grinned, eyebrows leaping. He said, "It wasn't me. It was Bianca."

Bianca, nineteen, her hair tucked into a black cap, wearing a huge black T-shirt. The officer thought she was another male passenger. Bianca rolled her eyes, furious.

The officer approached the other side of the van. "I need the male passenger to open the door. Open the door," he said.

My nausea rose again. Bianca rolled the door back slowly. I could see the officer. He was not holding a gun. A clipboard. I almost threw up.

He asked Bianca for her license. He didn't apologize for identifying her as a guy. He didn't ask her or Our Laurie to get out of the car. I stopped having visions of people lying on their faces in the dirt. He wrote the ticket. I leaned awkwardly on Gaila's window until it was done.

Three days earlier, I'd given one of our nephews a ride home after football practice. We'd spent a long time in the driveway, talking to General III, Derrick, three cousins, and a family friend. We talked about the police review of the 2006 shooting of our coach's brother. The commission had found no fault, though the brother was pulled over three times in thirty minutes, the first time because "he had a weird look" and the second time because after the patrol car continued to follow him, he ran a stop sign and made a U-turn. The official report said he had struggled when the officers put him in the back of the patrol car for questioning. Witnesses said he was trembling, his hands shaking. His brother had been shot by deputies when he was very young. The voice recorders were turned off. One officer said the man reached for his Taser; the other officer shot him. The witnesses, who spoke mostly Spanish, said he did not reach for the Taser.

Ben Tyson, the family friend, said he'd been pulled over the week before in the mostly white neighborhood where he'd lived for a decade. The officers said he fit the description of a robbery suspect. He gave them his ID. The suspect was described as six feet, 185 pounds, and in his thirties. Ben Tyson is five feet eight, rotund, and in his sixties. He was the first black man to work at the downtown post office in the 1950s. He was told to get out of the car and lie on his stomach on the sidewalk. He refused repeatedly, and was kept there for over an hour while the officers berated him and asked him questions.

General III had recently been stopped at 5:00 a.m. while riding his bicycle to work; he is a custodian at the community college. He was told drug dealers often use bicycles now. He was given a ticket for not having reflective gear.

The father of Delphine's basketball teammate was made to lie handcuffed in his own driveway for an hour by city police, who'd been called because his neighbors didn't recognize him when he sat on his own block wall, resting after gardening. He was wearing sweatpants. He is an officer in the Los Angeles Police Department.

It took two more hours to get to Huntington Beach and find a parking space.

We followed the van forever in the stalled traffic. We talked about July 5, seven days earlier. At 3:30 in the afternoon, Avery Cody Jr., sixteen, left a McDonald's with three friends, and was stopped in a crosswalk by a patrolman. They were ordered to put their hands on the police car. They did. They were ordered to lift their shirts, and Cody Jr. ran. After a two-block chase, he was shot in the back. Video footage from a 7-Eleven shows him running past with something small in his left hand. The police say it was a weapon. Witnesses say it was a cell phone.

"He shouldn't have run," Dwayne said, shaking his head. "You never run."

"But what if you panic? What if D— had panicked?"

He was quiet for a while. My van ahead rode low, with all those kids. "I was just hoping CHP didn't make him get out of the car," Dwayne said.

"What if the cop saw the cell phone and panicked?"

"You never run," he said again. "You just don't."

"Don't you remember Westwood?" I said, and he frowned.

"I don't think about that."

"I do," I said. "I tried not to until she started going out with D—. But now I think about it all the time."

My ex-husband looked at me like I was crazy. "What?"

When Delphine got her speeding citation, that January, D— was in the passenger seat of Thelma, the old red Honda. He was questioned at length, about his identification, his address. The patrolman didn't believe that he was seventeen. They were there nearly an hour. When our daughter called me, she was crying, afraid of what I would say.

She was right. I was furious, but not about the ticket. "When you get pulled over, you put him in danger," I shouted at her. "You're risking his life. Don't drive even four miles over the speed limit! He could have been shot and killed!"

Only some mothers say that to their children.

I said to Dwayne then, "It feels horrible to be the person watching, too. Okay? It's like that thing you get from being in a war."

"What are you talking about?"

I can remember scenes and dialogue from hundreds of books, but not acronyms because I hate them. "PTS something. Post-traumatic stress something."

For weeks after something like this happens, I want to sleep all the time, but I can't sleep until I know where everyone is. In their beds, at work on the graveyard shift, or in a gym.

At Huntington Beach, the six-feet-four Black Guy and the six-feet-five Black Guy arranged themselves on chairs. They were surrounded by us and six more girls on the blankets now, friends of Delphine, eating chicken and watermelon and cupcakes.

Dwayne didn't go into the water, as he always did. He loves to swim, and the girls love to jump on his back. But today, he dozed. He had slept only the two hours.

Our Laurie went in the water. He was alone for a long time, the farthest out in the powerful waves, because he was so tall the water only reached his chest. His baller shorts were long and wet. It's the braids under his ball cap that make white people nervous, the intricate tiny cornrows his mother plaits every week, that cross his skull in complicated patterns and end just touching his shoulders.

Rosette said, "Why does everyone make fun of watermelon and fried chicken anyway? Why did people always talk about Barack Obama and watermelon?"

Gaila said, "Oh, my God, could you be any more annoying? Learn your history, okay?"

Rosette was offended. "Why don't you ever eat watermelon, Daddy?"

"'Cause it's nasty," he said, opening one eye like a parody of a grumpy father. "Just like green peas. They made me eat it when I was a kid, and I ain't a kid now."

He was slumped in his chair, half-asleep. His feet were covered with sand.

That night, Dwayne called me at 11:15. He was on shift. "They make it back okay?" he said quietly, anxiously, in the echoing vacuum of the cement walls of the correctional facility.

We had left the beach in his truck after only two hours. He had to sleep before work.

"They came back about forty minutes after we did," I told him.

"For real?"

"I guess they got cold," I said.

Maybe they had been nervous. We didn't talk about it. "You working security unit?" I said. "You gonna fall asleep?"

He said he had court calendar, making the schedule for juvenile offenders who would be escorted in the morning. He would shackle and prepare them before he left for home, at 7:00 a.m. "I just wanted to know they made it back," he said, and hung up.

I stood in the kitchen doorway. Our Laurie was on the couch, with the little women heckling him while he took out his braids, which were full of sand. They had never seen his shoulder-length curls before, and they kept trying to take pictures with a cell phone.

IV

31

Switzerland, Loveland, Cuddyland

Always, January 12, 1950,
Always

To my daughters:

You'll have to imagine your father hiking up to a remote mountain in central Switzerland, to a wooden house perched on a nearly vertical slope, a chalet built in the early 1800s, in which lived a man we knew as "Uncle Willy," hermit and moonshine-maker who could have been in the classic novel *Heidi*. Theo Erb, nephew of my grandmother Rosa Erb Leu, took us to this mountain, where we drank homemade schnapps, distilled from apples and pears from Willy's own trees, the kind of alcohol you pour on a wound to sterilize it. Then, as your father says, "Man, I ate some hundred-year-old cheese!"

Uncle Willy accepted us immediately as family, because Theo brought us to him as such, and Theo's father, Fritz, was Willy's brother and Rosa's. Though Rosa Erb never returned to Switzerland, and we had no blood relation to the large network of Erbs, they have always considered us kin. I'll never forget standing there watching Willy tease your dad by offering him "mountain vitamins," a handful of goat droppings, Theo holding the goat, your dad cracking up. Willy looked exactly like all the roughly comic uncles in Riverside and Colorado—skin brown, olive drab pants exactly like General II, labor-thickened hands, and sly grin. The universal hardworking human in all our families.

This was a place my own mother never saw, a place that made a great story in the California driveway of the Simses, near the domino table, where Dwayne talked about the moonshine's power—we kept the one bottle Willy gave us, and if you threw a few drops into a fire, an explosion sparkled the most beautiful deep purple.

Your father and I stayed three weeks in Aeschlen, the village of Erbs, working in the plant before sunrise, sorting newly hatched chicks from the incubators into cardboard boxes to deliver hours later to farms all over Switzerland. Your father ate the brown bread and cheese in the dark with me, and the Erbs still talk about how his hands were so big he could hold up four chicks in each grip, for inspection. The rest of us could manage only two or three.

But your father and I, and you girls as well, would never have made it to the Alps if not for my stepfather, John Watson, from whom we inherited the traveling bone, as people call it. He bequeathed that bone to me as surely as if it were in my blood. No one else in our families had wanderlust like my dad John, or me, and now, you three. For we five, travel is always worth going broke. To see a new place is to make ourselves into different humans. Once, Delphine, you said to me that the most valuable thing I ever gave you was our travel, because when we were in the big world, we saw how insignificant we were. But it was my stepfather who gave the world to me.

———

Dwayne Sims, Theodore Erb, Willy Erb, Swiss Alps, 1985

John Paul Watson was born in Saint John, New Brunswick, Canada, in a blizzard climate (all three of your white grandparents survived thousands of feet of snow, and ended up living in one of the hottest places in America, and they sure as heck never went back.) He hitchhiked from easternmost Canada to California when he was seventeen, to visit an uncle. When he graduated high school, he came back to live in Montebello, California, following his parents, who had left those winters on doctor's orders because of lung disease. But his mother died not long after she got here, and his father passed away a few years later. My dad didn't go back to Canada. He joined the U.S. Army, then lived in a tiny shack with no bathroom, outside San Bernardino, and started building things—apartments, laundromats. He became a citizen, met my mother, and took all of us on the road—we kids standing up in the truckbed of his yellow pickup while he gunned the engine to make backfires that sounded like gunshots, causing passing motorists to look at us like we were insane. We pulled an eighteen-foot travel trailer.

My dad first gave us America: We rode down into the Grand Canyon on burros, we walked on salt formations in Death Valley; we saw Yellowstone, Zion, and Crater Lake. We hiked into the mist of Bridalveil Falls in Yosemite, where I held my wet face near the thundering power of the earth tossing water into beauty.

Then he took us to Mexico on second-class trains, where we met older women in rebozos, chickens in wooden cages, and kids with whom we drank the best Coca-Cola ever. In Chihuahua, we hiked into Copper Canyon caves where the Tarahumara indigenous people wove baskets. In Jalisco, we saw the cathedrals and zocalos of Guadalajara.

When I was sixteen, he took my two brothers, me, and my mother to Switzerland. She hadn't returned in twenty-eight years, since she first left, and he sold a laundromat to take her home.

We stayed with Rosa's brother Fritz in the Erb family compound—six sons, their wives and children, the chicken hatchery and orchard and vegetable gardens and a machine shop where the two eldest sons, Theo and Hans, fabricated metal parts. On that trip, my mother couldn't find her mother's grave, but we saw the Wolf Church, and the tombs of the Erb ancestral women who'd died in childbirth. By the end, the Erbs felt like my true family.

I went to Aeschlen alone in 1980, when I was nineteen, staying with Marie and Fritz Erb. We woke up at 3:00 a.m. to work in the hatchery, sorting the chicks, then ate a quick breakfast of bread, cheese, chocolate, and coffee, and traveled all of Switzerland in a panel truck. We delivered chickens to remote mountain valleys where I talked to farmers and their wives, drank schnapps and herbal tea, and learned Swiss-German dialects.

Then your father and I went in 1984, when we were newly married, and drank the schnapps, too. But he also hiked one day alone with Hans, up to the summit of a secret mountain; with Swiss Army knives, they carved their names into a stone. Hans, whose nickname is Hausie, told your father he was the only American to ever set foot on that mountain.

In 1995, my dad John and your father and I took the whole family to Switzerland, when Gaila and Delphine were six and four. But we'd planned the trip early—and by the time we went, I was seven months pregnant with Rosette. (Yeah, Rosette, I shouldn't even have been flying then. I sucked in your presence on the plane. You responded by kicking the crap out of my kidneys. But you ingested goat cheese and chocolate and Alpine air. You ended up quite Swiss.)

We went back three times since Rosette was born, just the

four of us, staying always with family. You girls swam in remote mountain rivers, hiked Alps and were butted by bell-wearing cows, and lit fireworks in the cornfields with Swiss cousins. You picked green beans with your great-aunt Marie. When I was nineteen, Marie taught me how to mix flowers, green beans, radishes, and herbs in the garden rows—something you all learned working in our garden, kneeling near the sunflowers, corn, and basil that grew so companionably. You knew the word *Bohnenkraut*, which means "bean herb," which Americans call savory. You knew the word *züpfe*, the braided bread, and *landjäger*, the dried sausage carried by young boys who tended summer cows in the highest Alps.

When your father and I got home to Riverside back in 1984, he told everyone in the driveway about Hausie and the mountain, and how all our Swiss cousins had nicknames just like our Sims cousins. No one but us could talk about how alike were the villages in Switzerland and in Cuddyland, where lived Nacho, Snooter, and Gato.

Cuddyland is the settlement across the Santa Ana River, on the west side, home of six generations of the branch of the Sims family begun by Mary Louise, eldest daughter of Daisy. For our family, the word *cousin* had evolved decades ago to *cuddy*, as in, "Hey, cuddy, give me a ride out to the Westside," and, "Leave her alone, man, that's my cuddy, she comes with backup you don't want to meet." If you do the math, and think about the people who came to California—ten siblings who marry into families with ten siblings, and then their own children marrying into families with six or seven siblings—the possibilities for cousinhood, and survival, are endless. It is the definition of Linda Hogan's lovely line: *We are the result of the love of thousands.*

When Mary Louise Morris was seventeen, she married Henderson "Gato" Butts, who was from a huge family in Rubidoux adjacent to the river, about two miles from the market where my mother bought my first Little Golden Book and my father bought the laundromat. Rubidoux, one of the first places granted to the Spanish Californios when the land was "claimed" from the indigenous people in the Riverside area, the Cahuilla and Serrano, had been settled in the 1800s. In the 1920s and 1930s, the Butts and Dumas families left Idabel, Oklahoma, after terrible race violence, and settled in a small area called Belltown, where Gato's father, a plasterer and builder, constructed a family compound of several homes.

You know the tales of Cuddyland. The cousins were tough—when your father was five, they put a wooden box over him, with rocks on top, in a vast field. He's still not a fan of enclosed spaces, like elevators. Cuddyland was where the deadly junkyard pig lived. When you'd see our cousin Snooter, he'd tease me about my first suit—a jacket and pants of sapphire-blue wide-wale corduroy that he sold to your dad when I was seventeen, after the suit fell off a truck. You three couldn't figure out that truck, which also dropped bottles of fine liquor and certain brands of shoes. I still have the suit. I still wear the jacket.

Your dad took each of you in turn, when you were sixteen, to practice driving on the dirt roads and fields in Cuddyland. He might have claimed there was less traffic out there, but I knew he loved to visit with Snooter and Rita and the other descendants of Mary Louise, and to show them your faces, because they ask about you all the time. "Where the girls now? Texas? Peru? What? They got the travelin' bone."

At night, after I visit with the cousins, I think of all the tiny villages I've seen, in Iowa and upstate New York, in Utah and West Virginia, small places made up of mostly kin. I think of Aeschlen, and Belltown, and wish I'd had cousins, wish I'd had the prairie of Colorado, wish I'd had my grandmother Ruby.

Not until I was twenty-two, driving across the country with my brother Jeff, to Nunn, Colorado, did we meet our father's cousins. We found a prairie town inhabited by our ancestors: our grandmother Ruby's sister's children. They were in their fifties. My brother and I stayed for three days, painting a barn for the widow of Carl Triboulet, Ruby's only brother. The town held about four hundred people. My brother and I sat one afternoon in an abandoned grain elevator, thinking we could move there, onto our family land. But he was nineteen, growing ten varieties of marijuana, and he sure couldn't grow that on the prairie.

No one talked to us about our grandmother. Not until I went back to Nunn in 2014, when I drove to Canada with my dog, did I see my cousins again, and then they thought I was old enough to hear the stories of my grandmother. By then I was fifty-three, and they were in their eighties. Dale and Kahla Barnaby, Ruby's nephew and his wife, fed me ham sandwiches, put me and the dog in the tiny second bedroom in the little wood-frame house, and took me out on the county roads raising dust to the lost places everyone had left, the land where my grandmother and her sisters went to dances, the abandoned ranches where they once grew white wheat and ate antelope they shot for supper.

But you, my daughters, have never seen those people, and now they are almost all gone.

I have lived longer than Frieda Roesti Leu, who died at thirty-nine, and Ruby Triboulet Straight, who died at fifty.

Ruby's sisters tried for years to save her. Her sister Hazel went out to Los Angeles, became a fervent member of Aimee

Semple McPherson's Church of Foursquare Gospel, when the famous Angelus Temple was built at the lake in Echo Park. Hazel sent for her mother, Amanda, and the youngest sister, Helen. They lived in Echo Park near the temple, and Amanda Baldon Triboulet was saved by the voice of Aimee Semple McPherson as it resonated through the radio upon which my great-grandmother laid her hands. She fell onto the floor, sanctified. She never returned to Colorado. Genevieve, the second-eldest, also went to California, and eventually became a Foursquare Gospel minister in the San Joaquin Valley. Amanda and Genevieve are buried in Lodi, California.

Ruby's sister Emma had married Frank Ball, and had two sons on a farm near Pierce. Vara had ten children out in Purcell. But when Ruby took her youngest child, my father, Richard, and fled the Rockies and Robert Straight, she didn't head east to the prairie. Three times, they went west to Hazel in California.

When my father was in first grade, they took the bus in winter down Rabbit Ears Pass, frozen highway and slipping tires, into Wyoming and then down through Utah, through the Nevada desert and over the Cajon Pass, onto Route 66, the way all seekers arrived. They stayed with Hazel first in Echo Park, and later, in Ontario, California.

Robert Straight was legend. Awful legend, in Colorado. He fought with his family, with neighboring ranchers, with strangers, with people he met accidentally in towns or on highways or other ranches. He was relentless and wiry and his anger knew no bounds. My father says he witnessed his father beat men to near death many times, and these pages are not the place to recall even worse.

My father's older brother, Robert Jr., and older sister Beverly were teenagers who left home early. His older sister Audrey, who had a heart condition, had been sent to California to recover; at fourteen, she took the train home, collapsed onto the station platform in Laramie, Wyoming, and died, in front of her mother, Ruby.

But each time Ruby took Richard to California, her husband—contrite, charismatic, frightening, her legal-wedded spouse—came to take them back. The last time my grandfather came to Ontario, he got a job as a foreman in a cement plant. My father was fifteen, in high school. After another night of violence, Robert Straight left for Fraser, and inexplicably, Ruby followed him. She abandoned my father. He was homeless, and his voice still tore ragged the few times he told me about it, when he was already in his eighties. He slept in the kitchen of the fast-food restaurant where he worked. He slept in cars. He rented rooms. At seventeen, he signed up for the military.

My grandmother Ruby chose her husband over her son, and that changed everything for him, and for us—his natural children and stepchildren—because my father never trusted anyone in his life. When I got into college, he wasn't happy for me; he said people who knew nothing of work would ruin my brain. He'd never even gotten to graduate from high school. For a freshman assignment, I asked him about my grandparents, and he said, "That's none of your damn business." I knew only the ice, the snow, and the grizzly bear. To me, he had been a child cowboy who was never a cowboy again—but always poised to flee, in his beloved 1970 Mustang.

Ruby was told by doctors never to live again at high altitude because of her weight, high blood pressure, and constant stress. But in 1950, Robert took her to Loveland, almost five thousand feet above sea level. My father was nineteen by then, married, with his first child—a son, named for him—and when he came home on leave from the Air Force, he and his wife Jean traveled to Colorado to show Ruby the baby.

They pulled up into the long dirt driveway of the house in Loveland, where my grandfather had been born. Ruby came outside to meet them, and my father handed her his son, and she collapsed onto the ground.

He has told me several versions of this. The cousins in Nunn have told me other versions of this, from their own mothers—Ruby's sisters. Ruby had been alone, in the mountains, with Robert. Who knows what had happened in the days before? My father grabbed the baby, gave him to Jean, and they called for medical help, a long time coming to a remote area in the Rockies. Sometimes, my father said that his mother already had bruises. Sometimes, my father said that he bruised her chest while he tried CPR.

Ruby's sister Vara's children say the bruises were the same as they always had been, since the beginning. They are resolute in their belief that her death was caused by her husband. Their mother, and the other Triboulet girls, lived very long lives, into their eighties and nineties. They were thin-faced, strong-willed, very religious women who preached, taught Sunday school, did not drink or smoke or dance, put up with nothing from their men once they decided that was it, and devoted their lives to their children.

Ruby had died almost instantly, in the gravel of the road that overlooked a beautiful vista of the Rocky Mountains and the pine forests and the steep, sheer drop of a cliff toward the river below.

There is not a single physical item anywhere in the world I have ever seen, or held, that belonged to Ruby. Not a small table or scarf or hairpin or recipe for cake, not a Bible or bracelet. I have her blood, and so do you, but we have nothing else.

———

My stepfather gave us this immense and insatiable wanderlust. As my friend Nicole says jokingly, *You all are just bagavonds.*

Our last trip with your father was 1997, when we went to Oaxaca. The day before we were to leave, we found out Rosette, at eighteen months, was too young for inoculations against cholera and yellow fever, so she stayed home with my mother. But Delphine, you had carried mononucleosis and a terrible throat infection from kindergarten to Mexico, and you were feverish and nearly unconscious by the second day, when we carried you down the historic streets of Oaxaca City to a doctor we didn't know. That night, I went with women I'd met to a nearby church for the patron saint of Oaxaca, La Virgen de Soledad, her black gown severe and triangular and scattered with stars. With the other women, I crawled up the cobblestones toward the face of the church, prayed for your recovery, and lit a candle. The women told me in Spanish who they were praying for—unborn babies, babies never arrived, babies who had died, babies who were ill at home. I told them about you. They told me to swear to La Virgen I would not drink alcohol—this was the land of mezcal—or smoke—my girlfriends were into fancy cigarillos then. (I didn't drink or smoke for twenty years after that night.)

Two weeks later, we celebrated your sixth birthday in a two-room cement-block house in a small village outside the main city in Oaxaca. It was named Santa Maria de Atzompa, where we'd met a mother with two girls your age. The four of you ate chicken with mole amarillo and mole colorado (yellow and red sauces) and then ran up the dirt alley to a backyard where two women made fresh tortillas on a heated comal, to buy another stack.

I carried home in my suitcase a two-foot-tall ceramic Virgin de Soledad, made in Atzompa, her gown covered with the distinctive green and blue flowers of the village. She has remained in my bedroom, along with the thread bracelet you wore then, and the candle I lit at that church, for all these years. Every night, I reiterate to her and all the other beings that I would sacrifice whatever required, for the three of you.

I tried to give you the world before the rest of the world took you from me. We went to Francis Ford Coppola's lodge in Belize, where I taught for ten days; you swam near the waterfalls, saw Mayan ruins and caves, learned about the Garifuna people, who were African, Mayan, Spanish, and spoke Creole.

The last two times we went to Switzerland, you hiked the Niederhorn and the Niesen, my mother's favorite childhood mountain, among bell-chiming cows and goats. You ate pizza in Thun near the Aare River blue-green as old turquoise, roaring under a bridge built in the 1600s, near a castle where your grandmother Rosa's sister Frieda's stepdaughter Lydia Staudenmann took you to see an exhibit of medieval china chamberpots, which made me think of all of us, the women.

You went to a farmhouse in Zwisselberg where your true great-grandmother Frieda's cousins still live, in the Alps. The village is near Wattenwil, where Frieda Leu's bones are lost now in that cemetery. The chalet was built in 1840, and three generations of your cousin's family live there, raising cows and pears and apples, harvesting wild honey, cooking you a four-course meal on an old woodstove. We all held hands around the lace-covered table while they sang grace in ancient Swiss-German dialect.

That is your blood. You can speak a little Swiss-German, some French and Spanish, and the language of Cuddyland—"Look at him! Cuddy still drivin' that old hooptie, ain't made no ducats this year. I remember when he had a new El Dog and them whitewalls would blind you."

You were all about clan. You gave up your beds for cousins and friends. You gave up your clothes and your money and your nights. As my mother had taught me, I taught you to make chocolate chip cookies, and they became Gaila's specialty, cookies far better than mine, the ones she made for everyone to say *thank you*, to say *I hope you feel better*. Rosette was very young when she decided she wanted her own cookies. She made lavender shortbread, with the three kinds of lavender—French, English, Spanish—we grew in the garden. Dough rolled on wax paper, flecks of purple in the rounds. She delivered them to a neighbor who had cancer.

Delphine's talent is the perfect gift, and she is the most bagavond of all of us. She brings silver hoop earrings from Mexico City, flowing pants from Thailand, olive oil from Umbria. She works everywhere, and when the cousins see my earrings, they say, "Where them girls now? Why they always gotta be so far away?"

You love to find the smallest villages. You know that the world thinks villages like our ancestral places—the driveway on Michael Street, the dirt lanes in Cuddyland, the ghost town of Nunn, Colorado, the family compound in Aeschlen—are not as important as the cities. But you know how kin keeps people like us alive.

Your father says he wants to be cremated, and his ashes taken to that Swiss Alp somewhere in the Bernese Oberland, the summit of Hausie's mountain. That would take our California blood to Switzerland forever. Hans Erb and Dwayne Sims.

We'd better find out where it is.

32

Bring Me Your Smartest Girl

Riverside, California, 2008;
Tulsa, Oklahoma, 1925

Dear Gaila,

You always said if you ever had a daughter, you'd name her Callie. You know this story—because you are the historian. You are the legacy.

In the spring of 1924, General Roscoe Conklin Sims went to visit Booker T. Washington High School in Tulsa. "Show me the smartest girl you have in this school," he told the principal. "I want my children to be smart."

The principal obligingly brought to the office Callie Rollins. She was thin, with the round-shouldered posture of her time, with large cautious eyes and full lips, with wavy hair parted on the side and pressed down along her head. She was very pretty, and seventeen. I tell you this again because she is your blood legacy—you are the echo. Your great-uncle John Prexy Sims told us about Callie, his mother: "Her greatest love was learning. Her idea of a great time was spending all day in bed reading."

That is you, my eldest daughter—you read in bed, under the table, in a tree, just like Callie, just like me.

General Sims was twenty-five. Though his father, Stanford, had been a teacher in Muskogee, General liked farming and building. His mother, Minerva, clearly preferred her lighter-skinned son Lanier, who lived in the city of Tulsa. But General was determined to make his farm work.

Callie was in Tulsa because her half-sister, Jennie, had taken in Fine, Callie, and James, after Zach Rollins died in Texas. Eventually, Fine rented a small house on Latimer Street. Callie had excellent grades, and was headed to college in the fall.

Imagine what it must have felt like to be in the principal's office, looked over by this stranger: short, self-possessed, and judgmental. A farmer. Callie Rollins refused his offer, probably with immense politeness. She went back to class. In the fall, she went off to Langston University.

Langston was near Guthrie, about one hundred miles from Tulsa. Originally called the Oklahoma Colored Agricultural and Normal University when it was founded in 1897, it's the westernmost historically black university in America. It was re-named for John Mercer Langston, who was born free in 1829 to a white plantation owner and an enslaved woman of African–Native American heritage whom he freed after she bore him a child. At fourteen, John Langston enrolled at Oberlin College in Ohio; his brothers were the first black students admitted to Oberlin, in 1835.

Callie did well in her classes at Langston, that fall of 1924. But the deal she'd worked out fell apart. She had deferred tuition payment. Fine had been expecting money from the sale of the land in Denton, but by January, there was still no money for college. Callie came home after that first semester. She married General Sims.

He took Callie out to his land in Fry Township, near Rentie

Grove, where he was farming sweet potatoes, watermelon, and cotton.

Callie had five children—Minerva, Stanford, Robert, General II, and John—between 1925 and 1937. General worked the children hard on the farm, but no matter what they did, he beat them. He worked himself even harder, plowing and hauling until he gave himself a hernia. He had what he'd wanted—five intelligent, handsome children—but he mistreated them and himself all day on a piece of land he was determined to conquer, during the Depression.

In 1937 he had an operation to repair the hernia, and was told to go home and rest. In the morning, he got out of bed, beat one of the children, went outside, beat one of the mules, and began to plow. The stitches ruptured, and he died.

Callie, the smartest and prettiest girl, picked cotton, worked fields, cleaned houses, and went hungry so often trying to feed her children that eventually she was near death. She was thirty years old. Her children were shooting wild game and collecting wild plants, and still it wasn't even close to survival. The older boys plowed with the mule until the mule had to be sold; then they plowed with their own bodies, drawing furrows in the earth. Callie collapsed, eventually, and was taken to the hospital. She was probably severely anemic, close to starvation.

Her mother-in-law, Minerva Sims, had moved to Callie's home by then, according to the 1930 census. She decided that the children should go to orphanages. It didn't seem likely that Minerva Sims would plow, but why she didn't try to send the kids to relatives in Rentie Grove or Tulsa is a mystery.

One morning, while Callie was in the hospital, Minerva took her five grandchildren to two separate institutions. Robert Sims told us, "They gave Sister a doll, gave me skates, and gave us some cookies. We were so hungry." Sister was the only name ever used for the eldest daughter, Minerva Kathryn, named for the very woman who took her only granddaughter to an orphanage and left.

That night, when Callie's mother, Fine Kemp, came home from work to her house in Tulsa, she was told that her grandchildren had been given to the state. Fine was near sixty-five then, still working. She had been a small girl taken from her home by strangers, beaten and hungry and not a single human to rescue her. There was no chance she'd let her only grandchildren spend a single night believing the same.

Fine's oldest daughter, Jennie, never had children. Fine's son Mack had been buried back in Denton. Her son Floyd had served in World War I, contracted tuberculosis in the military, and died when he came home. (Fine was given by the United States an American flag so big it covered her tiny front porch when she flew it on Memorial Day.) James remained disabled, and died at thirty-five.

Fine went immediately to find Callie's children. She retrieved them so quickly that Robert remembered they were still holding the doll and skates, though they had to give them back. He remembered the taste of the cookies. General II remembered the fury on Fine's face. She took all five children back to her house on Latimer Street, and then she got her gun and went to find Minerva.

She told Minerva that if she ever tried to take Callie's children away again, it would be over somebody's dead body, and that body was not likely to be her own. She had more than a bullet in her head.

You know that today Callie would have been the kind of woman who went back to school. Callie was forty-five years old when she came to Riverside to live near your grandfather General II. She did domestic work. Years later I met a teacher

Stanford Sims, Callie Sims, General Sims II,
Riverside, California, undated

who loved and praised Callie for watching her own four children while she was at work. I bit my lips, thinking Callie would probably have become a teacher if she'd graduated from Langston. What were her favorite classes? Would she have been a historian, like you?

You wanted to go to Kenyon, having worn that T-shirt since you were one year old, and you did so well on the SATs (having begun practice at nine) that you got into several universities. We went to visit Kenyon, but no—when we went to Oberlin, that was it. "The first college to admit black people and women," you told me, excited. "So it seems like a good place for me. You know—as a black woman."

John Mercer Langston, as an adult, led countless slaves along the Underground Railroad in Oberlin; you took your father, who spent many childhood hours with Callie Sims, to Langston's house. You both walked some of the Underground Railroad Trail. Freshman year, you tutored kids at Langston Middle School. I put your graduation portrait next to Callie's graduation photo from Booker T. Washington High School. Bring us your smartest women, every time.

You were the first girl we sent off into the world. You received a summer research fellowship from Caltech, one of the few nonscience students there, and wrote about the journey of the Sims family in 1950s Los Angeles. A year later, you wrote your Oberlin honors thesis on the black men in Walter Mosley's novels—who reminded you of your father and uncles. You exist in the world because of Fine's indomitable loyalty, and Callie's devotion and pain. You were our pride.

Gaila, Delphine, and Rosette Sims, Arcadia, California, 2018

(*Photograph by Cassandra Barragan*)

33

Kin—White House #1

We were three generations staring at the white bungalow home on Twenty-First Street, just around the corner from Central Avenue, in historic South Central Los Angeles. This house was just inside the boundaries of the original "rancho city lands of Los Angeles" on an historic map, established in 1869. We were making the young woman who stood at the wrought-iron fence a little nervous. She stared at us, and we waved.

It was July 2009. Dwayne stood with the two surviving Sims brothers, Robert and John Sims. Uncle Bobby wiped his large red freckled face with a handkerchief. Maybe sweating. Maybe a little tearful. His wife, Lee Myrtle, watched from the car. Toni Sims Scott, John's daughter, my age, a renowned artist, was there, elegant with straightened black hair, pink lipstick, and amber skin. Gaila, just turned nineteen, Delphine, just turned seventeen, Rosette at thirteen, and me—the short white woman who probably looked like a random real estate agent, except that my hair wasn't styled well. This house wasn't for sale. It had once belonged to Jennie Stevenson.

"Aunt Jennie taught me to tie my shoes right there on the steps," Toni Sims Scott said, pointing to the potted flowers near the porch. "I was five."

An older woman came to stand beside the girl watching us from the gate. They spoke to each other in Spanish.

"I slept right up there, in the attic," her father, John, said, pointing at the dormer window. "Damn, it was hot up there in the summer!"

Bobby said, "All of us boys slept up there in the attic. You, me, General, Stanford, Bill Bagley. All those cardboard partitions! And Jennie put us to work! We worked at the ice house, right there on the corner."

The old ice house was a recycling center now, with Latino men wheeling carts full of aluminum cans and bottles.

"She charged us rent," Bobby said. "We had to haul ice all over town, on Robert's flatbed truck. Those ice picks!"

"But there was always food at Aunt Jennie's," John said, turning to my daughters. "We were so hungry in Tulsa that my mother lost the marrow in her bones. She was close to death."

I looked at that house, a classic style of bungalow found all over America in downtown or historic areas, built anywhere from the 1880s to 1925 or so: deep eaves over a concrete porch, redwood frame or shingles, lath and plaster, dormer windows in the attic, maybe three bedrooms, wavy original glass in the living room window facing us. My own house looked exactly like this when Dwayne and I bought it.

But our house was only a mile from where we'd been born.

The purchase of this house was the culmination of Jennie Stevenson's badass life, as a woman who never bowed to any man. Jennie made this place a harbor for all her kin. I felt a thrill to see that porch.

———

Later that day, we went to the California African American Museum, only about five miles from Jennie's house, for the multimedia installation *Bloodlines*, created by Toni Sims Scott. In an exhibition room at the museum, about fifty relatives gathered to walk through the history of their lives.

At the entry was a large ship hanging from the ceiling, fabricated from translucent photo images of enslaved people, survivors of the Middle Passage across the ocean, moving slightly in the air. Nearby was a wooden slave cabin built by Uncle John, who'd left his initials in the eaves of the rough-shingled roof of the single room. There were cotton plants lush with bolls nearby. Farther into the room was an elaborate and massive family tree, an actual tree with branches and leaves upon which were hung translucent reproductions of historic photographs of Hardimans—Minerva and her formerly enslaved parents—and Simses, Stanford and his formerly enslaved parents, along with Fine, Jennie, Callie, and other relatives, along with the forebears of Toni's mother, who had been pioneer black residents of Los Angeles in the early 1990s.

People touched the faces of their ancestors, who dangled there twirling in the breeze created by our movements. Uncle Bobby and Uncle John sat on a long bench and began to speak. Bobby, a large man, his white guayabera shirt pleated down the front, cried, his cheeks glistening with tears. He said haltingly, "We used to lie in bed in the back room, all of us in that bed, head to toe so you'd be smelling the other fella's feet, and the wall was so thin I could hear our mother just crying, praying to God, asking him to give her strength to work one more day so we could eat. She was begging God right there on the other side, and I'll never forget hearing her."

Callie had worked as a domestic six days a week for a white

family in Tulsa, making $250 for the entire year; the children were teenagers, finishing high school at Booker T. Washington. I remember one day in the driveway, General II and his brothers declaimed the poems they had to memorize, as did high school students back then. Their resonant voices and beautiful diction were amazing. I remember Uncle John joking with me, "Even the gangsters back then had perfect English! We all did, because we learned how to recite poetry and speeches in high school. You could see a guy in a ba-ad suit and hat and he'd be a real gangster, but he'd sound just like the president."

Callie sent her children one by one to Jennie's house in Los Angeles. Once again, Jennie had gone ahead. She had gone as far west as possible.

Jennie left Tulsa in 1927 because her husband, Robert, miscalculated the depth of her badass. He messed up big time. After one moneymaking night in their home—a "hush-hush," where people could drink, dance, and gamble—during a disagreement, he'd pushed Jennie around. The way the cousins tell it, he didn't hit her, but he shoved her. Jennie wasn't having it. She still kept her gun in the bosom of her dress, even in her own house—but she didn't pull it on Robert. She took her money and got on a train for Los Angeles.

Robert's brother, Steve Stevenson, had been shot in the knee during the Tulsa Riot, in 1921, and he was done with Oklahoma. He'd moved to L.A. and bought a small house and piece of land, where he operated a junkyard with his flatbed truck. Jennie stayed with Steve. She worked, ran numbers, and made money, while from Tulsa, Robert repeatedly begged for her forgiveness. Finally, she allowed Robert to come to Los Angeles, and eventually, they bought the white house on Twenty-First and Central.

Robert got his own flatbed truck. Los Angeles was segregated then, in the 1920s and 1930s, though some Americans forget that; there was only one hotel for black people, the Lenox, on Central Avenue, the artery bisecting the heart of historic South Central Los Angeles, the broad street of jazz clubs, barbershops and salons, clothing stores and—my father-in-law's favorite word—*haberdashers*. Every day, Robert went to Union Station downtown, near the historic Pueblo de la Reina de Los Angeles, and waited for black people to get off the train. He took their heavy trunks onto his truck, and drove people to the Lenox or to the boardinghouses catering to black arrivals—including Jennie's house.

Jennie's house was full of her kin, and the people she considered her kin. Two years after General died, Callie had a baby girl with a man in Oklahoma. This daughter, Loretta, was sent to Los Angeles when she was only two, in 1941. Sister followed, then each boy—but Jennie also housed boarders and other people who needed a home.

Minerva married at eighteen, Stanford married at nineteen, and Robert married Lee Myrtle, who had graduated from nearby Roosevelt High, when they were nineteen. General II came to Los Angeles in 1950 and joined the Marines. Callie traveled to California just after that with John, who was sixteen. Everyone remembers General's rebellion: Once he stole Callie's last dollars and ran down the alley behind Jennie's house, while his mother chased him with a shotgun and shouted, "Are you going crazy?"

"He turned, spread out his arms, and yelled back, 'Yeah, you want to come?'" everyone used to laugh, retelling it in the driveway. "Then he climbed a tree and hid. 'Cause Callie and Jennie didn't mess around."

———

That day, with Gaila taking notes for her history project, we crossed the street finally, to greet the young woman at the wrought-iron fence. She spoke Spanish and English, and I speak English and Spanish—in the order of our fluency.

We told her about Aunt Jennie, and she opened the gate and led us all to the driveway, past the profusion of flowers. The resonance of history was miraculous. Her aunt owned the house, a woman in her forties with a round kind face, voluble hands that swept the vista of house and attic and driveway and shed, and a story of her own. She had immigrated from a tiny town outside Guadalajara, worked two jobs, and bought this house, probably not long after Jennie lost it to foreclosure before she died, in 1982. This aunt was raising her own family and also a host of nieces and nephews who had come from Mexico.

Everybody had a job. An elderly man and a middle-aged man and a young man sat on folding chairs in the driveway. They brought more folding chairs for Uncle Bobby and John. We all sat in the shaded concrete driveway, two clans speaking different languages. Our uncles asked her uncles about the layout of the house, and discussed the outbuildings constructed back in the 1930s. The niece said the attic rooms were still hot, and everyone laughed. I couldn't believe we were sitting there, nearly eighty years after Jennie arrived in Los Angeles, smiling with the present iteration of women who made this city home for those who had to leave a different home. Slavery, migration, borders, violence, poverty—clan will always reclaim humanity.

Gaila presented her paper on black Los Angeles in the 1950s at Caltech. Delphine wrote her college entrance essay about Aunt Jennie and the legacy of Sims women; when she moved to Los Angeles, to attend the University of Southern California, her dorm room was on Jefferson, about fifteen blocks from Jennie

Stevenson's old house. Delphine hung on her wall an original painting by Toni Sims Scott, a portrait of a young woman in blue.

I met Jennie once. Teri Andrews, daughter of Minerva "Sister" Sims, lived with Jennie in the white house; Teri says we were both at Fourth of July 1981, at Uncle John's house off Crenshaw; in the line of older women sitting in the shade, Jennie was there. She would have been close to ninety. I was twenty. It was the first time I saw the aunts as minor goddesses, arranged like the chorus in their folding chairs, talking about dancing days gone by, studying us bemusedly as the younger people snuck into the alley to drink and smoke weed and flirt, as if no one else had ever done those things. Aunt Jennie had black cat's-eye glasses, with the same slant as my blue ones from the past, but she looked cool. Glossy pressed curls. I had not seen the haughty fur-collar portrait of her yet. That day, her elegant cheeks were soft, collapsed like cake at the sides of her mouth, but she was smiling.

Teri told me that Jennie had a boyfriend then, and teased that there's still time for us. Lying awake at night, hearing the faint sounds of eight or ten teenagers in my living room laughing at YouTube videos, my girls and their cousins making popcorn, I think to myself, "This is nothing compared to Aunt Jennie." I write about fictional men who look like Michael Ealy and Idris Elba and A Martinez and Daniel Craig. Maybe Teri is right. I might get a boyfriend when I'm ninety, like Jennie did.

I learned about kin from General II. Though he'd been the wild brother, by 1958 and until his death in 2008, General II was the anchor for three more generations of Simses. At the house on Michael Street, he and Alberta never turned anyone away. They helped raise nieces, nephews, young cousins, and neighbor kids. General could be brusque, and he made all the young men work on the truck, hauling those branches and pushing those mowers—just as Jennie had. Alberta did biblical miracles with food, especially during her famous Sunday breakfasts: chorizo, scrambled eggs, and monkey bread.

Later that same year, 2009, I found a beautiful word—*biraderi*—to encompass what Jennie and General had done, what Sims meant, and how I'd tried to continue the legacy at my own house when I could. My cell phone rang at 1:00 a.m. My nephew Sensei said, "Auntie. You told me to call."

"Yup," I said. "And?"

"I'm alive."

"Excellent."

Only two serious rules, my daughters kept telling Sensei, when he came to live here: Don't eat chocolate or red foods on the beige couch (why I bought a beige couch was a matter of eye-rolling conjecture). Call at night so she knows you're alive. Don't blow that one.

I lay there in bed, two phones beside me as always—the cell phone, and the purple Target cordless landline that always died. I never knew which number someone who needed a ride might call. Sometimes I fell asleep with a flannel shirt on, a phone in each hand, sitting up against a pillow, like someone with important clients, except I looked like a sad small lumberjack. But that night, I stayed awake, thinking about clan. The tribe. Your people.

I learned the word *biraderi* from a vivid essay on Pakistan by Daniyal Mueenuddin. "An untranslatable word," he wrote, "something like clan but more visceral and entailing greater responsibility and connection."

I loved this word. I told my daughters about it, and they told their friends. I've spent my life writing about the biraderi of black America, the way diaspora and clan and unshakable devotion to blood family and chosen family have kept children alive. Gaila's friend Carly, whose mother is Mexican-American and father Scottish, said they should all get the word tattooed on their shoulders.

The massive biraderi of Simses means I am called Auntie by maybe a hundred nieces and nephews, young cousins, second and third and maybe cousins, great- and great-great-nieces and -nephews, and kin of geography.

I am called Auntie by Eddie Chandler IV, the son of Eddie Chandler III and Revia Aubert, whose mother, Zerlie, lives on the corner of Michael Street; but also by Stacy, Revia's brother's daughter by his first wife. I am called Auntie by Keshae, the granddaughter of Margaret Chandler, who is raising her after the murder of Margaret's daughter Maisha. I am called Auntie by Aashanique Wilson, whose mother, Tina, grew up a few doors down from the Sims house, and went to school with me, and is family.

My own daughters call those same adults Uncle and Aunt— and for them, people would drop everything and drive for ten hours to help.

It seems complicated to outsiders. But it's not. If you have ever been close to anyone in our huge extended family, we will feed you. Give you clothes, a bed, a car. Help you find a job. We have your back. Even after divorce—as is evident by the fact that Dwayne ate two or three meals a week at my house for years, and slept in his truck for a few hours, parked at my curb, if he'd gotten off work at 7:00 a.m. and we had a basketball tournament at 11:00.

Shirley, the woman Sensei still calls "Mom," is not his mother; she had a daughter, Ericka, with General III. She is my sister-in-law, even though she and General III were never married; she is Mexican and black, a tough woman shot at twice when she rode with a motorcycle club. She is the woman who kept Sensei most, even when she wouldn't speak to his father, and that is hella biraderi, as we put it in my house.

The biraderi aunts and uncles provide graduation money, rent money, baby-shower gifts, tuition for college or cosmetology school. Sensei is a skateboarder; he eats a lot of tacos and breaks a board every ten days or so. But lying awake at night, doing the math on new skateboards and shoes (what the heck do boys *do* to Vans?), worrying about whether I could handle having him here, paying his community college tuition and realizing I'd have three kids in college and Rosette in high school, I shrugged. He is a direct descendant of Jennie Stevenson.

I remember so vividly all those summer midnights when all three of my couches (even the one outside) were draped with sleeping teenagers, when I waited for the last of my daughters to come home, or for Sensei, the unmistakable clack-clack of his wheels on the sidewalk cracks, then the skateboard parked by the front door; my girls hollering that Sensei had clearly applied too much Axe.

I hope we are enough. I could never be as brave as Aunt Jennie, her cheekbones like shields under her velvet skin. But we will always honor kin—the faces around our table, in the candlelight, the ones with whom you can lay your head down by your empty plate and even cry, you are so relieved to be with them again.

34

A Place of Style and Refuge—White House #2

Riverside, California,
December 2011

Dwayne called me one morning, his voice rough and clotted with pain. "Grandma's house burnt down last night. I just drove by. There's people standing everywhere."

The two-story Victorian house was much more grand than Jennie Stevenson's or mine. It was white wood frame with elaborate fretwork and scallop-shingled gables on the second floor, with cedar closets where kids used to hide under her immense collection of elaborate hats; with windowsills where hundreds of sweet potato pies and teacakes had cooled until they were delivered by Daisy Carter's grandchildren to customers who swore there were no other pies like those; with a long upstairs bedroom where Daisy Carter's last husband received her grandchildren "like he was a king," according to General III. The house burned in the way newspapers report as "spectacular." When I went the next day, people said flames had shot out of the second story, which collapsed onto the first floor in a huge sparking sag. The side porch, where two benches once faced each other, where young men used to walk past hoping for a sight of Daisy's daughters, was gone.

"They used to sit on them benches, two and two," Mrs. Zerlie Aubert, who is ninety-five now, born in Lutcher, Louisiana, said to me from her white wire chair on Twelfth Street, just around the corner. She pointed to where ashes were now heaped. "The four sisters. Oh, all the men were in love with them four girls, yes they were."

That day in December, a post-quinceaneara party had been in progress in the yard, with guests of the Mexican-born residents who rented the house. The crowd escaped to the sidewalk to watch the fire burn. No one was inside. The flames appeared to have begun in the attic bedrooms, where two teenagers were living. There had been candles.

Most of American history had come full circle, in this white house. Built in 1910, when white people lived on Kansas Street and black people could not; bought in 1947 by Daisy after she married Ernest Carter Sr., decades of black history resided there: slavery, reconstruction, railroads, migration, munitions, reinvention, and generosity.

Ironically, in 1940 Daisy and her daughters and Aint Dear were living in a tiny cottage on Denton Street, only a few blocks away. Eventually, when their children fell in love, Daisy met Callie, whose life had begun in Denton, Texas. (One of Dwayne's favorite childhood memories is Sunday afternoons, after church, when the men were in the driveway, and three women would sit inside the living room to share a single bottle of Miller High Life and one surreptitious cigarette each: Callie, Daisy, and Alberta.)

———

Daisy and Aint Dear (Annie Tillman) and the four small girls had arrived in 1936 at the house of Margaret Henderson, Annie's sister, on Ninth Street, until they rented a place. Daisy worked around the clock; Aint Dear and Margaret Henderson watched the children. Daisy worked days in a munitions warehouse, as a Rosie the Riveter, getting a ride to Mira Loma with other women. When she came home, she rested for a short time, and then she worked with a crew at the turkey plant, with Margaret Henderson and other family members, plucking pinfeathers in the terrible smell.

But on the weekends, Daisy Morris, radiant and lovely, with shining cheeks and luminous smile, went to a club in San Bernardino where the railroad men liked to dance. There, she met an older man, twice widowed, with seventeen children who were grown. Ernest Carter.

General III loves to say this: "When she married Mr. Carter, our whole family ascended into the middle class." Ernest Carter had worked for decades for the Southern Pacific Railroad in San Bernardino. In the early 1900s, Ernest Carter was the first black man authorized to carry weapons on the trains, as a security guard working with the legendary Pinkertons.

With her savings, and the help of Mr. Carter, who was never called anything else by anyone in my generation, Daisy bought the house on the corner of Eleventh and Kansas. They all moved in: Daisy, her daughters, who were entering junior high and high school, Mr. Carter, Aint Dear, and a succession of families who needed refuge.

Daisy Carter's boardinghouse became a beacon to women arriving from the South during the 1940s and '50s. (When Daisy's cousin Eddie Chandler II, whose father had been hanged in Sunflower County, Mississippi, turned eighty, we went to a community party where he told the crowd, "You know, we were refugees from a third-world country. A war zone. Nobody calls it that, but that's the truth.") In Daisy's house lived Hattie Davis and her three children, who came from Georgia. Hattie married Reverend L. B. Moss, and moved into her new life—at ninety-eight, she still lives in Riverside. Hattie's daughter Judy Davis married Tommie Chatham, who was a child himself when he came to California from Gary, Texas. The Chathams moved onto Twelfth Street, and their four children are called cousin by the Sims family. My daughters have only ever known Trent Chatham, who is two years younger than me, as their uncle.

Daisy built a private entrance to one room for Floyd Walker's mother-in-law, known as Big Ma, born in Georgia just after the Civil War.

Daisy and the four girls worked every moment of the day and much of the night. Mr. Carter got cleaning contracts for local markets; the women cleaned at Butcher Boy, the meat-packing house that sold ground beef to the first McDonald's restaurants, in San Bernardino. They worked seasonally at the turkey plant. At home, Daisy made sweet potato pies and tea-cakes and pound cake to sell. She was famous for her skill with clothing. "Daisy could launder shirts like no one else in Riverside," her cousin Jesse Wall told me. "Lawyers and business-men all brought their shirts to her. And they took home pies and cakes."

Imagine now the pies cooling and the white shirts hanging starched in the kitchen, the people coming in and out, the hundreds of plates. The four sisters were always there, working outside or inside the house, rarely allowed to go anywhere else, taking breaks to sit two and two on that side porch, with all the men of the Eastside watching.

They were still under the charge of Aint Dear, whose

temper and suspicion had only amplified now that the girls were teenagers.

"She wanted all of them to get married right away, so they wouldn't be like her," Jesse Wall, Daisy's cousin, said to me when he was eighty, sitting in his pastoral office at St. James Tabernacle, the church his father started back in 1936. "Aint Dear had lived a life—boy, she didn't want them ever living that life," he said carefully.

But Daisy had made it this far, and her entire life was about Mary Louise, Myrtle, Alberta, and Rosie.

Mary Louise's oldest daughter, Rita Butts Sweeney, said, "All the older men used to say that—they'd tell me, your daddy, Gato, got the prettiest one out the whole bunch. He had her face painted on a rice scroll when he was serving in Korea." Mary Louise, at seventeen, married Henderson Butts, nicknamed Gato. They lived near the Santa Ana River. Mary Louise had seven children.

Robert Anderson, who is eighty-nine now, a former Golden Gloves boxer, surprised me one day, saying offhandedly: "You know who my first love was, when I was only sixteen? Myrtle. I worked at the market with Mr. Carter, cleaning the meat cases. Myrtle was so beautiful, I wanted to talk to her all the time. But Aint Dear, she was mean as a snake. She kept asking me, 'When you gonna cut some cake?' I was sixteen! I kept thinking, *Where is this cake?* Then I figured it out—she wanted me to get married!"

One Sunday afternoon, Robert talked Myrtle into coming out the side door of St. James, which was Pentecostal, where the services lasted for hours. Myrtle slipped out into the dirt alley, walked around the neighborhood with Robert for an hour, and then went back up the steps. "She opened that door and Aint Dear was right there! She cold-cocked her!" Robert said,

Rosie Morris, Mary Louise Butts, Myrtle Samuel,
at the Top Hat, Riverside, California, undated

holding up his hands in boxing stance. "Knocked her out, right there in the aisle!" He shook his head.

Myrtle was eighteen when she married Clifford Samuel, had three children, then married a man I always knew as Big Earl, had Little Earl, and finally married Bill Bagley, who had lived in Aunt Jennie's house in Los Angeles, leaving Tulsa with the Sims men he considered brothers. Full circle. Myrtle had three more children, eventually buying a house on Kansas Avenue, five blocks from her mother.

John Sims loves to tell us: "Oh, I just kept trying to talk to Alberta, she was so fine. I had just gotten here from Tulsa, with my mother, and we made it out to Riverside. I was a senior in high school, and Alberta was the one for me. But she kept saying, 'Don't you have a brother named General? I heard he can dance.'"

In Alberta's 1952 high school yearbook, her gym teacher wrote, "Hope your married life will be happy and that the best will always be yours." Two days after graduation, she married General Sims II. She had her first son, General III, in 1953.

They lived in a small stucco duplex on Eleventh Street by 1958, three houses down from Daisy. One of General III's first memories is this: "Mr. Car-*ter*! He treated my grandmother like a queen, and he defended her girls like his own, man! One night, Daddy didn't like the tacos Mama cooked, and he threw everything on the floor. She called up there to her mama's, and Mr. Carter came walkin' down the block. He came inside and pulled himself up—he was only about five-five, you know, and he moved his coat, and I saw that .45 pistol." General III laughed. "I was about five years old, and I had *never* seen my daddy just close his mouth and not say a word. But he did that night!" Mr. Carter suggested that his son-in-law always treat Alberta with respect, and that she should never have to call again.

Daisy Carter's house became one of the most elegant in the community, with leather wing chairs, a piano, a formal dining set. Her church dresses and hats were floral and epic. "She was the style-setter for the whole Eastside," said Jesse Wall.

Alberta and General II had bought their house on Michael Street, near the corner of Twelfth, and that is where Alberta lived, all four of her homes within a six-block radius of the rest of her life. Mary Louise died in 1980 of leukemia, at only fifty. Daisy Carter passed away the following year. And in 1982, Myrtle died of liver disease, also at fifty, an illness brought on, her family thought, by years of using harsh cleaners as a domestic worker. Daisy's youngest daughter, Rosie, had two sons with Al Terraciano, an Italian-American man, and moved to Las Vegas in 1980. She ran the wedding chapel inside Circus Circus casino, and perhaps from above, Aint Dear watched all the midnight marriages.

When she was forty, Daisy had a son with Ernest Carter. This was Mr. Carter's eighteenth child. They named him Ernest Carter Jr. By the late 1980s, Ernie Carter Jr., who'd gone to college and had an impressive job at the Naval Weapons Center in Seal Beach, California, sold the house to a rental company. The maroon club chair came to us when Alberta died, the leather smooth and oddly slippery to my children, the rounded upholstered arms worn by hundreds of hands.

I miss the chair. The arms finally wore out, cotton batting exposed like sheep wool under the fingers of my daughters, and Dwayne took the chair when he moved to his own place. I think of Alberta's lush beauty. I think of my own absolutely ordinary face and flesh, and how my daughters inherited through Alberta and Daisy their defined cheekbones and dimples and high-set hips, along with the resolute skills of survival that are required when you are a black woman with beauty and intelligence, and no mode for subservience.

Just as with Jennie Stevenson's white frame house in Los Angeles, Daisy Carter's house was lived in by the newest arrivals to California, mothers and aunts and children from Mexico. After it burned, everyone parked there to gaze at the black-satin alligator char of the wood frame and scalloped shingles. A month later, a bulldozer took down the remnants.

I stood there on the sidewalk, the acrid scent wafting in the wind, while Dwayne, his brothers General III and Carnell, General's son Sensei, and their cousin Eddie Chandler III walked the land looking for relics. Bottles and pennies and shards of crockery. Dwayne found his favorite doorstop, one he remembered from kindergarten afternoons when the nuns at Catholic school pulled him by the ears, and he ran away to Daisy's house for consolation and teacakes. A heavy bronze square with a ship etched on the side.

How many hundred-year-old Victorians burn in America, never to be replaced? Who can build a house like that now? And who would, in older neighborhoods like ours, in Detroit or Albany or Baltimore, anywhere in America where the mortgage crisis gutted communities that had resisted urban renewal and other assaults? All over this nation are Victorian and Craftsman homes of women who fled their birthplaces—Italy and Ireland, Greece and Armenia, Nigeria and China, Mexico and El Salvador and Honduras.

There were four beautiful sisters. My favorite photo shows

Alberta, anchoring a fragment of one night. A good night. This woman who changed my life—she is bemused and regal and slightly mischievous, sitting beside Rosie at a table where they are clearly at a formal dance. Are they with husbands? Are they with their two sisters? It doesn't matter. They both know they're lovely, that men are staring at them while they gaze at us.

Here are Daisy's descendants, walking across her land days after the fire. If you add up the Americans begotten from Daisy and her daughters, fed and clothed from the labors of plucked turkeys and starched shirts and rolled pie crusts, munitions for war and ministrations for love, there are more than 150 people in the world who exist solely because she made her way here, having been thrown over a Mississippi roadbank, threatened with firearms and more, packed up again and again in the dark to start over.

Dwayne Sims, Eddie Chandler III, General Sims III, Carnell Sims, Sensei Sims, on Daisy Carter's land, 2011. *(Photograph by Douglas McCulloh)*

Here are Daisy Carter and Hattie Davis and Aint Dear, on their way to church. Daisy remains radiant. Do you see her wearing this hat and these gloves, her elegant cheekbones and eyebrows, her smile not dimmed?

Hattie Davis, Annie "Aint Dear" Tillman, Daisy Carter, undated

35

Letter to My Nephew— Our Dungeon Shook (After James Baldwin)

Riverside, California, 2012

Dear Sensei:

I began this letter in 2011, when you lived here, and then put it away because I was too afraid of how it would end. I rewrote it four more times and it wasn't finished, because more of our people died. Then your son was born, at the hospital down the street. You stayed awake for two days, in the delivery room, and then you came here to sleep. You walked, you got the key from under the pot on the porch, and went to your old bed; when you'd called to let me know, I told you to take off your hooded sweatshirt before you went inside, in case someone who didn't know you was watching.

You look like the reincarnation of Bob Marley, your dreadlocks like black coral, your face angular and jaunty, your eyes the color of sycamore leaves, even your mouth and teeth somehow like his. But you are six feet two and that makes you frightening even to some white kids who listen to Marley while they smoke weed. When white people see you on the sidewalk they often think you want something from them, even though you are only on your way to the skatepark, because you are a master skateboarder whose favorite song when you lived here was "Midnight Rider" by the Allman Brothers. When you sang the lyrics, *I got to run to keep from hidin', and I'm bound to keep on ridin', I got one more silver dollar,* I went into my bedroom to cry, because that song was how my brother lived his life, and how he died. He was a stocky powerful white guy with long blond hair, and yet it felt like you were his reincarnation, sitting at the same maple table where he and his best friend used to hatch plans not legal.

Back then, you were obsessed with the Doors, Jimi Hendrix, and Janis Joplin. Your tattoos were not gang identifications, but a devil-grin skateboard clown and the inscription *One Love.*

In your face is all the world. Maybe Ethiopia or Haiti, via your father, General III, maybe Cherokee and Irish; Samoan and Mexican and black and white, via your mother, a woman I've never met. She lives in another state; she let you go when you were a baby, to be raised here with the clan of Simses. Gaila was eight months old when you arrived in California in 1990.

I named you accidentally, when your father called me and asked how to spell *Sensei.* I said, "Like the marijuana?" and he said, "Like the teacher in *Karate Kid,*" so I called Ed, a Japanese-Filipino childhood friend, to make sure about the spelling, and then I called your father back. He said, "Thanks, sis, you just named my fourth son," and I said, "What?" and he said, "I was going to name him Malachi, like *Children of the Corn,* if you didn't know how to spell Sensei," and I said, "Thank God, Ed was home."

———

You wrote your will at thirteen. Two of your best friends, Anthony Sweat and Markess Lancaster, also thirteen, were shot and killed in separate incidents in the summer of 2003. It was the last thing any of the generations before us would have imagined—Oscar Medina and your grandfather, General II, who were like brothers. Your friends were targeted and pursued by a Latino gang, Anthony running to hide on a porch a few blocks from Daisy Carter's house, but shot by the front door; Markess riding in a car with his friends, coming from a store near my house, and shot in the passenger seat. (In trial testimony, documented conversations showed the gang referred to finding black targets as "snail hunting.")

You were arrested at eighteen for felony burglary, when you walked to the store one morning from Michael Street, in your slippers, and you should have been at school, but two friends caught up with you, one carrying a duffel bag. When the police car pulled alongside, and you were all handcuffed, it turned out the bag contained stereo equipment the friends had taken from a house. The older woman who lived at the house testified that she'd never seen you, only the other two boys. She said you were not there. Even so, you were in jail for weeks. You explained to us when you were finally released that you used family donations to buy candy bars in jail.

You turned twenty-one living here, and burst through my front door one night with your hood up to keep Rosette and me from seeing your eyes—you were crying, and you buried your face in the dog's fur for a long half hour before speaking. You'd been skating near the hospital, on the metal rails beloved by all your skater friends, and two older guys came through the parking lot to rob you. (Who expects skaters to have any money?) Angry that you were broke, one man demanded your board, and when you held it up as if to hit him, he pulled a gun, pointed it at your chest, called you a name and laughed when you used the board as a shield and ran. Your fingers were invisible in the fur around the dog's neck, and your forehead on her skull. We made you taquitos and waited.

It is fifty years since James Baldwin, my teacher, my mentor, wrote a letter to his nephew James, a boy named for him, the son of his younger brother. I have read that letter countless times. James Baldwin wrote other words that I have on Post-its taped to this desk, where you worked on your essays for community college English class. You saw Baldwin's words every day, and told me so often how much they meant to you: "*I imagine that one of the reasons people cling to their hates so stubbornly is because they sense, once hate is gone, they will be forced to deal with the pain.*"

It is thirty-five years since he was my teacher. I was twelve when I first read his novel *Go Tell It on the Mountain*, and I cried when David, the unloved elder brother, watches Roy, the beloved younger brother, dying in the arms of their mother; Roy has been talking shit on the street, confronting other young men, and he's been stabbed. Roy, my brother, you—all the young men who cannot be confined inside, who have to be out on the sidewalk and the dirt road and the freeway, moving and moving, while other men are angry at your joy and freedom. Fifty years since James Baldwin wrote the letter to his nephew: "*You were born into a society which spelled out with brutal clarity and in as many ways as possible that you were a worthless human being. You were not expected to aspire to excellence. You were expected to make your peace with mediocrity.*" And now, when I see "aspire to excellence" as an academic or marketing phrase beloved by large institutions and by politicians, it comes as a sudden shock that I only wish for you to live. Just to stay alive. That is not exaggeration. That is how we women pray every night—we women who love you and men like you all over the nation. Fifty years later, and we are still praying, and staying awake, and startling at every siren, every backfire that sounds like a gunshot, every phone call after midnight. I have gotten those phone calls. Those hours take a toll.

Baldwin's letter says, "*There is no reason for you to try to become like white men and there is no basis whatever for their impertinent assumption that they must accept you. The really terrible thing, old buddy, is that you must accept them, and I mean that very seriously . . . They are in effect still trapped in a history which they do not understand and until they understand it, they cannot be released from it. They have had to believe for many years, and for innumerable reasons, that black men are inferior to white men.*"

The first Sims I can find is Cary Sims, born enslaved in Grenada, Mississippi; his son was Stanford Sims, born free, also in Grenada; Stanford's son was General I, born free in Grenada and died in Tulsa, Oklahoma; General II's son is General III, and you are the sixth generation. You are a Sims man. Inferior to no one.

Your father, your uncles, don't write you letters, but they tell you, in the driveway and on the porch, what you have to know. *Two of you can ride in the car. Three is a gang. One of y'all has to get in another car. Don't fool around. No standing out in the yard at a party. Don't be getting gas late at night. Don't be speeding drinking laughing singing rapping walking. Don't.*

You've heard Dwayne and me tell our daughters the same things. We partied in front yards and backyards and orange groves and fields of wild oats—*No, you can't go to that party, we don't care if you get mad, we don't care that other girls can go, we can't take that chance with you. You're all we have.*

The countless times your father and uncles and you were stopped while driving. *Hands out the window. No hands. No moving. No. No. No.*

We women never tell you this part—that we think we will have heart attacks when we see the sirens, see you sitting so still, standing with hands up—I have seen that, the muscle inside my chest hurting so bad that I imagined the small red heart I saw once when I was a child, excised from a bird by a cat on the sidewalk in front of my house, the muscle leaping four more times on the cement, but not bursting.

It is 153 years since the Emancipation Proclamation. You are free. You are free to skate down the street, to ride in a car, to walk down the sidewalk toward the taco place two blocks from here, where everyone knows your name. You wear a hood when it is cold. Your dreads are legendary. You wear an old Hawaiian shirt with two buttons missing because your grandfather General II left it behind when he died, and you miss him. You wear a sharktooth necklace. The tattoo you got in his honor reads SIMS. You do not fit the description.

Some things were easy when you lived here—the taco, taquito, enchilada part, when I made hundreds of them and you lined them up on your plate with unabashed glee; the part where you and your cousins watched *Dazed and Confused* and *Fired Up*, which contributed mightily to our weird family language. "All right, all right, all right," we would all say in our best Matthew McConaughey. And "unless you're an old lady gardening or a baby on the beach, you shouldn't be wearing Crocs." The part where the dog loved you best. The part where we had really good shampoo and lotion.

Some things were not easy—the part where you had to go to college classes and actually do homework; the part where everyone else in the house was female (my three daughters, and sometimes three of your sisters, their innumerable friends, all the chattering and laughter and gossip like sparrows in the wisteria vines), and when you brought home laconic tattooed skaters of all races and sizes who tried to watch endless skate videos and the single television in the house was clearly not enough for you all, and I got tired of making taquitos and went on strike; the part where we put a timer in the shower because you used all the hot water and we screamed at you because we were freezing.

We fought briefly over curfew and the absolutely required phone call every midnight to let me know you were alive. This is part of life when people have children, but it's different when the children are brown-skinned with dreadlocks. I achieved victory with you by shamelessly using the heart—I told you that if you didn't come home one night I might have a heart attack and your uncle Dwayne would have to raise you, which entailed the end of taquitos, nice shampoo, and everything else you loved. You did not come home late after that.

In March 2012 you put on your grandfather's shirt and I drove you and two other nephews to the funeral of your cousin Lareanz Simmons. He was fourteen years old.

He is the great-grandson of Arthur Ford, Daisy Carter's

brother. He was being raised by his grandmother Bernice Hobdy, Arthur's daughter. You are the great-grandson of Daisy Carter. Lareanz was shot on Georgia Street, near Twelfth Street. A few blocks from Daisy Carter's house.

Lareanz was halfway through his freshman year of high school, and Rosette was a junior, both at the same school where Daisy Carter's daughters went. He was in ROTC and the band; he wore skinny jeans and a blond-streaked Mohawk. He lived as far from gang life as possible. He had gone to a neighbor's house to borrow a DVD, and he was at the edge of his grandmother's driveway when a car pulled up, and a young Latino man shot him. He was hunted, in the driveway. He was shot six times at close range. His grandmother Bernice kept him alive long enough to donate his organs, and his heart went to a young white man.

You and your cousins joined more than four hundred people lined up outside the church on Kansas Avenue, within sight of the street where Lareanz died: the military-uniformed ROTC members in formation, white and Latino and Asian and black kids from the band who loved him, crying and holding hands.

I took enchiladas and money to the church hall for the repast. I had to work. Then I drove two blocks to Pennsylvania Street and sat shaking for ten minutes in my car. You and Delphine and Rosette were here, two streets away from Georgia Street, at the exact time Lareanz was shot. You had talked them into driving to another cousin's house to visit—my two girls in the red Honda, putting up an umbrella through the open sunroof for a joke while you and your cousin stood in the driveway talking, and fifteen minutes later, a car turned down Georgia Street and someone saw Lareanz walking.

The geography made me cry. Five generations raised in these six blocks. The fallen. Our fallen. America's fallen. The heart of Lareanz beating in another human.

My dungeon shook. My ribs shook. My eyelids shook. You were all on my couch that night, lined up like panelists on a dating show, when the phone call came about the shooting. You were all sitting up straight: Delphine, Rosette, you, your brother Evan, his girlfriend Stephanie, who is Mexican-American, all trying to talk me into letting the five of you go out, and me shaking and saying, *No*. Dwayne and Uncle Trent calling and saying, *Hell, no, everyone stays in for three days. Like always.*

What people from elsewhere have always said to me, when I write about these deaths: *But it can't be that bad out there in California! The sun is out. You have palm trees. Everybody has a yard. The cute little bungalows. That's not the ghetto. That's not the projects. You have all that sunshine.*

Bullets fly through sunshine as well as snow. In the shadow of palm trees the same as elms and ginkgo. Blood soaks into grass differently. We feel the same, except that we are not national news, because it's different *out here*.

Is our fear different because our forebears went west?

Your son, Dustin Ozzy, is six years old now. At our most recent Memorial Day gathering, there were about forty children under the age of twelve, and about forty young people in their teens and twenties. In 2018, the "American birthrate" was reported as the lowest in history. We laughed.

James Baldwin's letter says: "*Try to imagine how you would feel if you woke up one morning to find the sun shivering and all the stars aflame. You would be frightened because it is out of the order of nature. Any upheaval in the universe is terrifying because it so profoundly attacks one's sense of one's own reality. Well, the black man has functioned in the white man's world as a fixed star, as an immovable pillar, and as he moves out of his place, heaven and earth are shaken to their founda-tions."* Barack Obama, the president your grandfather wanted to vote for, if General II hadn't died twenty-one days before the election, the president whose face your uncles wore on T-shirts for years, was a moveable star that rose. His forebears went west, all the way to Hawaii.

The dungeons shake.

You named your son Dustin Ozzy. Yes, for Mr. Osbourne. Your half-grin, your dreads tied back with one of Delphine's basketball shoelaces, your foot iced again with my last bag of frozen corn because you skated off the rails. Now you've stopped skating full-time and started working as a bar bouncer and at the skateshop. For Dustin.

You have to stay alive. You often skate at the park directly across the street from Daisy Carter's burned house. From those concrete ramps, you can see the foxtail weeds growing tall against the chain-link fence around the empty piece of land.

"You come from sturdy peasant stock, men who picked cotton, dammed rivers, built railroads, and in the teeth of the most terrifying odds, achieved an unassailable and monumen-tal dignity. You come from a long line of great poets, some of the greatest poets since Homer. One of them said, 'The very time I thought I was lost, my dungeon shook and my chains fell off.'"

I read my teacher's words again, again.

Your dungeon shakes differently—it trembles, it is iCloud and permeable and Twitter and purposeful, intended to demon-ize you again. It is not the bars of the slave jail, the barracoon; it is not the metal bars around which civil rights activists wrapped their fingers while James Baldwin wrote to his nephew. You have a son. This is my letter to say we love you, and we want to see you walking up our cracked sidewalk, holding your son's hand when he looks for the dog and the chickens in my yard, every year until there is silver hair in your dreads tied back with a shoelace.

Love,
Auntie

36

American Human
Not Interested

I looked up and Gaila was gone to Ohio, Delphine was gone to Los Angeles, and Rosette's eyes shimmered with held-in tears.

It wasn't the actual day Dwayne, Rosette, and I dropped off Delphine at USC that broke my youngest daughter's heart. It was the morning of Rosette's first day of high school, and she was abandoned. Disconsolate.

"I'm Beth," she said, her voice shivery and then given over to crying. "I mean, I'm not dying."

She meant that of the sisters in *Little Women*, she was the one left home. Alone. With me. "All your laserlike intensity can be focused on me now. Great."

I spent years defending their choices to leave—Rosette as well when she went to USC, too. I raised them as Alberta had whispered: to run the world. I told them not "I want you to be happy," but "I want you to make a difference." Cheesy, but spoken as the child of immigrants, married to the child of people once enslaved. Their father and I left, and then we came back home.

We knew our girls might never come back.

I looked up and they had been gone for two years. Speaking to groups of women in Miami or San Francisco, in Austria or Turkey, I said I had never met another mother who had three daughters all working in museums. Gaila was an education specialist at the Carver African-American Museum in Austin, Texas, running programs on black history, art, and culture for children and visitors. Delphine was a curatorial assistant at the Santa Barbara Museum of Art, preparing shows featuring Latin-American Women Photographers and exhibits about nature and image—writing text about cicadas, France, and the intersection of science and art. Rosette was working at the California African American Museum in Los Angeles, giving tours, while majoring in Classics.

Of course, our family and friends said, "But how are they gonna meet any men at museums?"

I rolled my eyes.

They moved through the world as women most men could not classify. We did not do castas.

My daughters told me stories about people who approached them and asked, "So what are you?" or declared, "I can guess what you are." Delphine told us about a young black man at a bar who said to her and three girlfriends, "I can tell each one of you exactly what you are. You—you're Puerto Rican. You—Dominican and Cuban." To Delphine he said, "You? You're straight Latina. You don't have any black in you." He was wrong for each girl.

My daughters would at times hear Algerian, Samoan, Saudi Arabian, Hawaiian, Dominican, Cuban, Puerto Rican, Mexican, Colombian.

When Rosette played on the high school tennis team, someone said to her, "You're the only black girl on the team," and when Rosette replied that there was another black girl, and the white teammate said, "Oh, she's not black, she's Egyptian."

One night, a young man pressed Gaila at a bar in Ohio, "No, really, where are you actually from?" and she said, "California," then "America," and he said, "But what are you?" and she said, "American, human," and he said, "But you know what I mean, what are you really?" and she said, "Not interested in you."

37

Braid/Züpfe

Dear Rosette,

You called me after you had your hair braided this fall, by a woman named Ermaline, from Ghana, which took seven hours while you listened to the voices around you. For years I kept a photo on the refrigerator of you with your grandfather General II when you were six, wild-shining curls springing like a headdress around your forehead, like an Egyptian goddess painted on a wall. But in kindergarten boys pulled on the curls, and people only talked to you about your hair, so on regular mornings you always asked me for two braids.

Your hair, so overwhelmingly impressive when you were a college freshman that it rose in a thick corona of spiraled blackness all around your face and down half your spine, so much hair that you finally decided you had to cut some of it off just to be able to breathe and be noticed as a whole human, for your face and brain and your words.

You had asked me and your sisters about where you should

part your hair, for the braiding, and I flashed back to the mornings when I'd take the comb through your long wet hair when you were small, making a center part down the middle of your skull all the way to your nape, actually looking at the gradation of thin skin along the crown of your head, the bone casing of your brain, and how the demarcation from skull to spine was a hollow where suddenly the flesh was softer and plush. I would gather all that hair and begin your two thick braids down low, by your ears, when you asked for Pocahontas braids. The single high braid springing from the top of your skull was the Jasmine braid. Oh, the years of Disney. And every now and then, we'd wrap the braids around your head and add flowers—that was Heidi.

But while you sat patiently and I twisted, you asked how much Indian was in you. How much Swiss. How much of your grandmother Alberta. You knew you were the child who had Alberta's dimple, her eyebrows, and the shape of her smile.

Now you were twenty-two, in your first year at a new job. On that fall Sunday, Ermaline parted your hair on the side, braided tiny sections along your head, and plaited your hair with additional hair from a bag until tiny braids hung down your back. Exactly what you had wanted when you were very small, looking at the hair of your sisters.

The next day, you said on the phone, "I was sitting at my desk today and someone saw my hair and said, 'Oh, I didn't know you were black.'"

I said, "What were you before?"

You said, "I don't know. I don't know what they thought. I feel like it's much more apparent to people that I'm black. Like, if I'd been flying under the radar, now I'm not. I feel more like myself than ever."

That night, I sat on the porch and imagined you, in the salon chair in the living room of the house of Ermaline, who came here from Ghana. You didn't tell me about you. You told me about her—how she spoke to her children, a twelve-year-old daughter, a ten-year-old son, and triplets(!) who were five. You told me she never sat down, that she stood for the entire seven hours, that her husband and children came and went, that she never took a single break to eat. She was working. You were listening, the way you have always listened.

When you were two and three, you had no bed and slept mostly with me, because your dad was gone and you were sometimes worried about corraling your world, and you'd heard so many things from your sisters the night before. You'd awaken me with strangely murmured quizzes that you were trying to pass: "Mommy. The white one is salt and the black one is . . ." "Sidewalks are made of . . . cement." "My new bunny's name is . . . Blaze." And if I asked you a question, you'd sigh and say, "I haven't the famous clue what I want to eat."

You listened when I was braiding the hair of your older sisters, when your aunts and cousins were braiding hair. I saw strands of long hair divided into three sections, woven thousands of times with thumbs controlling the movement. Over and over, over and over.

Women braid hair no matter the color or texture. Women braid grass into baskets—Gullah women descended from Angola women, in South Carolina and Georgia. Women braid palm and agave fibers into baskets and hats and bowls—Cahuilla women and Kumeyaay women here in Riverside County, and over the artificial border into what is now Mexico but was only home for centuries. Women braid corn husks and palm fronds into sombreros and sleeping mats here, in southern California, because they did so in Oaxaca and Michoacan. Braid jute and string and cotton fibers into rope. Braid dental floss and embroidery thread and plastic wire. We have braided these things into lanyards and necklaces and bracelets and hair ties.

In the 1880s, my great-grandmother braided tiny threads of silk and wool into an edging for a small folder with pages of green handmade felt, to tie closed the little cloth book that holds hundreds of needles, of all sizes. That is the book I untied to retrieve a needle for your entire childhood—the thicker needles to repair holes in your shirts or dresses, the finest needle to tease out the splinters in your fingers. My great-grandmother made this book in rural Switzerland, and gave it to my mother, who gave it to me.

Our entire lives are about weaving. In the Swiss Alps, my mother sat while her hair was braided into two tails that dangled at the front of her blouse, tied off with ribbon, maybe one of the last things her own mother did before she was bedridden.

I remember wincing at the bathroom counter, my mother yanking the comb through my blond hair that reached the middle of my back, my mother whose hair was short and brown by then. My hair would be contained in two braids. I wonder if anyone touched her hair with patience after her mother died.

The braid my mother loved was züpfe, a loaf of bread whose dough was divided into three ropes and plaited, painted with egg yolk, and baked to puffed glossy brown, with a soft pale yellow center. It was special, for Sundays. *Züpfe* was our favorite word as children, because it means "braid" and that meant bread. My mother loved to braid dough, which was not the hair of children. She loved to give you and your sisters this bread, and you loved to say the word again and again, it was part of your Swissness, but my mother did not braid your hair. Even now, she does not touch people with tenderness or maintenance or casual gesture. She cannot.

———

I learned to braid hair in typing class. (I learned my perfect cursive handwriting, which people still comment on when I sign books, from the graffiti artists in my remedial math class.) I was a high school freshman. Our elderly white teacher hated us. It was 1975, and we were boisterous and poor, those of us in typing class. Our male compatriots were in shop—wood and metal and auto. We were in Home Economics and Typing. The social class divisions were strict.

I loved typing in a room full of girls who painted nails and did hair and sang, as the teacher ignored us. She really hated me, because I could type so quickly I should have received As, but I steadfastly refused to use my little fingers on the outside keys, so she steadfastly awarded me Cs. If I weren't stubborn, I would be dead by now.

My friends and I finished typing our ridiculous meaningless sentences. Then they taught me to cornrow, to French-braid, and to be in the easy company of girls who didn't mind touching hair and laughing. My hair was useful for experimentation. I sat next to Vicky Winn, who teased that any style she attempted on me fell out immediately. But she French-braided the hair around my face, a small improvement. Then she turned her back so I could practice on her. Vicky's hair was exactly like yours, long thick shoals of black wave and curl. Soft and smelling of Afro Sheen. You have met her—one of my oldest friends. Her only son runs a salon, and flat-ironed Delphine's hair for prom. Vicky's hair remains thick, black, and wavy, her son styles her, and her smile remains unguarded. We know each other as women who lost our younger brothers to drugs. When we hug each other, we know the past in our bones.

———

The braid is among the most beautiful patterns in life, I thought that night after you called. I grew up with girls whose grandparents were from Mexico and New Mexico, whose hair was braided and arranged around their heads for folklórico dancing, twined with thick red and green and white ribbon for the hat dance at the Shrine of Our Lady of Guadalupe; African-American girls whose braids were fastened at the ends with pastel barrettes and glass beads; Japanese-American girls whose braids were glossy and so black they gleamed blue in the light. And my braids, like Heidi's.

The day your dad and I got married, I braided my brother's long hair for the wedding after he put on his tuxedo, something he'd never worn and hated passionately. He and I looked exactly alike. Center part, single weave down the middle of his back. Rosa, our Swiss grandmother, used to say sarcastically about us, "Which is the girl and which is the boy?"

Hair is keratin, as I always told you when you were little. A collection of dead cells. Hair and nails. The features by which women are judged are those which are not alive.

Your hair would have been a great joy to the ancestors you never knew.

A few days later, you called me again. You were crying like I haven't heard you cry for a long time. You had just watched, during lunch hour at the computer on your desk, the Vice channel footage of the violence at Charlottesville, Virginia. You said to me, "I can't believe this. They hate us so strongly they march and display their hatred and they're all around me and I'm terrified. I feel like I can never go to the South again."

I waited until you hung up to cry. This nation had broken your heart again. It had broken my heart again. The first and only time I ever took the three of you South was to

Rosette Sims, Los Angeles, California, 2018

(Photograph by Vanessa Feder-Johnson)

Gulfport, Mississippi, to rebuild houses one year after Hurricane Katrina. You were only eleven, technically too young to go, but you sweated and hammered and painted and met women and daughters who looked like you, growing up in rural Mississippi, where Washington Thomas's children survived and raised big families that built this country.

The other cannot win. You dried your eyes, you were shaking. You were in the office, your braids fresh, taking calls from actors and agents, casting television shows with women who are black, mixed, Asian-American, Mexican-American. With men who are Haitian-American, Nigerian-born, Iraqi, and Chicano.

That you worked then for Disney was not lost on me, every day when I walked past the old armoire holding our single television, the shelf holding DVDs of your childhood: *Beauty and the Beast, The Little Mermaid, Pocahontas, Aladdin, Snow White.*

I see you in Colombia, visiting the town of Palenque, learning to drum with descendants of West Africa. You told me the enslaved women in Palenque braided the routes to freedom in their cornrows. I see you at your desk; I see you move the braids out of the way so you can write something down. I see Alberta watching you, and Daisy Carter, and Fine. You raise your eyebrows at something someone says, and your ancestors, those beautiful women, they bite their lips at the perfect arrangement of tiny hairs that fly across your brow.

38

Ancestry

Riverside and Santa Barbara,
California; Ibadan, Nigeria,
2018

It was the last week of college for Delphine, and she'd been working two museum jobs and finishing finals, so she almost didn't go to the party. But she and her friends did. She was bored, about to leave when someone tapped her on the shoulder and asked her to dance. She turned and gave him the icy murderous glare we all hated—and for which I had to take partial credit, as I used a similar look for years. But I used my arctic glare only on people who threatened me and my girls, strangers or idiot men. Delphine was beautiful, and I was not. She frequently used her Sahara staredown.

"I don't dance to YG," she said, enunciating with evil clarity. (YG is an especially—well, nonromantic rapper. We may leave it at that.)

He was brave, this stranger from a different university. He asked for her number, and inexplicably, she gave it to him. He had a melodious Nigerian accent, played soccer for Caltech, was a mechanical engineering major also graduating that year. The kind of man she'd never dated before.

For their first anniversary, she framed a YG CD and hung it on the wall of his apartment.

"Ayooluwakunmi Oluwafemi Jeje," Delphine said to her father in August 2016, as we walked around the park at the end of my block.

"I gotta say all that?" Dwayne said, hitting the ground with the walking stick I keep for him, for these excursions when one or more of the girls comes home to visit, and they walk every day. (We have a sturdy former broom handle and a sawed-off pool cue.) Delphine and I rolled our eyes. He pounded that broom handle polished smooth by his hand with each step.

"Kunmi," she said. "You can call him Kunmi."

"And his name means something?" Dwayne said.

"His first name means 'I'm Full of God's Joy.' His middle name means 'God Loves Me.'" She hadn't told him yet that Kunmi's family had given her a name, too. Oluwamayokun, which means "God Has Topped Off Our Joy."

I can't think of a kinder name for future in-laws to bestow upon someone.

The Jeje family lives in Ibadan, Nigeria. Kunmi came to California in 2009, to attend Caltech; then he worked for Oracle. After two years, he went to Stanford, for his master's degree in computer science. Delphine was working at the Santa Barbara Museum of Art.

This walk, and many more, were how we were letting Dwayne do all his thinking, because for all these years, he and the uncles had been suspicious, downright hostile, and purposefully terrifying to prospective suitors for the girls.

(Still told in our house: Delphine was headed to prom with

a quarterback, and Dwayne sat in one of my chairs and said, "You have her back by midnight, young man, or I'll hunt you down like a dog in heat." We told him that was inaccurate, that the female dog was the one in heat, but he remained unmoved, and then mentioned his gun collection. That led Rosette and me to discuss with Dwayne how Ted Nugent uses the phrase wrongly, as well, while Delphine left with the quarterback.)

Delphine told her father that Kunmi was Yoruba, Christian, and about his family's house in Ibadan, Nigeria's largest city by surface area, third-largest by population, with more than three million people. His father's ancestral village is Erinjiyan Ekiti. Kunmi has more grandparents, aunts, and uncles than a Sims. That's impressive.

Dwayne listened. We walked. Delphine and her sisters had talked about taking DNA tests. I'd been working on this book, and we talked about what I found on Ancestry.com. Sims and Hardiman and Triboulet and Straight. Very little on Daisy Carter's ancestors. Nothing beyond the two names Fine had listed when she applied for a social security card when she was sixty-five, in Tulsa. Father—Henry Ealy. No birthplace listed. Mother—Catheran. Born in Murfence Bur, Tennessee.

"So you really like this young man?" Dwayne said, rolling his eyes. Then he said, "I wonder what they'd think about that. Nigeria. The ones that came over."

The ancestors.

We talked about everyone that day, walking near the Santa Ana River where he and I had once heard the pig, across the water from where we'd fed Floyd's pigs, walking below Mount Rubidoux where we'd walked for thirty years, where we made Rosette hike up the steep trail when she was seven to prepare her for Switzerland. We were within sight of the former landfill, now closed, where Dwayne was the human tarpaulin holding down the heap of palm fronds and eucalyptus branches in his dad's truck.

We talked about the DNA test. What if Delphine was part Yoruba? Part West African? Where was Catherine's mother from? Catherine, Fine's mother, died in 1879, so she might have been born around 1835 or 1840, which meant Catherine's mother might have come from the African continent. What about Catheran's Cherokee lover? Would DNA show Delphine as part Swiss, or just European? Were the Sims and Hardiman and Rawlings white men—overseers and slaveowners—really Irish, as family stories said? Who was the unknown father of Alberta?

But a year passed, and it was December 2017. We lost Loretta Preston, the youngest daughter of Callie. Delphine had modeled herself after her great-aunt Loretta. (She had written that Loretta was the imperious opposite of the stereotype assigned in early American history to women who looked like her and Aunt Loretta: the "tragic mulatto," the light skin, the light bright, the high yellow, the woman whose looks canceled out every other feature of her life.)

Loretta, who had worried I could not cook.

Since Dwayne and I lived in Massachusetts that first year of our marriage, and survived on pinto beans and rice, I had not been immediately tested. But it wasn't long after we moved back home that I knew I had to come up with a side dish. All the women had one. Sister made peach cobbler like no one else. Loretta did collard greens. No one really did rice. I don't remember which gathering was the one where I tried, in desperation, a variation of Hoppin' John, a traditional good-luck dish, and dirty rice, with the only ingredients I had at home for a New Year's Day gathering.

I browned hot red-pepper sausage with garlic, then added Mahatma saffron-yellow rice, black-eyed peas, and plenty of seasoning and black pepper. I have made it now for thirty-five years. It is called Your Rice. As in the cousins asking, "You fixin' to bring Your Rice? You don't bring it, Joe Killer and Eddie will be mad."

It was one of the most joyful accidents of my life. For our family events, I make my rice about ten times a year, enough to serve fifty people. Teri Andrews makes fried chicken and peach cobbler with her mother's expertise, and lime-green Jell-O cake; Margaret Chandler makes potato salad; Shirley makes macaroni and cheese; Carolanne, Myrtle's daughter, makes tamale pie and her own salsa; Christine Sims Stuckey makes corn salad, and her daughter E'chea makes barbecued beans. Our side dishes do not vary. They belong to us.

These were the dishes we made for the repast of Loretta Preston. She was seventy-eight years old. The memorial was at Tillman's, the historic black funeral home on Park Avenue and Tenth Street, still within our six-block radius. We lingered in front of a tiny wood-frame house across the street, with a railing porch and peaked roof. Callie Sims lived here when she came to Riverside; the women gathered that day had all lived there with Callie—Teri and Karen, Loretta and her only daughter, Nygia.

The elegy on Loretta's funeral program: "Elegant and Chic with a side of Sass. Well put together but will kick your ass." Delphine had written a piece for the memorial; shaking slightly, she read it aloud: "You always knew you were fine. I've waited a long time for my cheekbones to end up like yours but alas the greatest cheeks I've ever known have now left us . . . You threw shade before I even knew what it was. You always commanded your space and held it with such ferocity."

The repast—traditional meal served after a funeral service— was a block away, at Twelfth and Park. Orange Valley Lodge #13 was built by David Stokes with the help of his uncle, Robert Stokes, Riverside's first free black resident. Robert Stokes, a tall, powerful man, came to California from Georgia in 1870, bought land and raised pigs where the historic downtown Fox Theater stands. He was the first black policeman in Riverside County. The building was constructed in 1910; our relatives and friends hold parties, dances, and funeral repasts there still today.

I have a photograph of Orange Valley Lodge #13 from 1912; the palm tree in the sidewalk is about two feet tall. Delphine took a photograph of us, the women, after we served the food for Loretta; the palm trees are probably seventy feet tall.

We are true California. True America.

General III carried in my rice. For the first time, I had made it with something new. In my kitchen now is a plastic water bottle filled with a spice mix for meat—hot but with a different tingling from what we are accustomed to. A handwritten label: *Suya Pepper.* Kunmi's mother, Olubukola Jeje, had carried the bottle from Ibadan when she came for his Stanford graduation. We spent three days together. She handed it to me with care. It is my newest treasured inheritance.

"You put something different in the rice," the Sims cousins said, at the repast. "Damn, it tastes good."

My eyes burned with tears. Loretta had been so worried that I couldn't cook. She would have loved to meet Bukola Jeje. This was the best I could do.

Delphine and Kunmi were married in April 2018, at the courthouse in Santa Barbara, California. My daughters would hate it if this book ended with a wedding, having made vicious commentary for years about American movies center on marriage and fantasy, as well as the idea that we as women are complete only when married. This wedding was small, and very Sims transcendentalist. It was impossible for Kunmi's family to come from Nigeria; he had his best friends, two couples who are Nigerian, Cameroonian, Iranian-Nigerian, and

Lisa Sims Bennett, Teri Andrews, Karen Lark, Lynette Richardson, Nygia Preston, Susan Straight, Christine Sims Stuckey, at repast for Loretta Preston, Orange Valley Lodge #13, Riverside, California, 2017

Vietnamese-American. Delphine had Dwayne, Gaila and her partner Andre, Rosette, and me. The morning before the ceremony, Delphine and I cut hundreds of flowers from my Riverside garden—Queen Anne's lace, Spanish and French and English lavender, and tiny pink Cécile Brünner roses from a bush maybe eighty years old, the blossoms smelling of lemon pepper. We carried the blooms in an orange plastic bucket from Home Depot. I made candleholders from glass yogurt jars that I handpainted with her favorite wisteria vines, tiny brushstrokes of lavender, fine tendrils of green. I learned to paint this way in Switzerland. I wrote in calligraphy with a silver pen the names of my daughter and her husband on the glass.

On her hip, Delphine has a tattoo that she got knowing full well I couldn't object. In beautiful cursive script, it reads *Sang Mêle*. Mixed blood. I have been writing about people of mixed race for her whole life. For her wedding, Delphine wore her hair natural, as she has for years. Her millions of black slinkys, as she put it when she was small, are now threaded with some silver—the DNA of her father. Her freckles—the DNA of her grandfather General II. Her "bagavond" constancy of travel—the DNA of her grandfather John Watson.

From me? Maybe the love of cicadas and flowers and all the blue.

Down her spine, she has a long single stalk of delphinium tattooed in lavender blossoms, which rose from the deep V-back of the wedding dress. Kunmi wore a midnight-blue suit brought by his sister earlier from Ibadan. They stood before the court clerk, who read the vows. Then I stood beside the clerk and Dwayne, and read the two Bible verses sent to me by Kunmi's parents, to bless the union.

The ceremony was live-streamed to Nigeria by the two groomsmen. The Jeje family was assembled to watch the wedding. We faced the camera to celebrate with them.

Delphine Sims and Kunmi Jeje, Santa Barbara Courthouse, April 2018

(Photograph by Ashley Blakeney)

My daughters have not gotten around to the DNA test. Busy living as who they are, inhabiting their precise combination of blood and family and geography and unknown, the genetic family and chosen family.

On television shows about roots and identity, I've seen celebrities shout in relief that their DNA shows they are only 46 percent or 35 percent European or white. They hate their slave-owning ancestors. But the enslaved women who were forced to have children with men like Hardiman, Rawlings, and Sims didn't choose what they would pass on. They loved those children. They survived.

It's easy to say the letters casually—DNA—but the thousands of strands in the double helix are not all measured by Ancestry or 23&Me.

My father, Richard Straight, died on January 3, 2018, just after the funeral for Loretta. He was completely alone in the hospital, during his three days of coma, except for me and his longtime girlfriend, Barbara, who is very small and staunch and whom I resemble so much that nurses assumed she was my mother. My father died while I held him. Of his four natural children and four stepchildren, no one else was in his life. Not a single cousin or grandchild. His sister Beverly, eighty-nine, lives in Missouri, near her daughter and grandchildren. She is the last child of Ruby Straight. My father's story is for another book, but I felt deeply the sadness of this solitude. If he were a Sims, there would have been fifty people in the hospital waiting room, telling stories, buying food, dozing until it was their turn to sit beside his bed and whisper into his ear, the way Dwayne whispered to his mother, Alberta, that I was going to have another baby.

Alone with him, I whispered to my father while he took his

last breaths that he taught me to drive better than anyone else ever could have, that he taught me to fish, and once we grew a sunflower eight feet tall and ate the seeds.

In his previous illness the year before, having been tied with restraints to his hospital bed and given morphine, perhaps not knowing I was beside him, perhaps knowing, my father shouted, "Product of a rape! No one wanted you!" I was frightened. He was? I was? I was so scared I left the room and went to the parking lot. Opiates and DNA and memory: not a combination I wanted.

We send off saliva or blood, to ascertain who we are.

Saliva, the bodily fluid used as weapon of disgust and power, the power to spit upon enslaved people or poor women or immigrants or teenagers sitting at a Woolworth's lunch counter or walking into a high school in Arkansas, or my own daughter on the playground.

Blood, the bodily fluid used to classify and categorize us as humans, the one-drop rule, one drop of "Negro" blood and a human is a "Negro," a percentage of drops of blood to identify a human as Native American, all the phrases we hear as American history. Purity of blood. Bloodline. The cushions of blood and placenta that held my daughters inside and that was inside them and outside them. Their blood when rose thorns pierced their skin, when they fell on their chins (chins and foreheads bleed so much!), I'd look at the blood soaking the tissue and think about everyone who came before, always imagining a narrative.

I'd tell us both a story, while the child bled, because story was in their blood, too, and would calm them like nothing else. Just as story had calmed me. They were me. I was them.

And I realized that James Baldwin had added something to

my own genes—he affirmed for me what was instinct: Secondary characters save us, save not only our stories but our lives. The thousands of humans with their own narratives. I'd given that love to my daughters, telling them stories and then listening while they talked about friends and strangers. When they were teenagers, I told them that if they were reading, watching television, or listening to a human speak, they were working, and no one should ever assume interruption was welcome.

The world is narrative, and America needs to remember that.

It's the reason people tell my daughters the stories of their complicated lives, just as they have always told me—strangers, friends, people I meet once in a restaurant or on a train or in the park. It's happened to us all over the world. It is in our DNA, our eyes and ears. Last year, meeting Rosette in Los Angeles for an event at the University of Southern California, where we both received our degrees, she startled me by saying with sadness that one of the first people she noticed when she moved to L.A. was a flower-seller, probably from Mexico or Guatemala, a woman who stood at her freeway exit holding bouquets. That was four years earlier—the woman had been pregnant. Rosette said, "Now her little boy is standing next to her, and she's pregnant again, and she's standing in the same place holding the same flowers. I thought something might have changed for her." She narrowed her eyes and we both paused, looking out at the traffic. A bus passed—the same route on which I'd ridden when I was eighteen, where I'd set the first story I wrote for James Baldwin.

Maybe the pie charts and percentages tell us who we are in truth, as opposed to the stories and legends we've been told as family, the secrets we uncover in letters or historical records. We who have always thought we knew who we were. Our hair, eyes, teeth, the length of our femurs, the way our brains process information, our inherent tendencies toward sadness, fear, anger, humor.

It may be science. But science cannot change secrecy and survival.

No articles, no photos, no records of how many of the ancestors survived. Now even our cats and dogs have thousands of portraits. General III's daughter Pashion Sims, great-granddaughter of Daisy Belle Ford Morris Carter, has thirty-five thousand Instagram followers. Her hair, makeup, dresses, and shoes are daily art to friends and family and strangers. She is twenty-two.

Maybe we'll have a wedding for Gaila and her partner, Andre LeBlanc, with more roses, and maybe we won't. She met him in Austin, Texas, when they both worked for elementary schools with AmeriCorps. We kept hearing about this guy Andre, assuming he was black. We didn't know any white Andres. He is descended from the Acadians expelled from Nova Scotia, after fleeing France, and then arrived in Louisiana. His heritage is impressive. He is Andre the White. We find this hilarious. He is a patient teacher of history, student of American Sign Language, and lover of baseball.

Rosette at one time dated a young man also from Nigeria, whose heritage is also Yoruba. Her best friend, Ada, is Nigerian-American, born in California. Rosette and Ada talk about making a film wherein they go to Nigeria and document the way young Nigerian-Americans are changing American culture.

In December 2018, Delphine and Kunmi traveled to Ibadan for his sister Kiitan's wedding. Six hundred people attended the blessing ceremony. Toby, Kiitan's husband, presented the Jeje family with forty-two yams. He lay prostrate before his in-laws.

Delphine is now Jeje, and Sims. (Kunmi has not been required yet to prostrate. But yams sound good to Mr. Sims and me.)

Full circle. In the most ironic of ways to people who believe in narrowing the world, in closing borders and folding their arms and thinking only of the few people they believe deserve their love and meals, our family is still on Homeric odyssey time. From the enslavement of peoples, not only from the continent of Africa but of indigenous peoples in America, to women held hostage by law or fury or ego, to women who broke free and escaped and stood their ground.

They went west. Always west. My daughter will go to West Africa.

The daughters of our ancestors carry in their blood at least three continents. We are not about borders. We are about love and survival.

That day we said goodbye to Loretta, I sprinkled the suya pepper on the rice, and Bukola Jeje's hands were with mine, and she was for the first time with the biraderi of Simses. She has given us Kunmi, her only son. We have given her a beloved daughter.

I hope my daughters know this: You are the result of the love of thousands.

There is no other country I'd ever want to live in but this one. This country of women.

39

Saphina

Tennessee, 1870

And then, last month, I finally drew the four journeys on a paper map I got from the Auto Club, as if I were planning a trip myself. I used yellow marker for Rosa, pink for Daisy, blue for Ruby, orange for Fine. The nation is traversed by their wanderings and purpose. Odysseus has nothing on them. Scylla and Charybdis lurked in the clearing near the woodpile, and in their own homes. The Cyclops sat with a gun trained on a woman with a baby. The Sirens were men who did not sing from the ocean but told them if they were patient and leaped into the plow or the forest, life would be beautiful—and then tried to drown them with sadness. The lotus-eaters were those who told them they didn't deserve better, they didn't have the courage to run, to go to school, to buy a piano. The seas were asphalt and dirt. Wind did not move them more quickly toward a destination not the island of Ithaca, which was never home because home was something to flee, until they made California into home.

I put my finger on Murfreesboro, where Fine told a

government official that Catheran had been born. I remembered reading accounts of the Freedmen's Bureau, and how formerly enslaved people were moving, moving, trying to find food and shelter and work after Emancipation. The terror of roving bands of vigilantes. I remembered that free black men as well as Cherokee men were hunted down in Tennessee before and after the Civil War.

I'd been searching six years for Fine's parents. I tried different spellings of their names—Henry and Catherine—and widened the search area, and then a census record showed up. July 15, 1870. Civil District No. 2, the nearest post office in McMinnville, Tennessee, which was about twenty miles east of Murfreesboro. Henry Ely—Mulatto. Catherine Ely—Black. Five children: Mack Ely, eight; James Ely, six; Mary Ely, four; Irena Ely, three; Saphina Ely, one.

Saphina. Phina. Fine.

It was 2:00 a.m. I trembled. There is no way to be sure. But Fine named her sons Mack and James. She listed her parents with these names. It is so geographically close as to make sense.

I stayed up all night, trying to find more. Reconstructing her life—this woman with so many names in her lifetime. Saphina. If she was born in 1869, her mother died not long after, and she was given away to the white family that beat her, where was her father?

Mulatto. The family story was that he was Cherokee. But who can know what he told the census taker? Henry Ely was "illegal" whether Cherokee or free mulatto or free colored man, because of the Indian Removal Act and vigilante violence. Who could truly know how his wife died, and what happened to him? He could have been one of the thousands of men killed on the night roads and left in the woods.

Where was this house? Were they sharecropping? Did the landowner not want to pay them? Were they among the

Fine Ely Hofford Rawlings Kemp, Tulsa, Oklahoma, undated

hundreds of people attacked as those reported to the Freed-men's Bureau? Perhaps someone wanted those five children.

Near dawn, this piece of paper still gave me that feeling of water trickling down my breastbone. This little girl. A small child. Bereft. Alone. Resolute. They would not break her. The primal gathering of self. The odysseys.

Ruby Triboulet had her sisters and her parents. My mother, at fifteen, had not married the pig farmer in Canada, and she ran away. But her family existed, even if they were in Florida and then California.

Daisy had siblings who were separated, sent to different porches and pallets and kitchens. Pillar to post. But her aunts would not let her starve or die.

Fine had no one in the world. No one.

People tell their descendants, *I had someone to live for.* A child. A lover. A mother. Even a beloved horse, or faithful dog.

Fine had the tensile strength for survival absolutely alone in a landscape of terror. She was six or seven. Did she think these things? *I will live. I will see the sun. The moon. The blackberries. The bullet. The bones of my bare feet will take me down this road.*

40

The Work of Women—
Evaporation and Memory,
White House #3

Riverside, California, 2018

To my daughters:

Home is the place where they have to take you in. Your people would take you in there, in the Swiss Alps, and they would feed you here in the Sims driveway, below our windswept foothills. But since I'm never going anywhere, you will always have this white wood-frame house with redwood shingles, the third white house in the story, on our corner. Even though it's been painted green, some of that original white paint still clings to the underside of the windowsills you three always leaned out of, looking down into the yard to see the possum swerving along the gravel toward the apricot tree.

Two years ago, for the season of Lent, I was asked to think about this: What do we have that cannot be reduced to ashes? Our houses, our cars, our clothes, our money, our awards, our own bodies—all can be burned.

I thought of the few things that may belong to me: my

daughters, my books, my 108-year-old house, my nine-year-old car, my clothes, many that I've had for thirty years. (Delphine, who prefers to dress like Sofia on *The Golden Girls*, loves to pillage my closet for '80s looks, and Rosette wears as a tunic the batik dress I wore when pregnant with her.) My dog. My six chickens. My own body.

All of us, and those things, can be reduced to ashes. The ashes of my brother, Jeff, came to this house in 2002. They would be ashes reduced to further ashes. I will be reduced to ash and I hope my daughters will scatter the remains of me and the remains of my brother on Little Sugarloaf, the smallest of the three Box Springs Mountains where we grew up together, pushing through yellow brittlebush and the white trumpet flowers of hallucinogenic jimsonweed, listening for rattlesnakes and digging for fool's gold in the shadows of the granite boulders.

Maybe Dwayne's ashes will be on the Swiss Alp he hiked with our cousin Hans.

I washed dishes one night during Lent, thinking of what might be eternal. Then I washed clothes, washed the dog, washed my hands, washed the outside of the chicken coop, washed the kitchen floor, and sat on the cement steps outside. The cement would not burn.

Everything we did, as women, seems evanescent. Evaporated. Invisible except to memory.

Fine: She picked cotton and blackberries, chopped wood that burned and hauled water that dried, all of those things dissolved into the survival of people who hated her and then people who needed her and people who loved her. She cleaned the bodies and hair and clothes of Jennie and Callie. She cleaned houses. She cleaned the bodies of her sons. She went to Tulsa and washed clothes for white people, cleaned the tears of her grandchildren, plucked the feathers from chickens with her daughter, cleaned the blood from animals, and cleaned the pots of the oil and debris from meat.

Jennie cleaned the blood from her own body. She cleaned the blood of the man she killed. She cleaned the floors after hush-hush parties in her Tulsa house. She cleaned her pistol. She cleaned her white house in Los Angeles, and the clothes of all the people who lived there, and the plates and pots of the people she fed. Even when she was an elderly woman, as our cousin Karen Lark remembers, Jennie still ran numbers, which meant she kept figures in her head or on small pieces of paper, and she leaned over the fence in the alley behind her house laughing and talking to the people whose numbers stayed in her head until those daily numerals won or lost and they, too, evaporated.

Daisy made it to California and sorted the munitions of war, the agents of death. She and her daughters plucked and cleaned the bodies of turkeys and washed the floors of blood and feather and guts and bone. They cleaned the floors at Butcher Boy, the beef and guts and bones and fat, the meat that ended in hamburgers and cheeseburgers in thousands of bodies moving along the new freeways. They washed and bleached and dried and starched and ironed hundreds of white dress shirts. They made hundreds of pies and cakes, fried hundreds of chickens.

Alberta told me the story of washing diapers and clothes for her six children in the early 1960s when salmonella tainted the city water supply. She mentioned the wringer washer. She grinned and said it was the worst, children lying half-naked on the floor while she hung rows of wet cloth on lines outside; she said this while we folded the thick cotton diapers and washcloths we used to clean the bodies of my two baby girls. "Go on and rinse that cloth one more time," she said to me, looking down at Gaila's face. "Look at that little bit of sweet potato on her mouth."

Rosa Erb Leu washed the blood and bone and vomit and fluid and diseased cells and soiled equipment and linens of thousands of humans, beginning with the inmates of the krankenhaus for the insane, to the body of my grandmother, to the bodies of the steelworkers in Fontana, the origin of Kaiser Permanente Healthcare System, but who remembers her touch on their forehead or shoulder? Her hands so twisted by arthritis when she was ninety that her fingers resembled splayed feathers, as if she would fly from the chair on the square of artificial turf, and even then, blind, she would work her way around the earthen plots surrounding her mobile home, planted with tomatoes and chard and grapevines, telling me she could feel which were the weeds and she would pull them out, and she could feel which were the vegetables and when they were ready for her to twist them from their stems and bring them inside for the boiling water.

Ruby Triboulet Straight must have washed the hair and clothes and bodies of her four children, washed the blood from sheared sheep and castrated cattle from the clothes of her husband. The oil of machine and truck and gun. No electricity or running water in the ranch homes and cabins of the Rocky Mountains—creek water so cold they broke the ice to bring it up. Ashes and ashes of wood fires. The water of boiled beans. Melted snow. The sawdust of hundreds of pine trees felled and dragged by horse, in the hair and clothes of my father.

Only memory cannot be burned.

I made thousands of cupcakes for your birthdays and the birthdays of everyone who came to stay in this house. I made thousands of brownies for basketball snack bars. Thousands of chocolate chip cookies. I washed thousands of socks. I wrote thousands of words. I pulled out the weeds and fed them to the chickens and gathered the eggs and scrambled them for you and your friends and crushed the shells and put them into the dirt and new weeds grew.

Now Gaila is getting her PhD in African-American/ American Studies, at University of Texas, Austin. Delphine is getting her PhD in Art History/African American Studies at UC Berkeley. Rosette has just taken a new job with Amazon Studios in Los Angeles.

When I knew none of you would come back here to live, and I cleaned out the bedroom dressers, I found thirty-eight pairs of jeans. The Sisterhood of the Stay-Home Pants. I had never seen many of these jeans. They'd been left behind or traded by the multitudes of girls who slept here, cousins and basketball teammates and school friends and college roommates and neighbors. There are so many sizes, I haven't bought jeans for six years. Whether I gain or lose weight, I wear the pants of your past.

Everything else can be reduced to ashes—the money, the things men cared about, the houses and cars and hats the men wanted, the dresses and coats and hats the women wanted. The wedding rings they had or didn't have, never received or lost or took off, wouldn't burn. Our finger bones will turn to soot. But on Daisy's corner lot, Dwayne found the bronze doorstop from his childhood. Maybe our brass doorknob, original to my house, would survive. The one that Delphine points out is so loose and twitchy after being touched by hundreds of hands that it can be opened only by the experts: Delphine, Rosette, and me.

I sit every night on this porch, staring at the grass where we used to sleep when it was so hot, where we lay looking up at the sky, the bats, the whoosh of an owl, the blur of night moths, the abrupt midnight songs of mockingbirds.

"You taught us how big the world is, and how small we are."

Delphine, you told me this two years ago, when we walked on Little Sugarloaf, amid the white boulders.

"You always let me read in a corner and didn't make me wash the dishes right away or talk to people." Gaila, you told me this when you had found your beloved bench on which to read at Oberlin.

"I was trying to explain to someone how we grew up." Rosette, you told me this last year, in Los Angeles. "I was like, Wait—what's below humble?"

When I started writing this book, I typed until two or three in the morning, as if I were someone with much younger eyes, and on the evening after my first draft was done, I was cleaning in the garden—reflexively, genetically incapable of letting the branches and weeds advertise my slovenly weeks of writing, as if my mother might walk up the path. I lifted a big river rock and then I saw a piercing light, like a tracer bullet curving around the edge of my left eye.

I had a detached retina, in exactly the same place as had happened two years ago to my left eye, after I'd worked too hard on a novel. Delphine came home to take care of me. She drove me to the retinal specialist for laser surgery, the pain of which felt like intense green stitching I observed deep inside my brain, my eyes held open by plastic. I recovered sitting in the darkened living room while we watched our favorite television shows. I was berated if I attempted to pull a weed.

Then Delphine went home.

I am here alone, masses of dark retinal debris clouding parts of my vision. In the left eye, the debris is a gray jellyfish that swims back and forth, as if a windshield wiper moves it with my glances. In the right eye, the new debris is two black spiders hovering in the vitreous at the deep right edge of my sight, and then a black chiffon scarf that moves diaphanous over my sight, as if drifting in a gentle wind.

I feel like a failure. I contemplate cleaning the garage. The walls are ridden with termites, my brother's old workbench filled with his bullets and Dwayne's, with nails and screws from our former lives. From the rafters hang every Big Wheel, tricycle, training bicycle, and beach cruiser my daughters and nieces and great-nieces have ever ridden.

Then I realize I'm an idiot. I hold six generations in the handlebars of this Big Wheel. Fine and Ruby would marvel at this Big Wheel, and the tiny fingers that once clutched the plastic grips. The hollow wheels made the loudest sound imaginable on the gravel driveway and old sidewalks bordered by yellow irises brought to me the first year we owned this house by General Sims II, and purple irises brought to me by my mother, Gabrielle Gertrude Leu Straight Watson.

Some women considered this the promised land. Once they got here, they never wanted to leave. Daisy and three of her daughters, Callie and both her daughters, and Rosa are all buried or ashes here. Jennie is buried in Los Angeles. Fine's resting place is Okalahoma, and Ruby's is Colorado. But they are all with me.

I test my vision in the garden. Restricted to the sidewalk, I see everything close up. I hear a small repeated thump somewhere nearby. A little lizard is trying to leap back out of the metal watering can. Teenager-sized, the length of my thumb. A western blue-throated fringe-toed lizard. I know this because I was a nerd, a kid who identified all lizards, butterflies, beetles, rocks, and wildflowers in notebooks. A loser. My daughters know all the names of these insects and lizards as well, and know to shake out their high heels in the closet, cool cradles of baby lizards like this.

If I weren't out here right now, being a loser, the reckless teenager would have died in the hundred-degree heat. I tip the can over so the lizard can run into the sunflowers.

Your father comes by once or twice a week, to sit here on the porch, peeling and eating navel oranges from the tree we planted when my brother died. We talk about what we fear for your days and nights, what we hope for your weeks and years, and then he finds comfort in considering what items to deliver or purchase or move for you. (From the swap meet, he buys Kunmi and Andre cell phone accessories, which is a great improvement from eternal suspicion.) We talk incessantly about you girls. We know you might never come home, but we are human, so of course, our hearts race when we think we'll see your faces. We talk about Daisy Mae, the possum who died only this year, in my basement, having somehow made her way inside again.

When he leaves, I listen to the melancholy finches in the sunflowers. The night will turn to the deep blue of new denim.

All we women have to give you is memory. Everything we washed is there. Everything we cooked. Everything we said.

What we felt we might keep to ourselves, unless someone wrote it down.

Riverside, California, 2000

(*Photograph courtesy of Juli Jameson*)

Acknowledgments

Trying to thank all our family—blood and biraderi—feels impossible. But here goes:

Sims: John Prexy Sims, Lee Myrtle Sims, Karen and John Lark and family, Teri Andrews and family, Toni Sims Scott; General Roscoe Conklin Sims III, Lisa Bennett, and family; Shirley, Ericka, and Sensei Sims and family; Carnell Sims and family; Christine Sims Stuckey and family; Derrick Sims and family; Angela Sims; Nygia Preston and family; Margaret Chandler Cain and family; Eddie Chandler III and Revia Chandler and family; Rita Butts Sweeney, Anthony "Snooter" Butts, and family descended from Mary Louise Morris Butts; Carolanne Bagley and family descended from Myrtle Morris Samuel Bagley; Rosie Morris; the Wall family; Trent Chatham and all the Chatham and Hamilton family; the Wilson family; the Marshall Anderson and Robert Anderson families; the Aubert family; the Collins family; Dell Roberts and family.

Watson/Leu: John Watson Jr. and family; Chris and Barbara Leu and family; Mark Leu and family; Christine "Stini" Leu; Zoe Watson and Gervais Warren, Saint John, New Brunswick, Canada.

Swiss Familie Erb, in Oberdiessbach and Aeschlen, especially Beat and Annina, Theodore and Marianne, Hans and Ruth; Lydia Staudenmann and family, Hunibach; Daniel and Anne-Marie Roesti, Wasen in Emmental; Fritz and Susi Kiener, Zwiesselberg.

Straight/Triboulet/Barnaby: Dale Barnaby, Vara Helen "Toots" Barnaby; "Fuzz" Barnaby, Barbara Peary, Dean Straight.

The Jeje family—Oluwatunwamise Jeje, Olubukola Jeje, Ifeoluwakiitan Jeje, for new kin and kindness.

Sisters in the geography of love: Holly Robinson, Kate Anger, Nicole Harris, Tonya Jones, Elizabeth Eastmond, Kari Rohr, Juli Jameson, Dina Lisa Giustozzi, Susan Rae Lakin, Kim Chanta. Douglas McCulloh, honorary Sims; Eleanor Jackson, in the country of mothers; Pat Strachan, Andy Hunter, Wah-Ming Chang, John McGhee, Nicole Caputo, Jennifer Kovitz, Megan Fishmann, Sarah Jean Grimm, Elizabeth Ireland, and the Catapult family; Katie Freeman, honorary cousin, and Richard Parks. The writers whose generosity and love carried me all these years, with their own landscapes: Dorothy Allison, Judith Freeman, Michael Jaime-Becerra, Joyce Carol Oates, Walter Mosley, Karen Tei Yamashita, Alex Espinoza, Tod Goldberg, Stewart O'Nan, Patt Morrison, Jervey Tervalon, Jonathan Gold, Kate Moses, and Carolyn See. And all the people on the campus of the University of California, Riverside, who for thirty years have made family survival possible.

———

The most love and gratitude, of course, go to the people of my deepest heart: Dwayne Sims, Gaila Sims and Andre LeBlanc, Delphine Sims and Kunmi Jeje, and Rosette Sims.

In Memoriam:

General and Alberta Sims; Robert Sims and Crystal Sims; Stanford Sims; Loretta Preston; Margrett Sims, BJ Green, Corion Green; Lareanz Simmons; Eddie Chandler II and Lucy Segovia Chandler; Maisha Walters; Jesse Wall; Jeannette Sims; Tommie and Judy Chatham; Lewis Gainer Sr.; Floyd and Leonard "LB" Walker; Jesse Lee and Clarice Collins; Doriella Anderson; Waudier Rucker-Hughes; Sterling Stuckey.

Kahla Barnaby; Helen Triboulet Dixon; Galen Barnaby; Ed and Kate Barnaby. Paul and Della Watson, Ronald Watson.

My mentor: James Baldwin.

My father: Richard Dean Straight.

My brother: Jeffrey Paul Straight Watson, who I miss every day of my life. The next book is yours.

ABOUT THE AUTHOR

Susan Straight has published eight novels, including *Highwire Moon* and *A Million Nightingales*. She has been a finalist for the National Book Award and received the Robert Kirsch Award for lifetime achievement from the Los Angeles Times Book Prizes, the O. Henry Prize, the Lannan Literary Award for Fiction, and a Guggenheim Fellowship. Straight's essays have been published in *The New Yorker*, *Harper's Magazine*, *The New York Times*, *Granta*, and *The Believer*. She was born in Riverside, California, where she lives with her family.